THE
NO-DROP
ZONE

EVERYTHING YOU NEED TO KNOW ABOUT THE PELOTON, YOUR GEAR, AND RIDING STRONG

Patrick Brady

Foreword by Andy Hampsten
Tour de France stage winner

MENASHA RIDGE PRESS
www.menasharidge.com

The No-Drop Zone

Library of Congress Cataloging-in-Publication Data

Brady, Patrick, 1963–
  The no-drop zone: a quick-start guide to get you on the road and riding smart / by Patrick Brady. — 1st ed.

     p. cm.
  Includes index.
  ISBN-13: 978-0-89732-660-5
  ISBN-10: 0-89732-660-1
  1. Cycling. 2. Cycling—Training. 3. Bicycle racing. 4. Bicycles—Maintenance and repair. 5. Road bicycles—Maintenance and repair. I. Title.
  GV1041.B725 2011
  796.6—dc22
                              2010036806

Cover design by Scott McGrew
Text design by Larry Van Dyke
Cover photograph by Greg Page
All interior photographs by Greg Page and John Pierce unless otherwise noted.
Indexing by Galen Schroeder/Dakota Indexing

Menasha Ridge Press
P.O. Box 43673
Birmingham, AL 35243
menasharidge.com

Table of Contents

Acknowledgments   vii
Foreword   x
Introduction   xiii

Section I The Experience   1

Chapter 1   What Is Road Cycling?   3
Chapter 2   Basic Riding Skills   9
Chapter 3   Group Riding Skills   21
Chapter 4   Advanced Skills   29
Chapter 5   Challenges for Women   37
Chapter 6   Traffic   43
Chapter 7   Crashing   47
Chapter 8   Organized Cycling Events   53
Chapter 9   Racing   59

Section II The Machine 63

Chapter 10	A Detailed Look at the Road Bike	65
Chapter 11	Materials and Construction	69
Chapter 12	The Components of the Modern Road Bike	83
Chapter 13	The Geometry of a Road Bike	99
Chapter 14	Purchasing the Right Bicycle	109
Chapter 15	The Bicycle and Rider Combination	115
Chapter 16	Fitting the Bike to the Rider	121
Chapter 17	Helmets: Or Why Your Noggin Is Worth More Than $30	127
Chapter 18	Bicycle-Specific Clothing	131
Chapter 19	Accessories	141
Chapter 20	Tools and Maintenance	147
Chapter 21	Upgrades for Your Bicycle	163
Chapter 22	Gearing for Your Bicycle	169

Section III The Lifestyle 173

Chapter 23	Training: Why, How	175
Chapter 24	Diet	185
Chapter 25	The Fred	191
Chapter 26	Traditional Practices and Occupational Hazards	197
Chapter 27	Travel	203
Chapter 28	Cycling Clubs and Organizations	209
Chapter 29	Pro Racing	215
Chapter 30	Further Reading and Involvement	231

Lexicon	237
Appendix	249
Index	255
About the Author	265

Dedication

I dedicate this book to the members of my family who wrote works that contributed to the body of knowledge in their chosen field: my father, Gabriel Martin Brady, the author of *George M. Cohan, the Original Yankee Doodle Dandy* (2002); my grandfather, Henry Philip Gobie, the author of *The Speedy: A history of U.S. special delivery service* (1976); and my great-grandfather, Philip Henry Gobie, author of *Bellows Falls and vicinity illustrated: Designed to portray and perpetuate the attractions and historical facts of Bellows Falls and the surrounding villages . . . and Walpole and Charlestown, New Hampshire* (1908).

—P. B.

Acknowledgments

I consider the work contained in these pages to be the achievement of many. I alone could not have created what I hope will serve as a reference text for riders new and experienced alike.

First and foremost, Greg Page has earned my undying gratitude for his many photographs that illustrate the book's contents. As an accomplished cyclist who has competed in every cycling discipline there is, his insight into the concepts I needed to convey resulted not only in excellently composed photographs, but often revisions to the text that increased its clarity. My friend's tireless work and unflagging commitment to this project has resulted in a book better than I had a right to expect.

John Pierce of Photosport International took my laundry-list request of images of the sport's great personalities and ran with it, giving me images of such depth and perspective they inspired my desire to write yet another book.

Another cycling friend, writer and editor Alex Armitage, reviewed the entire text, letting me know when I was geeking out even too much for him. He devoted many hours to the book, acting as a reader advocate, prodding me to get to the point and to keep it clear. He was the human 800-grit sandpaper that guided me to polish what I'd left unfinished.

A number of people in the industry reviewed my work for accuracy. Without them, this work would be considerably less reliable. I owe beers to *Bike Magazine* editor, former pro, and *A Dog in a Hat* author Joe Parkin; Chris Carmichael of Carmichael Training Systems; Dotsie Bausch of Empower Coaching Systems; Scott Holz of Specialized; Catherine Page RN, MSN, WOCN, of Downey Regional Medical Center; Wes Wilcox and Doug Cusack of Trek; and Peter Easton of Velo Classic Tours.

Mike Sinyard and the staff at Specialized get an extra-special mention for their support for this project. They made every resource at their disposal available to me. Indeed, Nic Sims's tireless work on my behalf deserves greater credit than I can express here.

I have been fortunate to make many friends in the bike industry over the years, and they responded by sending me gear and images to help illustrate the genius and hard work that characterize the industry. I extend a very warm and special thanks to: Nic Sims, Gabe Sullens, Andrew Hammon, Josh Rebol, and Luc Callahan at Specialized; Harry Spehar and Scott Daubert at Trek; Bill Rudell at Cannondale; Andy Paskins at Zipp; Todd Linscott, Bill McGann, and Christian Feldhake at Torelli Imports; Larry Kohn at Assos; Gary Vasconi at Capo Forma; Rudy Reimer and Othon Ochsner at Ochsner Imports; Peter Kukula, Katie Humphrey, and Gary Medley at Castelli Imports; Sandy Nicholls at Gita Sports; Sean Coffey at Blackburn; Tom Petrie and Steve Owens at Cantitoe Road; Steve Blick at Oakley; Suzette Ayotte at Fi'zi:k; Dave Trendler at VeloPress; Peter Donato at Cervelo; Lorenzo Taxis and Brian Sarmiento at Campagnolo USA; Doug Martin, Jeff Soucek, Ty Buckenberger, and Jake Duehring at Felt; Mattison Crowe and Skunk at Seven Cycles; Armin Rahm at Sixtus USA; Richard Sachs at Richard Sachs Cycles; Kirk Pacenti at BikeLugs.com; Greg Townsend at Townsend Cycles; Dwan Shepherd at Co-Motion Cycles; Michael Zellman at SRAM; Andy Pruitt at the Boulder Center for Sports Science; Bill Armas at Park Tool; Roger Wotton, Jim Whitsett, and Randall Arakai at Cynergy Cycles; Jay Wolfe at Helen's Cycles; Pat at Pat's Cyclery; and Jeff Weir at Jeff Weir Photography.

The models contained in these pages are talented and knowledgeable riders I'm fortunate to call friends. I owe each of them my gratitude and a good meal to replenish the thousands of calories they burned while on duty for me. Thanks to Roger Wotton, Renee Fenstermacher, Nicole Keshishian, Noel O'Malley, Michael Hotten, Greg Castaneda, Michelle Orem, David Price, Eric Romney, Marcella Piersol, Greg Leibert, Mark Neuman, Ron Peterson, James Petit, and Vickie Castaldi. You're all the best. Peter Nistler gets a nod for his good nature and willingness to play the part of the Fred.

I must also acknowledge those who shared their knowledge with me. Thanks to Hal Mabray at the Peddler Bike Shop, whose conscientious work taught me about wrenching; David Deuber, who whipped my riding skills into shape over countless miles of New England roads; Bill Farrell at the New England Cycling Academy, who taught me how to fit someone; and Garrett Lai, my boss at *Bicycle Guide*, whose belief in my writing ability gave me the opportunity to serve a tradition larger than my life can span.

My editors, Molly Merkle and Richard Hunt, have earned my gratitude for their input, their guidance, their abundant patience, and their many helpful ideas. How this book would have suffered without them.

Finally, I reserve my greatest praise for my wife, Shana. No number of copies sold can adequately repay the lost weekends and evenings I devoted to bike stuff, bike people, and bike ideas. She persevered, planning a wedding, and endured pregnancy. She also served as my most challenging cycling student, and asked "Why should I do it that way?" to each new instruction I gave. She inspires in me a continuous desire to serve, to share cycling with the rest of the world. I'm a better person thanks to her.

Foreword

I **like to ride.**

That said, now that I am retired from competitive racing, I miss the peloton. It's a thrill to ride in the mass of speeding cyclists. Riding in a pack is the closest a human being will ever get to flying . . . flying in a flock of birds. It can also feel like a vacuum. On a flat, wide road with a good surface, riding in the peloton only takes half the effort of being at the front.

The downside of being in a mass is that you as a rider want to be in control of what's happening. There is a sweet spot near the front of the pack where there is a great draft, yet you can still see what is coming or going down the road. Being in a blazing-fast pack without working hard is very satisfying.

The sweet spot area in the peloton is very crowded, and riders are willing to take high risks to stay there. In the worst of times, it's like the Tokyo subway at rush hour. A lot of crashes happen in a massive peloton.

I was fortunate to win the Giro d'Italia [author's note: Andy is still the only American to win this Grand Tour] and the Tour of Switzerland twice. To do this certainly took a lot of training, experience, and perseverance. But having fortuitous weather, wind, and heat conditions, plus not getting mixed up in any crashes . . . those are things a rider can't control.

Both of those races include some very difficult mountain terrain. Racing in large packs and descending in the high mountains of the Alps and Dolomites requires great skill. And nerve.

Racing in a pack is like playing soccer. I am fine being with a lot of people, but I need to plan what I am going to do and when I want to make my move. It may be a stage where my intention is to just dribble along with everyone else. Or I might be looking for a clean shot to get away.

Racing down mountains is also like downhill skiing. While there may be other riders who may help or hinder my descent, frankly I'm more concerned about the feedback I am getting from my bike in regards to the road surface. Is my bike feeling like it wants to leave the road? If it is wet, I may think it is slippery, but is it really slick out? Wet or dry, the technique is the same: Brake only in the straights, and only lean in the turns.

Part of being able to ride comfortably and confidently in a peloton is the result of training and experience, but another crucial part is making sure your bike is tuned so it can handle whatever the race and road conditions are. I had the best mechanics in the world when I was on the 7-Eleven/Motorola team, and I can say that because I also rode for enough Euro teams to appreciate how good they were.

When I was a kid, I worked in cycle shops to earn enough money to afford my bikes. I knew I needed to know how to fix my bike or at least understand how it worked to know what to do in a race if equipment went south. So I paid attention.

I fixed and maintained my bikes when I was at home. When I went to a race, I pointed out what my bike was doing wrong and right. And maybe I was dumb enough to suggest to the mechanics what they should look at. I took every opportunity to offer them a coffee or beer and just watch them coax the bikes into perfect order.

I remember one day in 1979 Eddie B. thought he had better crack the whip on the Junior Worlds team kids by forcing us to mount our own bikes to prepare for a time trial. He was sure we all knew nothing about bikes, and I got lumped in with the other racers in his diatribe. It sucked, but it was part of the fun being a junior racer.

So you need to learn what how to maintain each part of your bike, and by doing so, you'll better understand how all those parts come together. That information is crucial for a rider—the same way you monitor your legs and not push things too fast too soon, you'll be able to monitor your bike to see if there's a problem that's developed with a gear, a brake, or the steering.

Bikes have evolved a lot since I first entered the pro ranks. Nowadays, the gears always shift and the brakes work, even in the wet. My feet are comfortable even on hot days, my eyes don't get blasted by rocks, I can fall on my head and probably be okay, and Fi'zi:k made a saddle that is better than okay.

The bikes are lighter, but that makes no relative difference to racers. Frames are still diamonds and the best wheels have spokes, so in some ways, I don't think things are all that different. I used to race on rims that weighed 280 grams, which is lighter than rims are today. I replaced those rims pretty often too.

With the bike company I started after retiring as a pro cyclist, I put all that knowledge I gained to work for myself . . . and others. With Hampsten Cycles, I think about what the bikes are doing. For instance, now that I ride on a variety of roads, as unlikely as it sounds, I sometimes design bikes around tire preferences. Larger tire diameters offer less rolling resistance and more grip on descents. Those are major advantages at the cost of a minor weight increase. And they are great for rough or nonpaved roads.

It is better to go to your local bike shop on a quiet day and spend some time telling an interested salesperson how you ride, and how you want to improve or change your terrain and distances. If what you hear back is about how such-and-such a bike won a race or is newer than anything out there this week, then try to get the conversation back to your riding. Ideally, you want to hear about how a bike will be fit to you, not you to a bike.

We build bikes specifically for each rider. We have no agenda to try to "move" any material because there are no bikes in inventory. And we get into some very interesting conversations with our customers. For instance, many people want to avoid the harsh ride of aluminum, yet don't initially follow our suggestion to use tires larger than 23mm. Yet a bike with 27mm tires and an aluminum frame could give them just the ride they are looking for, at a lower weight they also might insist on. Titanium and steel are our most popular materials, but we like to get them thinking about all of the possibilities.

It is better to have a less expensive or older bike that fits than a bike that isn't the right dimension. Keep in mind that most bikes available are what racers ride. If you are 20-something years old, very flexible, ride at 30 mph, and have all day to ride . . . well, most of us aren't that lucky.

Do you use the drops on your bike? That is an indication of your bar height; that is, if you don't use them, then you could probably benefit from raising your bars and using the drops more. So what I focus on when I fit a rider is the stem length and handlebar height. The seat position is fairly easy. The stem is a lever acting as the "steering wheel" that transmits all the directional feedback to the rider. When we are rushing down a mountain hoping to beat a rain shower and wondering if perhaps we were a little too liberal with that morning's tire pressure, it is the stem that is transmitting the "Should I or shouldn't I brake here?" data. It is simple to decide what length stem we feel a rider would need, and with all the great frame materials to choose from now, we can decide how long the top tube needs to be to get the right reach for the rider.

I look at a rider and ask about her or his riding habits/preferences, decide on a stem length and height, decide on a top tube length, and send it off to the wizards at HampCo Towers to do the math. These are the types of things you'll learn more about in the *No-Drop Zone*. Good for you for picking it up.

Cyclists have so many great frame materials and equipment options to choose from now, it is amazing. These choices also let you focus more on getting the bike to fit just right. That sounds easy, but discussing stem and crank length and seat, handlebar, and tire options is a crucial part of fitting the frame. Which is why all the information in this book is so important.

I also like using my racing strategy of wanting to be fresh for the last two hours of a race in the bikes we build for our mostly nonracing customers. For some conditions, this means riding a light and stiff bike. But more important is having a bike that does not take energy out of the rider. Bikes that are too stiff or rigid make riders tired and cranky. The great Eddy Merckx told my team in 1989, "Never select a bike that might help you gain seconds on a climb if you might lose minutes in the descent."

Understanding the geometry of a bike, or in my case, not understanding it, is another lesson I learned from Eddy Merckx, who is the world's fitting master. My input in design always revolves around the bikes' need to have neutral handling: Lean a little and the bike turns a little; lean a lot and the bike turns a lot. I understand that different angles change the steering effect at the front wheel, so the fork rake has to adjust to the angle. Fortunately, our frame builders all understand the math behind this. And the math has been in place since the Wright Brothers were wrenching bikes.

Late in my career as a pro, I joined the U.S. Postal team, and part of my role was to mentor the younger riders. I hope I helped some of the guys; it was very nice for me to end my racing days with a green American team, and one coached by Eddie B., who was my first coach.

Some days I needed to be the captain on the road and decide how we would race as a team. Most days I preferred to let the race happen and have the strongest riders lead us.

I tried to tell appropriate race stories and see who might be learning from them. The riders on that team were very talented, so it was fun making the most of our race days together.

The other thing I've done since I retired from racing was starting a tour company that focuses on tours in Europe, especially Italy. In most places that have good roads to ride on, there is also a good climate for wine and great food. There is a bit of a theme there. So there's really no surprise with the tour groups—I like to ride and I like to eat.

I like to eat a balanced diet with olive oil being my primary fat—pasta when it is good, a nice piece of meat or fish five times a week or so, and not so much sugar that I am buzzing. Math helps out here too: Our bodies are tops at converting food into energy and storing it in our liver and muscles in the form of glycogen, and the rest is converted to fat.

The *when* of eating for riding is important to focus on. Rehydrate well after riding; eat some but not too much in the first hour after a race. Then at dinner eat well but don't stuff yourself. Breakfast just isn't going to add much more glycogen if you had a good dinner, so go fairly light. I was told how Sean Kelly would eat lightly before a race and refuel well during the (long) race. A strategy from Formula One racing: Start light and fast, get in the lead if you can, and fuel during the race.

I love designing fun rides in great areas. It is not a mistake that interesting people choose beautiful places to grow great food and wine. Of course, there are quiet roads in many of those places to ride on. In Italy you have great roads, great food, great wine . . . and the rednecks drive three-wheeled pickups and like bikers. The roads in Europe were made with donkey carts in mind. To riders, that means gentle grades with lots of turns. Come on, let's ride!

—Andy Hampsten,
Tour de France stage winner

Introduction

I always wanted a life defined by adventure. As a child, my bike delivered the thrills. Unfortunately, playing drums in rock bands, driving a car, and dating short-circuited my adventure chip in my teenage years.

One day in college, I swung my leg over the saddle of a friend's new bike. With less than a mile beneath me, I found myself grinning and thinking: "This is terrific. Why did I ever stop?" Weeks later, I purchased a used Specialized Expedition, a bike meant for touring. Everything about it, from the brakes to the handlebars to the shifters, seemed exotic and geared for adventure.

On my very first ride, a nail punctured the rear tire's tread, tube, and sidewall in one impressive thrust—a humbling end to my maiden voyage. I had no clue what to do next other than to visit a bike shop. Clearly, such a lack of knowledge would undermine my freedom. I had a lot to learn.

I immersed myself in cycling culture. I wanted to know about touring, about bicycle racing, about the funny clothing, how to work on my bike; heck, I wanted to know everything. I bought magazines. I annoyed the mechanics at the local bike shop. I asked friends.

I learned about group rides, metric tools, sew-up tires, Campagnolo, Eddy Merckx, Greg LeMond, the Tour de France, clipless pedals, panniers, indexed shifting, bike computers, and more. Each new piece of information made my world that much richer.

Even though I had a voracious appetite for my new sport, what I lacked was a guide. My education was spotty, so I began working at a bike shop and entering races. Somehow, riding with more experienced cyclists and rubbing elbows with knowledgeable mechanics filled in the gaps as if by osmosis.

I rode, a lot, first with just a few friends, then with larger groups. Experienced racers taught me how to ride in a paceline and often dropped me as suddenly as a cell phone call. I began racing, did a solo tour in the Rockies, and rode a host of centuries.

Because of the amount of time and effort it took for me to acquire this knowledge, I wanted to save others the trouble by sharing what I had learned. I taught classes on bike maintenance, gave riding-skills clinics to newer riders, and helped formulate an instruction program modeled on the system used by the Professional Ski Instructors of America. But because I was a writer, I wanted to reach a broader audience, so I began freelancing for magazines.

During my interview with *Bicycle Guide* magazine, I was asked—point blank—how much interest and ability I had to write content aimed at new riders. My response: I welcomed the chance. One day in the office, we were having an editorial meeting when a coworker lamented that we were compiling an impressive array of articles for new riders but there was just one problem: Missing an issue was like missing a class for which there was no textbook. The answer seemed simple: collect the articles into a single book. And so this book was born. In my years of writing about cycling, I have been called upon many times to assess who the average roadie is and what will constitute an interesting article for that reader. Too often, people both inside and outside the bike industry make the mistake of believing that the foundation of the roadie lifestyle is racing. Well, it's not.

Racing can be great fun, but week in and week out, incredible group rides take place all across America. Roadies spend the majority of their bike time on group rides. You don't have to drive to get to them. There's no entry fee. They tend to be safer than races. They feature known routes (at least to the regulars) and start at the same time each week. For people with families, pets, and honey-do lists, every one of those features is a selling point.

But there's an even better feature that keeps people coming back: Group rides are fun. Sure, there's usually some very fast, very intense time on the bike, but the fast portions don't last all that long. The best part is that group rides give you a chance to ride at a firm tempo nestled in the group at speeds difficult to sustain on your own, and they leave you with enough energy in reserve to chat with friends.

We're social creatures. Enjoying the company of like-minded people can make any day better. Being able to share an experience with others makes it that much more enjoyable, much like the conversation over a good meal. I frequently tell people that I don't exercise; I just go out to play with my friends. No matter how fast a ride is, it never really feels like work, as the doing is so fun.

Back to that notion of a guide. It used to be that each bike shop was affiliated with a local club. The club elders were steeped in cycling lore and taught the new riders the ropes. Before novice riders had cycle computers, heart rate monitors, wattage devices, and training manuals, they had to depend on tips from a club's most experienced riders. You listened or you got dropped—at first, both. Today, with so much information to be found in books and magazines and on the Web, anyone can find training advice enough to achieve great fitness. But information on what is necessary to ride in a group is still woefully lacking.

The body of knowledge necessary to be a competent roadie is surprisingly broad. I've agonized over what and how much to include. From an array of riding skills to basic maintenance and training, there are some basics every rider needs to master. There are far more that many cyclists find interesting, though aren't necessary to the experience. I've chosen to include what is truly necessary—choosing a bike, riding skills, maintenance, diet, etc.—as well as a bit of material that isn't life or death, but that which many riders may find pretty fascinating, such as bike geometry, gearing, and a who's who of the great racers and events.

Cyclists who ride road bikes have practices and phrases all their own. They're called "roadies"; call one a "biker" and they're apt to correct you. Hang out with a bunch of them at a coffee shop after the ride is over, and you'll hear talk of attacks, blowing up, gaps, and holding wheels. This funny code holds meaning for those engaged in the rides and races of the sport. Each ride begins with a warm-up and every week includes a recovery ride. *The No-Drop Zone* was written to decode the terminology, explain the practices, and get you up to speed more quickly to make the sport as enjoyable and safe as possible.

I asked a number of experts for their input. In each instance, what I told them is that the book would serve as Road Cycling 101. *The No-Drop Zone* isn't the last word on anything, but it should serve as the first word on everything a rider needs to know.

Rather than present my own views on everything from frame materials to etiquette, I have attempted to convey the attitudes and opinions broadly held by industry leaders and strong riders in the peloton. I've done my best to avoid anything controversial while accurately portraying some of the hard-won experiences of cyclists with whom I've ridden.

In social situations, when people find out I'm a cyclist, they naturally start asking questions. What is the attraction to cycling, given that I shave my legs, wear Lycra, and share the roads with SUVs? I tell them that riding in a peloton is as much fun as you can have with people you're not married to. The No-Drop Zone is that perfect spot in any group where you're sheltered from the wind, chatting with a friend and seeing the beautiful world around you. It's the ideal reward for experience. I hope that you'll find groups to ride with, make new friends, achieve new levels of fitness, and find a fresh way to explore the world around you. Good luck!

—Patrick Brady

Section I
The Experience

Chapter 1
What Is Road Cycling?

One spring day 20 years ago, I met some friends for my first-ever group ride. I'd done plenty of riding with other people, but this was different. There were eight cyclists and most of them were racers, a distinction to me as significant as doctor or lawyer.

Rather than a leisurely cruise through the country roads at the edge of town, I learned that this would be a serious training ride complete with pacelines. What a paceline was, I had no idea, but the guys were patient with me and showed me how to slip in behind another rider to take advantage of his draft, which saves an incredible amount of effort. Later, they taught me how to ride in the paceline's rotating formation, where each cyclist leads the group for mere seconds before ducking back into the shelter of other riders.

I ventured a brief look down at my bicycle's speedometer and realized I'd been riding at speeds I could scarcely reach on my own, much less maintain for miles at a time. The coordination was fluid grace, like a ballet on wheels.

To say I was hooked is an understatement. For me, the experience wasn't just a bike ride—it was a triumph. The ride was physical and got my heart racing, yes, but it also required the fine motor control of a gifted performer. Then there was the camaraderie that came from enjoying the company of other riders, sharing the workload, coordinating movements that were both strenuous and taken with the utmost care for our mutual safety.

Amusement parks can only wish they were this exhilarating.

What I flashed on during my drive home was the first day I rode a bicycle on my own. When I realized that the adult holding me up had let go and I was actually pedaling a bicycle fast enough to balance it on my own, the adrenalin electrified my body. It was, relative to my short life, the coolest thing I had ever done.

Riding in a group was that thrill all over again.

For many of you, learning to ride your bicycle also changed your life immeasurably. Your first mastery over a machine. Parental limitations notwithstanding, the big world became noticeably smaller. Plus you got your first big, deep breath of freedom. Like starting school, learning to ride a bicycle was a big step toward your entry into the world.

Your first taste of the independence that cycling offered was probably not your last. From a single-speed bike with 16- or 20-inch wheels, you graduated to a multigeared bike with 24- or 26-inch wheels. Your range grew beyond the neighborhood to school and farther.

And then you learned to drive.

Following your 16th birthday, if you rode a bicycle, there were only two reasons: Either you didn't have access to a car or you really loved cycling. That you are reading this now says a lot about the power of that first experience all those years ago.

Okay, so we have all ridden bicycles, but what is it that differentiates the road experience from other forms of cycling?

First, road cycling is a social activity that no other sport can match. You can chat with friends, eat and drink, and learn about upcoming features in the route.

Second, road cycling is a aerodynamic adventure, as the group forms a pack, known as a *peloton*, so that some riders can take shelter from the wind behind the other riders in a move known as *drafting*.

Drafting is the defining experience of road cycling. The simple act of following another rider's wheel speaks of trust, skill, and a workload shared. When you follow another rider's wheel, it is possible to save more than a third of your energy output. Most of the energy you expend is devoted to overcoming wind resistance, so when riders work together they can increase speed and conserve energy. This gives you the opportunity to go farther and faster.

To the uninitiated, drafting looks both difficult and dangerous. It is neither. With the information contained in this book, you will be able to develop the knowledge and skills necessary to ride with groups and take the draft.

The drop handlebar offers three primary hand positions so riders can vary their position on the bike to increase comfort as well as respond to changes in riding conditions. The multigeared drivetrain lets a rider optimize his or her pedal cadence over a broad range of speed and terrain. And the high saddle position and aerodynamic position seating enable a rider to pedal as efficiently as possible.

These features define a road bike as we know it today, but it wasn't always so. The high-wheelers of the 19th century, the great-grandfather of our road bike, were remarkably different. The rider sat nearly upright, and the bicycle had but one gear. The earliest bicycles even lacked brakes. To stop, a rider had to attempt to pedal backward, exerting force in the direction opposite the motion of the pedals. The frame was constructed from steel tubing that might be used in plumbing; it was heavy-gauge and yielded such a harsh ride that such bikes were often referred to as "bone rattlers." Unfortunately, the early tires afforded no refuge; they were solid rubber.

But time marches on, or in this case, rolls on. Over the decades, with improvements in design, manufacturing, materials, and, it should be said, road surface, the road bike has evolved to its current sleek, efficient form.

What Is a Road Bike?

The contemporary road bike is as different from other bicycles as a Formula 1 race car is from a sport utility vehicle (SUV). Stripped down to its most basic characteristics, the road bike features the following:

❶ Large-diameter (roughly 29-inch) wheels equipped with skinny (less than 1-inch-wide) high-pressure tires

❷ A drivetrain with 18 or more gears

❸ A high saddle position that allows significant leg extension

❹ A "drop" handlebar that is often equal to or lower than the saddle height, resulting in an aerodynamic upper-body position.

Certainly, the details are more numerous than that, but these features are necessary in order to allow cyclists to meet the criteria necessary to ride in a group. The large-diameter wheels with narrow (25-millimeter), high-pressure (100–130 psi) tires offer the low rolling resistance that leads to maintaining speeds above 20 miles per hour (mph).

A top-of-the-line road bike: the Specialized Tarmac with Shimano's electronic Di2 group.

Other Types of Bicycles

There are more types of bicycles than you might imagine. In addition to road bikes, there are bicycles with a variety of purposes.

BMX

With its 20-inch wheels, single speed, and unforgiving saddle, the BMX bike is truly the domain of kids. Nimble and meant for riding out of the saddle, it got its start in short races; BMX is shorthand for Bicycle Motocross. They were designed for competing on dirt tracks that mimic those raced in motorcycling motocross. It gained immortality in the film *E.T.* and has since become a preferred tool of the antigravity set competing at the X Games.

BMX bikes were conceived as the kids' bicycle answer to dads' motocross motorcycles.

Cruiser

If your idea of a bike ride is going for an easy pedal through the neighborhood, the cruiser is as relaxing as cycling gets. With one gear, a coaster (or "kick") brake, a relaxing upright position, and handling like a limo, the cruiser is the perfect antidote to the blahs.

Cruisers are ideal for leisurely rides.

Mountain Bike

The mountain bike was invented as a way to ride terrain too rough for lightweight road bikes. The mountain bike took the broad gearing and powerful brakes from touring bikes (more on those later) and combined them with a flat handlebar, shocks to minimize the bumps, and fat, knobby tires. *Voilà*—a whole new sport.

For off-road riding, nothing is quite as much fun as a proper mountain bike.

Hybrid

Bike companies introduced hybrids to combine the plentiful gears and upright riding position of mountain bikes with narrower, high-pressure tires to yield a bike truly appropriate for road and bike-path use. With its upright bar, soft grips, and a big saddle, a hybrid is a bike anyone can ride comfortably.

Part road bike, part mountain bike, hybrids combine plentiful gears and powerful brakes with smooth, high-pressure tires.

City

Bikes styled like the old English three-speeds are making a comeback for short-range commuting and errands. In this modern incarnation, city bikes have been updated with aluminum frames, lightweight components, internally geared hubs, fenders, and racks or baskets to make carrying a load easy.

For those who love traditional three-speeds, today's city bikes combine easy functionality with around-town convenience.

Road bikes combine a comfortable fit with aerodynamic efficiency for an ideal blend of speed and endurance.

Why It Is Designed the Way It Is

The purpose of a road bike is to give a rider the optimal tool for riding as efficiently as possible both alone and with a group. Today's road bike resulted from intense competition among riders and among manufacturers. It's a Darwinian example of descent with modification. Advances in metallurgy, engineering, and knowledge of aerodynamics, and even our awareness of biomechanics and improved training methods, have produced an amazing result. Road bikes today weigh less, include more gears, stop better, handle more nimbly, are easier on the body, and increase efficiency when compared with bikes made at the beginning of the last century. For proof, check the average speeds of the Tour de France: in 1903, the race averaged 16 mph; in 2005, Lance Armstrong set a record average speed of 25.9 mph.

Chapter 2
Basic Riding Skills

It sounds strange, but there's more to riding a bike than riding a bike. That is, while nearly anyone can swing a leg over and pedal off down the block, certain skills make riding the bike easier and safer, both in groups and/or solo in traffic. Cyclists and drivers alike find sharing the road easier if your movements are smooth and predictable.

To have complete control over your movements, you need to be balanced on your bike. You should feel as secure sitting on the saddle and coasting along as you do when you are standing on solid ground. The more relaxed you are on the bike, and the more second-nature your movements are, the less riding a bike in traffic or a group will seem death-defying, which, as it turns out for most of us, isn't something we always equate with fun.

Combining a bicycle's symmetry with the rider's tendencies, many operations such as starting, stopping, coasting/descending, and drinking will be performed favoring either your left or right side. Rather than try to perfect ambidextrous operation of the bike, it's more helpful for most riders to become comfortable with their own preferences. To find out which foot you are more comfortable positioning forward, try a little experiment: Go kick a ball. Unless you happen to play for Manchester United, you probably prefer to kick with one foot rather than the other. Just as most people are either left- or right-handed, most folks are left- or right-footed.

Most people prefer to stand on their left foot and kick with their right. Most riders with this preference also find that they are more comfortable positioning their left foot forward when the cranks are level. This will make a difference when starting, coasting/descending, and stopping. Knowing which foot is dominant will increase your comfort and confidence while riding your bicycle.

Balance

Many people mistakenly believe that you must balance a bicycle to keep it upright while riding. The centrifugal force generated by two spinning bicycle wheels creates a significant gyroscopic effect. Once a bicycle is in motion and going more than 5 or 6 mph, it is inclined to stay upright and to keep rolling in the same direction. Even if you find yourself in a situation that tests your confidence, the combination of momentum and gyroscopic effect will keep your bicycle upright and traveling straight.

On a road bike, your center of gravity shifts constantly as you shift position. This ever-shifting location can generally be defined as just forward of your navel. It is lowest when your hands are in the drops and highest when you stand with your hands on the tops of the brake levers, or "hoods." As a result, applying pressure at your feet in order to shift your weight at your pelvis gives you more control over the bicycle. That's because whether on or off a bike, wherever your pelvis goes, you go.

When you stand on flat ground, you center your weight between your two feet. On a bicycle, you do the same thing when you put your weight on both pedals and the cranks are level (parallel to the ground).

Weighting your pedals is a critical part of controlling your bicycle. If you've ever seen someone try to start by pushing off without either foot on the pedals, it's generally a wobbly affair. Of the three points of contact you have with a bicycle—at the bar, the saddle, and the pedals—the pedals are the most critical for control, as they allow you to establish how your weight is distributed on the bike. The more you can do to control how your weight is distributed on your bike, the more confidence you will feel as you ride.

Determining which foot you naturally balance on will tell you which foot should be positioned forward any time you coast for optimal weight distribution and handling.

How to Start, Clip in, and Stop

Riding with clipless pedals is a lot like skateboarding with your feet duct-taped to the board. Clipless pedals take some getting used to, but once you feel comfortable "clipping in," you'll be amazed at how much more power goes directly to the bike. The first thing you have to do is learn how to clip in and clip out. A stationary trainer that holds your bike steady while allowing you to pedal can be helpful. Alternatively, you can position your bike in a doorway and practice by backpedaling. Try pedaling for a minute, stop, turn your heel outward, and clip out. Each time, slide off your saddle and touch your foot to the ground before starting again. This practice will serve you well on the road.

The first place you'll see your increased efficiency is in starting from a standstill. New riders will frequently push off multiple times, with one foot kicking at the ground as if they were using a scooter. There's an easier way.

Clip your dominant foot into the pedal—we'll assume it's your left. Bring the pedal up to the 11 o'clock position. Now, rather than kicking off with your foot that is on the ground and trying to find purchase with a decidedly slippery cleat, push off slightly with your right foot while making a forceful pedal stroke down with your left foot. This will quickly generate enough momentum so you can pedal a few strokes and then clip in your right foot.

Clipping in your second foot should be done with that pedal positioned at 12 o'clock—the top of the pedal stroke, which means that the foot already clipped in will be at 6 o'clock—the bottom of the pedal stroke. This pressure on the opposite pedal will make clipping in easier.

Clipless pedals increase a rider's safety and control.

Many pedal systems (such as Look, Time, and Shimano) work by hooking the front lip of the cleat into the pedal and stepping down to overcome the retention spring and lock the cleat in place. With these pedals, the rear of the pedal is weighted to keep the front of the pedal up and easy to catch with the cleat. To engage the cleat, start with the toe of the shoe behind the pedal and slide it forward across the pedal. The lip of the cleat should catch the pedal; begin the downstroke of the pedal and the cleat should engage.

Other pedal systems (for example, Speedplay and Crank Brothers) work by simply stepping down on top of the pedal. With Speedplay and Crank Brothers pedals, just line the cleat up on top of the pedal and step down squarely.

With a bit of practice, clipping in the second foot becomes automatic.

No matter what pedal system you use, it's important to avoid looking down at your pedal when rolling out. Keep your head up and eyes forward so that you can avoid obstacles as well as other riders if you are on a group ride.

When stopping, clip out your nonleading (or -kicking) foot. Because your leading foot is the one you balance on when kicking a ball, leaving it clipped in will give you more control and balance when one foot is clipped out. Many new riders fall over as they ride up to stoplights

Clip out before you come to a stop and you'll never fall over.

the first few times because they are indecisive about which foot to clip out. If you know that you will always clip out your right foot, that moment of indecision at low speed will be eliminated.

The art of efficiently clipping in and out can sound a bit complicated, but remember, just like the steps involved in starting a car and pulling out of a parking spot, all those seemingly complicated steps become a fluid sequence after a few rides.

Hold Your Line

Most of your time on a bike is spent going perfectly straight. Today's road bike, though, is a marvel of agility. It can handle instantaneous changes in direction for turns tighter than cars can handle, no matter the speed. There's just one issue: Making swoopy turns doesn't apply to the straight road.

Most of your time riding will be spent pedaling down straight roads or at least roads with only slight to moderate bends. The ability to ride in a straight line without constantly weaving left or right like a drunk heading for the door of a bar is called "holding your line."

Because a bicycle must share space with cars when on the road, it is important to show drivers that you can and will control your bike by behaving reasonably and predictably. The more you do to inform drivers of your intentions, the less stressful sharing the road is. The more predictable your riding is, the calmer everyone around you will be. It may seem counterintuitive to use such an agile instrument for going straight, like using a scalpel to cut butter, but road bikes are designed to do what you need when you need it.

If you are riding to the right side of the road in a straight line, a driver might reasonably expect that you will continue to do so. If a

The ability to ride in a smooth, straight line is called holding your line.

rider is swerving in and out of driveways and occasionally veering into the second lane of traffic, most drivers won't know how to interpret the cyclist's erratic riding and will take the first opportunity to speed by.

Here are some tips to keep in mind as you work on holding your line:

- Keep your upper-body (arms, shoulders, neck, and back) relaxed; avoid moving your shoulders in rhythm with your pedal stroke.

- Grip the handlebar or lever hoods lightly; don't do the death grip.

- Look up the road; don't stare right ahead of your front wheel.

Pedal in Circles

Pedaling in circles requires some practice. Most of us learned to ride a bicycle equipped with traditional platform pedals. As a result, we learned to pedal a bicycle by pushing down on the pedals. The vast majority of all road bikes are equipped with clipless pedals that allow you to generate power through a much greater portion of the pedal stroke than if you just pushed down on the pedals.

If you were to watch a rider pedal with platform pedals from his right, you would see the rider's leg muscles begin to tense to apply power at the 2 o'clock position. Maximum power is achieved almost immediately and continues until the 5 o'clock position. Beyond 5 o'clock, power wanes severely. Because the rider is limited to pedaling on the downstroke, cyclists refer to this as "pedaling boxes."

If you were to watch a rider pedal with clipless pedals from his right, you would see the rider's leg muscles begin to tense to apply power at the 11 o'clock position. Power would increase through the pedal stroke until maximum power is achieved around 2 o'clock and continues until the 5 o'clock position. Beyond 5 o'clock, power wanes some but doesn't drop off completely, and most riders will continue to generate power through the 7 o'clock position. Highly experienced riders experience only a slight dead spot in their pedal stroke between 9 and 10 o'clock.

While it's not necessary for you to pedal perfect circles, using this pedal technique results in certain benefits. First, by using more and different muscles in your legs, you can reduce fatigue and generate more power with each pedal stroke.

No one has a perfectly circular pedal stroke, but applying force through as much of the pedal stroke as possible saves energy.

Here are some tips to keep in mind as you work to pedal in circles:

- Practice moving your feet through a circle; don't just push the pedals down.

- At the bottom of the pedal stroke, visualize yourself scraping mud off the sole of your shoe; don't let your foot just hang.

- Try to visualize your pedal stroke as applying continuous power through the entire revolution; don't think of it as alternating left, right.

Watch Your Cadence

A high pedal cadence is beneficial for many reasons. Having a computer with a cadence meter can quantify your pedal stroke. Studies of trained cyclists have shown that the most efficient pedal stroke—one that generates the most power relative to heart rate and lactic acid production—occurs between 80 and 110 rpm.

By riding with a high cadence that you can comfortably maintain, the workload is on your aerobic system—heart and lungs—rather than your muscles. This preserves your strength and helps to increase your endurance.

Here are some tips to keep in mind as you work to increase your cadence:

- Concentrate on maintaining a smooth pedal stroke rather than pedaling boxes.

- Try to increase your speed by increasing your cadence; don't just shift.

- Watch for "hopping" in your pedal stroke; don't allow your rear to rise off the saddle.

When to Shift

Knowing when to shift will increase your efficiency. Because most road bikes are equipped with 20-gear drivetrains, the average rider has enough gears to maintain a reasonable cadence from 8 to 40 mph. Effective shifting capitalizes on your momentum so that you can generate power as smoothly and efficiently as possible. One of the quickest—and surest—ways to rob yourself of momentum is to wait too long to shift gears.

No matter what road bike you are on, the left shifter will always operate the front derailleur, shifting between the two or three chainrings next to the cranks. The right shifter will always operate the rear derailleur, shifting among as many as 11 cogs on the rear wheel. How each type of shifter operates is covered in Chapter 12.

The key to shifting is anticipation. If you wait to shift until you feel your cadence slow, then you will already have lost momentum. The point behind having a 20-gear drivetrain is to make each shift the smallest possible change in gearing.

The terminology of shifting can get a little confusing. *Upshifting* is what you do when you want to accelerate. Upshifting is shifting into a

With the shifter controls placed right where your hands are, you can change gears any time you need.

smaller cog on your rear wheel, which generates greater speed if you maintain the same cadence. *Downshifting* is shifting into a larger cog, which means less speed, and less effort, at a given cadence. Downshifting is what you do when you get to the base of a climb.

Here are some tips to keep in mind when you shift:

- When upshifting, shift only one cog at a time, and wait until you feel spun out of that gear before shifting again. The shifter for the rear derailleur is at your right hand.

- When downshifting, shift before you experience a noticeable loss in momentum; as soon as you feel an increase in pitch, downshift.

- Shift chainrings (either up or down) any time there is a significant change in terrain. Reaching the foot of a big hill or beginning a descent are natural times to shift from one chainring to another. The shifter for your front derailleur is at your left hand.

Brakes on today's road bikes offer much more stopping power than they used to.

How to Brake

A road bike can stop in a short distance if you know how to brake properly. Today's brakes are significantly better than the brakes that the pros used only 20 years ago. In those days, brakes were considered a way to alter speed, not stop on a dime. Today, stopping can be more easily controlled, thanks to the increase in mechanical braking power and pad technology.

Most of us had a childhood experience that taught us the power of the front brake, an experience that may not have ended well, as flying over the handlebars is neither safe nor fun. As a result, many riders tend to favor the rear brake over the front. ***This is exactly the opposite of ideal braking technique.***

As you brake, your momentum shifts the majority of your weight onto your front wheel. As a result, most of your bike's braking power is concentrated on the front wheel.

Consider an example in the extreme: If a rider moving at 20 mph locks up his rear wheel, the bike will skid to a stop because most of the rider's weight is already ahead of the rear wheel. The rear wheel will,

in effect, be dragged behind the rider like a plow. Effective, but hard on tires.

If that same rider locks up his front wheel, due to a relatively high center of gravity, the bike will simply pivot on the axis of the front wheel, unceremoniously depositing the rider on the ground.

For maximum control in the shortest possible stopping distance, the best approach is to apply the brake levers with equal pressure. At a certain point under hard braking, the rear wheel will lock up. Once you have experienced this a few times, you will be aware of approaching that point. Once you have a feel for it, if after slowing you still need to increase braking force, try increasing pressure only on the front brake. Or increase the weight on the rear wheel—which will allow you to brake even harder—by pushing your butt back off the rear of the saddle.

Here are some tips to keep in mind when you brake:

- Light to medium braking: Apply both brakes equally.

- Hard, fast braking: Increase force on only the front brake.

When to Use Each Hand Position

A road bike's drop handlebar has three primary hand positions: the bar top, the lever hoods, and the drops. The various positions offer riders three different options for optimal efficiency for multiple kinds of riding, as well as the opportunity to move their hands to avoid discomfort caused by keeping your hands in one spot for too long.

Lever hoods

The hoods of the integrated brake–shift levers offer the most versatile of all hand positions on a drop handlebar. First and foremost, the position gives riders excellent control over the bike with shift and brake controls right at the fingertips. The position offers a fairly aerodynamic ride while maintaining a high enough body position to see adequately. This is the most comfortable position for long, flat miles.

The hoods are the ideal location from which to make out-of-the-saddle efforts such as climbing and brief accelerations. They also offer a good position to work from for shallower climbs.

In a survey of Tour de France riders, the vast majority of riders said the lever hoods were their favorite position, offering the greatest versatility. If they had but one position to use, the hoods would be it.

Bar top

The top of the bar offers riders the most upright seated position. Ultimately, it is also the most comfortable position, but it does sacrifice some aerodynamic advantage. This position also sacrifices some leverage and control of the handlebar, making it less than desirable for situations that require fine control over the bike, such as when riding in a speeding pack or going downhill.

The position also lacks the ability to reach the shift and brake levers. To shift or brake, a rider must move a hand to the lever, and any delay can make even an ordinary situation a little dicey.

Though the position compromises control, it is popular with riders who are doing slower recovery rides and when climbing. The more-upright position reduces stress on the shoulders and neck but also increases a rider's ability to deliver power to the pedals for climbing. Climbing is further aided by the rider's upright position as it opens the chest, making deep breathing easier.

Out-of-the-saddle efforts from the bar tops result in a position that is compromised in both handlebar control and weight distribution, making the bike difficult to control. It's a bit like trying to drive a car from the roof.

To most riders, the most comfortable place for your hands is on the lever hoods.

Riding on the bar top is comfortable thanks to the upright position it offers.

Drops

The drops are the least used of all handlebar positions. They are the most specialized of the positions, offering excellent control at high speed. Of the three hand positions, the drops distribute more weight on the front wheel for maximum traction in hard cornering.

Riding in the drops is useful for hard efforts on flat terrain where aerodynamics can make a big difference in speed, on descents when fine control is necessary at high speed, and during out-of-the-saddle sprints when maximum finishing power is needed.

The shift and brake levers remain an easy reach from the drops.

The drops are the ideal hand position for aerodynamic riding, sprinting, and descending.

How to Climb

With a road bike, the saddle is the place to be. Unlike a kid's BMX bike in which the saddle is really only used when the rider isn't moving, roadies don't stand much. Remember, the road bike is all about efficiency, and staying in the saddle is the most efficient way to ride. The more you conserve your energy, the more energy you'll have either later in the ride or later in the day once you are off the bike.

Seated climbing combines great power with a relaxed upper-body position.

On all but the shortest hills, you can generate sustained power most efficiently if you stay in the saddle. Keep your hands on the bar top, and sit up as much as possible to enable deep breathing. Use a small gear to keep your cadence up; if you use too large a gear, your speed will drop.

Many new cyclists become frustrated on long climbs when they see their speed cut by half or more. Be patient as you climb. Climbing is a matter of finding the highest pace you can sustain. If you go all-out at the bottom of a hill, you are likely to blow up—that is, reach the aerobic limit of your muscles—and then need to slow way down so you can recover. Avoid this mistake by starting at a reasonable pace. Then gradually increase your pace until you feel you are at your limit.

When to Get Out of the Saddle

Standing up requires a lot of energy, which is why you will spend most of your time in the saddle. When you stand, your heart rate shoots up, so it's not the sort of effort that can be sustained for long periods of time. There are times, however, when it's appropriate to stand up and deliver a big burst of energy. Generally speaking, most cyclists can only sustain a full-power out-of-the-saddle effort for 10–15 seconds.

The two reasons to get out of the saddle are for powerful bursts of climbing or for a sprint on flat ground.

Climbing

Standing up on a climb gives you the opportunity to use your full body weight to turn the pedals over. Short, steep hills and short, steeper sections of longer climbs are where this technique can be useful.

Position your hands on the lever hoods to keep your chest open for deep breathing. This position also offers optimal weight distribution for maximum control. Position your shoulders over the handlebar to keep your hips back and sufficient weight on the rear wheel. If your shoulders move ahead of the handlebar, you risk spinning the rear wheel on steeper terrain or any hills with loose sand or gravel.

For maximum power on a short hill, standing is the way to go.

Sprinting

An all-out sprint is generally reserved for the end of the ride or race. Many group training rides have a known sprint line that allows riders to practice sprinting in a group. A sprint effort can also be useful for bridging a gap to riders who are ahead of you or for leaving a group you are with.

Position your hands in the drops and keep your shoulders down and over the handlebar for maximum aerodynamic efficiency and optimal weight distribution for maximum control. If your shoulders move ahead of the handlebar, you risk bouncing the rear wheel.

Even if you never hope to win a race, a good sprint will help you accelerate the bike to near-traffic speeds.

How to Corner

Cornering on a bicycle is a pretty intuitive process. Your body figured how to maintain control while turning ages ago; however, you may not understand the principles at work. The fact is; when cornering, you don't actually steer the bicycle. That is, unless you are moving at very slow speeds—for example, less than 8 mph—speeds low enough that the bike remains almost perfectly upright. When cornering at typical riding speeds, you are, in fact, countersteering.

Countersteering is just like it sounds: It is the opposite of steering. You've probably noticed that any time you turn you lean in the direction of the turn. This is the primary effect of countersteering. Suppose you want to turn right. By turning the handlebar slightly to the left, the front wheel is shifted left of your center of gravity. This initiates a lean to the right. Once the bike is leaning to the right, it turns right, the same way a skier or skateboarder would. Ending the turn requires steering the front wheel back under you to bring the bike upright, something we learned to do unconsciously years ago.

The turn's radius (its tightness) is controlled by two factors: your countersteering and your weight distribution. How you weight the pedals will help determine how the bike corners.

The most common mistake new riders make in cornering is to drop the inside pedal. A rider who doesn't understand the principles of countersteering will effect a weight shift to lean the bike in the direction of the low pedal. Unfortunately, this can result in the pedal hitting the ground, which can result in a crash. Even when it doesn't result in grinding the pedal on the ground, with so much weight shifted in the direction of the turn, oversteering—turning too sharply—can result.

Before you can take a corner at speed, you need to figure out how you prefer to coast. This is another reason to know which of your feet is

Countersteering is the art of turning the bike away from the corner in order to make a sharp turn.

dominant. By putting your dominant foot forward, you can better shift your weight from side to side to control the lean angle of the bicycle.

Keeping the cranks level will help you control your weight distribution as you corner. If you have ever ridden with no hands on the bar, then you already know you can control the bike by shifting your weight on the pedals and saddle.

How to Look over Your Shoulder

To get the fullest picture of what is behind you, you need to be able to look over your shoulder. Looking over your shoulder accomplishes two things: First, it gives you a clear picture of how many cars are present. Second, it shows drivers you are aware of the traffic and will be less likely to make a sudden turn into traffic.

The trick to looking over your shoulder is to keep the bike pointed straight while your head and shoulders are twisted to the left. Sounds easy enough, but the hardwiring in our brains is such that where your eyes are pointed, your head tends to follow. And wherever your head points, the body tends to follow.

To overcome this tendency, pick a road with little traffic and a painted shoulder line. Try riding a few inches to the right of the shoulder line with your hands on the top of the bar. Next, twist your head and shoulders to the left

When you look over your shoulder, keep your hips straight and the bike won't turn.

while continuing to look forward. Remove your left hand from the bar and keep your body centered over the bike—do not lean as you twist. Many riders will put their left hand on their hip as they twist.

You will likely drift to the left as you twist your head and shoulders. With some practice, you'll find that you can twist without drifting. The next step is to simply look back quickly, just like checking the blind spot when you drive. If traffic is heavy or moving quickly, you may want to look back twice in quick succession. Your first priority, of course, is to remain aware of what is directly ahead of you.

Your peripheral vision is absolutely key to this maneuver and riding safely in general. Compared with driving a car, you have more unobstructed view, and remaining both vigilant and observant will make this move safer and increase your awareness overall. Likewise, along with the unobstructed view, your sense of hearing is heightened because you're not encased in a car. You'll soon learn to recognize the sound of traffic approaching from the rear and can steer accordingly. Supplementing a look back over your shoulder with vigilant listening will dramatically improve your safety on the road.

Chapter 3
Group Riding Skills

Cycling is a marvelous solitary activity. It can offer a way to get away from life's stresses and give you more than just a workout. Group riding, however, is when life as a roadie really becomes fun.

Riding with a group presents cycling as almost a different sport. While riding alone your nose is always in the wind; riding in a group presents a number of benefits:

- You will cover more ground in the same amount of time.
- You will learn new routes.
- You will make new friends.
- You will be pushed to a new level of fitness.
- You will hone your bike-handling skills.

How to Ride in a Paceline

The first step toward riding in a group is learning to draft another rider. Drafting can cut your effort by a third—sometimes more—depending on how close you follow the rider ahead of you and how large that rider is. The bigger the rider, the better the draft. The best way to learn how to draft is to ride in a paceline—and they come in three flavors.

Single Pacelines

The simplest form of group riding to learn is the single paceline. Single pacelines are usually made up of a small group of riders—they can be hard to keep organized with more than 10 or 12 riders. Your turn at the front is like playing locomotive to a train and it is called "taking a pull." This isn't literal, of course, but your effort is referred to as your "pull."

After pulling at the front for a period of time (some groups might choose 30 seconds, a minute, or more depending on speed, fitness, or other factors such as traffic), the rider will "pull off," meaning the rider moves either to the left or right out of the line and drops to the back of the group. In this version, riders line up single-file and the rider at the front pulls the group for a period of time (again, the length of time may be dictated by speed, fitness, or road conditions) and then rotates off and drops back. For the safety of the group, it is generally best to pull off to the left after checking the traffic behind the group.

The pace should remain consistent when you get to the front. If the pace is high—higher than you are accustomed to—it is preferable to take a shorter pull at the higher pace than a longer pull at a slower pace. Do not slow until you have pulled off, that is, until you have moved far enough to the left or right that the rider just behind you may pass unimpeded. When you drop back, begin to accelerate when you are even with the last rider so that you move smoothly into that rider's draft. If you wait to accelerate until that rider is ahead of you, you are likely to have trouble getting back into his draft.

Riding in a paceline is easier to learn if the other riders are experienced. Initially, the most difficult skill to learn is how to keep a constant pace that matches the speed of the rider in front of you. Many riders try to learn with other inexperienced riders; it's nearly impossible to learn how to maintain a consistent pace if the rider you are following doesn't know how to do it either. A single paceline is an easier circumstance to learn in because if you find yourself gaining on the rider in front of you, you can move either to the left or right of the rider.

Try to maintain a distance of 3–6 feet behind the rider you follow. As you become more comfortable drafting, you can shrink that distance. Experienced cyclists can ride inches from the rider ahead of

Teamwork! A simple paceline can save you roughly one-third of your energy.

them. Most skilled riders will maintain a safety margin of a foot to the rider ahead. Try to limit your side-to-side distance from their line to a maximum of one foot to either side.

Peel off before you feel you need to. Until you have a clear picture of your fitness, keep your pulls short. If you wait to pull off until you feel tired, there's a good chance that you'll get spit out of the group rather than making it back into the paceline.

Double Pacelines

In a double paceline, riders are assembled in pairs. It is essentially two single rotating pacelines assembled side-by-side. The rider on the left will pull off to the left while the rider on the right will pull off to the right. After pulling at the front for a period of time (some groups might choose 30 seconds, a minute, or more depending on speed, fitness, or other factors such as lane width), the two riders will pull off simultaneously. They slow and allow themselves to be passed by the group before moving back into the rotation at the back of the group. Double pacelines are the best way to keep a large group orderly.

Maintain your pace when the rider in front of you pulls off. The big mistake new riders make is to accelerate when the riders in front of them pull off. Just as with the single rotating paceline, unless the group has agreed to accelerate, etiquette requires that the effort remain consistent. So while your effort will go up slightly because you no longer have a draft, the pace should not increase. Changes in terrain, such as what riders call a false flat (a slight uphill grade, almost imperceptible to the eye, but noticeable to a rider) or a slight downhill, can result in a change of pace; the point is to keep the effort level consistent.

Maintain a consistent distance to the rider next to you. Experienced riders will ride 1–3 feet from each other side-to-side. This distance is easy to maintain if you follow the line of the rider in front of you.

Stay even with the rider next to you. If you pull ahead or fall behind the rider next to you, that is called "half-wheeling." It is, in short, one of the cardinal sins of cycling. That disparity in distance will radiate through a group, making a mess of a previously orderly paceline. Worse yet, half-wheeling by pulling ahead can cause the group's pace to rise because as the rider being half-wheeled tries to pull level, the half-wheeling rider will often increase pace, perpetuating the problem.

Rotating Paceline

The rotating paceline is the most advanced of the pacelines. As a result, it requires the greatest care to execute. Like the single paceline, it is used with a smaller group of riders. This kind of paceline works best if the riders in the group are relatively evenly matched in ability. If there is a wide range of ability, it will be difficult to keep the rotation smooth.

The rotating paceline starts the same way as the single paceline. Riders begin in a single line. The difference is that riders pull off sequentially, with riders pulling off as soon as there is room to move to the side without brushing the front wheel of the rider dropping back.

One side of the rotation will move faster than the other. The rider at the front of the faster side

A rotating paceline takes a bit of skill and practice, but it's a terrific way to ride safely at speeds you can't maintain on your own.

will only pull as long as it takes to pass the rider in the other line, at which time he pulls off gradually. The rider he passes will call out "clear" when the passing rider's rear wheel is ahead of the passed rider's front wheel. Once in the slower line, the rider will gradually drop back until he can move into the other line. In particularly fast rotations after moving into the accelerating line, the rider will call out to the nearest rider, "last." This will help the rider anticipate the acceleration that is required to get back into the faster line.

As you move forward in the faster line, the rider ahead of you will become the rider you pass as you pull off. This rider will call "clear" to you. After you pull off, the rider that pulls in front of you will be the one you call "clear" to. When you get to the back of the rotation, the rider that previously called out "clear" to you will now call out "last." You will call out "last" for the rider ahead of you, the

one you called out "clear" to. When the procedure is done correctly, you'll always call out to the same rider and will be called to by the same rider.

If the rotation becomes disorganized, allow riders to rest briefly by going single-file. Once everyone has had a breather, you can begin the rotation again. Any accelerations should be gradual—don't increase the speed during your pull by more than 0.5 mph.

How to Ride in a Pack

A pack is what forms when a group of cyclists is too large to ride in an orderly paceline. Unless there is uniform consent about the kind of paceline, what the pace is, and how quickly the group should rotate, some rider will tire of riding sheltered in the group and head for the front with the desire to spice things up. One man's pleasant conversational pace is another man's funeral march. Likewise, one man's tempo pace is another man's absolute limit. Things get interesting in packs. Your first goal is to stay safe. Your second is to have fun and get fit.

Riding in a pack isn't as orderly as a paceline, but it can be as exhilarating as flying.

Hold your line. Holding your line is one of the most essential skills to riding in a group of cyclists. When riding alone, holding your line is considered relative to the construction of the road and obstacles in the road. In a pack, holding your line is considered relative to the rider in front of you. Picture how a school of fish swims—they turn as one and somehow, miraculously, do it without bouncing off each other. As the pack moves left and right relative to any roadside obstacles and through turns, it is important to follow the line ridden by the riders immediately in front of you.

Protect your front wheel. The easiest way to go down when riding in a group is to allow another rider's rear wheel to come into contact with your front wheel.

One of the most important skills when riding in a group is the ability to maintain your position relative to the riders to your left and right.

Imagine drawing a half circle with your front wheel that describes the bike's steering radius. Consider that roughly 3-foot-radius arc from left to right around your front wheel sacred. If someone moves into it, back away to protect your front wheel.

Getting dropped is part of life. Most riders gets dropped on their first few group rides. Many experienced riders will get dropped from early-season rides if their fitness is off. If you are new to a group ride, ask if there are regroup points and try to find out what the route is before you roll out. If you are unfamiliar with the roads in the area, carry a map with you, just in case. Be aware that most group rides don't sustain a high pace for all that long. If you can, maintain a high, but manageable, pace after you are dropped; it is possible the group's pace will drop and you'll be able to catch on to the group even before reaching a regroup point.

By protecting your front wheel you will be able to avoid contact that could cause a crash.

Don't worry; everyone gets dropped; don't give up, because most groups ease up, giving you a chance to rejoin.

Some positions in the group are better than others. Where you choose to be can determine how hard you work.

Beware the accordion effect. As the group accelerates and slows, the overall shape of the group will change. A group of riders 4 abreast and 8 deep can quickly become 16 riders in double file, or worse yet, 32 riders in single file. This is because not all riders will accelerate at the same time or the same pace. Delays in reaction time will result in the riders at the back beginning to accelerate after the riders at the front. To stay with them, the riders at the back must accelerate more sharply in order to make up that lost ground.

When slowing, the delay in reaction will cause the group to bunch up because the riders at the back will begin braking later than the riders at the front. For this reason, it is important that the riders at the front slow no more than necessary and stop no sooner than necessary. Should even one rider stop short, that lack of stopping distance for the riders behind can result in a crash.

Learn how to backslide. One way to avoid being dropped is to move up in the group before a big acceleration or big hill. This requires some knowledge of the ride, of course. By being near the front when the acceleration or hill comes, you have the ability to drop back through the group, much like pulling off the front of a paceline, and then hopefully the pace drops before you reach the back of the group, and the end of your rope. Many riders use stoplights to move near the front of the group in anticipation of a fast portion of the ride. Be aware that

Closing a gap to another rider can keep you from getting dropped.

many of the fastest, most experienced riders will object to you moving to the very front of the group if you aren't strong enough to help maintain the pace. When pulling up to a stoplight, it is better to move *near* the front than *to* the front.

Learn how to move up. For new riders, the easiest places to move up are at the edges of a group. It takes some time to begin to feel confident that you can move through gaps in the group as they open. Rather than trying to ride up to the front of the group with your nose in the wind, move to the outside of the group and wait for another rider to come by. Once a cyclist passes you, check over your shoulder quickly to make sure that rider's wheel is free, and hop on the express to the front.

Choose your position in the group. Where you position yourself in the group will determine how you need to ride to stay in the group. The strongest riders tend to ride at the very front of the group (the first 10 riders or so). If you are up there, you will be expected to take a pull and to be able to close a "gap." A gap is what riders call a space that is equal to the length of a bike. If there's room for a rider between you and the rider ahead of you, you are said to have left a gap.

The area near the front but out of that rotation of riders at the front is the position with the most even pace. Many riders will work just

hard enough to try to be near the front without actually being at the front for this reason; this also happens to be one of the safest places in the group. The middle of the group can be crowded but offers a terrific draft. Accelerations in the group's pace are more noticeable here. The back half of the group offers the best draft, but changes in pace can require violent accelerations.

Close gaps left by others. If you are in a rotation and the rider ahead of you pulls out, thereby leaving a gap of more than six feet, a quick way to make friends is to try to close the gap, provided you are strong enough to do so. If the pace is too high for your ability, give the rider a quick wave to indicate that you need some help. After signaling, pull out of the rotation and drop back.

Drink on the bike. If you are going to ride for more than an hour, you will need to drink some water to replace the fluid you lose through perspiration. If you are riding on your own or in a small group, there's nothing wrong with waiting until you stop to take a drink. If you are riding with a fast-moving group that seldom stops, it's important to drink as you are moving.

Drinking with one hand means you will be steering, shifting, and braking with the other hand. More than almost any other skill in this chapter, it is important you are comfortable grabbing, drinking from, and replacing the bottle without looking at what you are doing.

For maximum control, it's a good idea to drink with the left hand while controlling the bike with the right hand. Keeping your right hand on the bar gives you more control than you'll have with your left. If you need to shift gears as you drink, the rear derailleur (which is shifted with your right hand) offers finer adjustments in gearing. Similarly, if you need to brake suddenly, the rear brake offers more easily modulated braking power; a big fistful of rear brake won't send you over the bar the way the front brake can.

To meet your hydration needs, you will need to drink frequently as you ride.

Chapter 4
Advanced Skills

As you begin to do faster group rides with more challenging terrain and conditions, you will also find yourself riding in closer quarters to other riders. Some additional skills will be helpful to keep you safe and with the group. Developing these skills can be a lot of fun. Think of these as the E-ticket rides for roadies.

Descending

Descending uses the same countersteering technique you use to corner. It adds to this an extra dimension in speed. To control your bike at speed, you need a position that blends great control and aerodynamics. The ideal position is a tuck with your head low, your rear in the saddle, your hands in the drops, and your cranks level.

As your speed increases, so does the minimum radius of any turn you make. Put another way, the faster you go, the bigger the arc. For this reason, you need to choose your position in the lane before entering a turn. For a right-hand turn, set up as close to the center yellow lines as possible before entering the turn. Once you enter the turn, aim for the apex, the actual corner to your right; as you pass the apex, gradually allow yourself to swing back out to the yellow lines, thus giving you the

gentlest line through the corner and allowing you to carry maximum speed. For left-hand turns, the process works just the opposite: Set up as close to the edge of the road as possible and then apex at the center yellow lines followed by a swing back to the right edge.

Descending a mountain road can be terrific fun. Image: Patrick Brady

Joe Parkin is a former professional cyclist who spent four years racing in Europe and holds the distinction of being the only American to contest the World Championships on the road, mountain bike, and cyclocross. He says, "I like to keep my elbows bent and actually bend them more as I get closer to the apex. As I come out of the corner, I allow myself to sit up just a bit more. Using your inside leg as an outrigger of sorts helps get your bike and body set up for S-turns too—tossing the knee toward the corner really helps reweight everything before entering into the turn."

Make your turn as smooth as possible, because sudden turns or adjustments to your course can cause you to lose traction. You can use these same apexing techniques for corners you take above 20 mph.

Echelons

An echelon is a paceline for crosswinds. Think of it as a paceline blown sideways. The goal of any paceline is to keep the rider in front of you between you and the wind. The front rider stays in the same position as with a paceline, but the rest of the paceline shifts to hide from the blowing wind.

To perform an echelon, start with a rotating paceline (explained in Chapter 3). If the wind is from the right, riders will overlap wheels with the rider ahead of them to the left. Rather than a static response, an echelon is an on-the-fly response to the wind. As you feel the wind on your right side, you move left and up. In an extreme crosswind, where the wind is at almost 90 degrees to you, riders may be lined up almost side-by-side.

Think of an echelon as a paceline that has been blown sideways.

"It is important to keep yourself in the rotation," Parkin says, "even if you're not feeling up to it." As soon as you're back at the tail of the echelon, you're done for. Rotate to the front as smoothly as possible. In other words, don't up the pace—just keep it steady. If you speed up, the rider behind you will (or should) let you keep your nose out in the wind longer than you want. Similarly, as you're coming off your turn at the front, slow your pace just enough to fall back into the rotation as quickly as possible. Most importantly, if you find a hole in the echelon big enough to stick your front wheel into, do it. Do not wait for an invitation. Remember, the tail of the echelon is hell.

In a standard paceline, the direction of rotation doesn't matter much; either line of riders can be the line moving up. In an echelon, the idea is to rotate into the wind. The "front" line of riders moves in the direction of the wind, while the "rear" line of riders is moving away from the wind.

Because an echelon usually involves riding three—or more—abreast, it is illegal to perform on most roads. On closed courses such as can be found at organized events and races, it is legal. On country roads with little traffic it can often be performed safely, but riders should keep an eye on approaching traffic.

On a closed course, echelons can have as many riders, as the road's width can accommodate. For most amateur riders, though, an echelon usually starts to break down once it tries to accommodate more than 6 riders in width (about 12 riders total).

Touching

Strictly speaking, cycling is a contact-free sport. There are times, however, while riding in close quarters when riders may touch. Just as on dates, some touching may be welcome, while other touching isn't.

Tapping

There are times in the peloton when you may overlap wheels slightly. Should a rider begin to move toward your wheel, it's okay to give the rider a warning tap with your hand on their hip. Because calling out may not get the rider's attention or let the rider know where you are, physical contact makes the point clear. Don't shove; just a light tap with few fingers from your open hand to the let the rider know you are there is all that is required.

Pushing

On hilly rides, experienced riders will sometimes help a struggling newbie and offer to give a push to the top of the hill. If you get such an offer, remain seated, hold your line, maintain a firm grip on the bar, and keep pedaling. The acceleration will be a little sudden, but whatever you do, don't hit the brakes. Little pushes like this can make a huge difference on a long ride and can teach you more about riding in a group than getting dropped will. The first push is sometimes tough on the pride, but almost everyone has been there.

Parkin recalls, "As a *domestique,* I would often wait and ride with my various sprinter-type teammates on climbs, if the course profile suggested that the race might end in a big bunch-sprint. Even if they were riding well on the climb, I might give them a little push for the last kilometer or so before the summit. Every little rest counts."

If someone offers to give you a push, just remain seated and hold your line; the rest is easy.

Shoving

Cycling, like any sport, gets its share of overly aggressive athletes. In exceedingly rare instances, one rider will give another rider an angry shove. This behavior should never be tolerated by any group or club. Touching a rider anywhere other than the hips or lower back is unacceptable as it can cause a crash, which could bring down many riders. Should you receive a shove, make your first priority to stay upright. Following that, don't engage; just backslide through the group away from Mr. Aggro.

Parkin knows the feeling well. "I was in the front echelon of a semiclassic in Holland one time, rotating back to join the front line of the thing. A well-known pro, Jelle Nijdam, hesitated a bit too long so I jumped in front of him, causing him to nearly fall out of the rotation. The ensuing shove was followed by a punch that was so hard I think I still have the shape of his hand imprinted on my right butt cheek."

It is possible to bump into another rider and not fall down immediately.

Bumping

Bumping is different from touching in that it isn't usually deliberate. It usually occurs at the hips and handlebars. Hip-to-hip contact isn't usually much of a problem unless you receive a bump from a rider much larger than you. Stay loose and try to correct your line as quickly as possible. Handlebar-to-handlebar contact can be more problematic, as bars can become locked, sending both riders down. If you sense that riders are being squeezed together, move your hands to the drops, where the presence of your hands and forearms makes it harder to hook bars. Hip-to-handlebar contact is the most dangerous because a good bump from someone's hip can turn your bar, causing a crash. Should you get bumped in this way, try to keep your weight centered over the bike and steer the bike back under you immediately.

"The biggest mistake people make here is when they try to move away from the rider they have bumped into," says Parkin. "Try to lean toward the contact until you're both under control. Bob Roll and I used to ride so close together on training rides that our handlebars were almost always touching."

Touching Wheels

In rare instances, riders touch front wheel to rear wheel. The basic rule is that if the two riders are riding at roughly the same speed, the rider in back, whose front wheel has made contact, is the rider who goes down. If the rider in front is moving noticeably slower than the rider in back, they can both wind up on the ground.

Riding Hands-free

Riding with no hands on the bar is an essential skill every rider needs. On its own, the skill is a great education in how a bike corners and how you can control your bike simply by shifting your weight at the saddle and pedals. It is handy for adjusting zippers, glasses, and helmets on the fly.

When learning how to ride with no hands, make sure your speed is at least 15 mph. Move your hands to the bar top and then simply sit up straight. With practice you'll find that you can turn and even do upper-body stretches.

"My favorite *domestique* moment occurred during the Tour DuPont in 1994, when I was riding for the Coors Light team," Parkin reminisces. "One of my teammates wanted a Coke, but not in the can. In a very compact peloton going down a long descent at about 45 mph, I sat up and poured the contents of the can into his water bottle. I'm sad to say that I've probably done that kind of thing more times than I've been able to raise both hands high over my head for a victory salute."

The ability to ride with no hands can come in handy when you least expect it.

Eating

Once you know how to ride no-hands, you can eat while riding, which is an important skill if you want to avoid bonking. Begin by removing the bar or gel from your jersey pocket. Sit up quickly and tear the wrapper open. In the case of a bar, pull the wrapper down enough to expose the bar and then put one hand back on the handlebar.

Some rides don't stop much, so you may need to open a bar on the fly.

Dressing and Undressing

In many places, temperatures can change significantly over the course of the day. Morning riders may find themselves stripping off arm warmers and vests as the day heats up, while some riders may find a need to add these pieces in the afternoon. Similarly, you may need to strip off pieces at the bottom of a long climb or put them back on at the top when you begin the descent.

Frankly, undressing is the easier of the two. With arm warmers, hook your thumb over the top hem and pull it down to your wrist. Sit up briefly and pull it off over your glove. Put one hand back on the bar and stuff the arm warmer into the nearest pocket. Repeat. Be careful to pull the arm warmer forward off your hand and not sideways. If you pull sideways you risk hitting another rider and crashing.

In some places, temperatures can go from hot to cold and back again based on the terrain. Sometimes it can be most helpful to just push the arm warmers down to your wrists for the climb and then pull them back up for the descent if the climb isn't too long and you don't anticipate stopping at the top.

Removing a vest requires sitting up a little longer. Begin by unzipping the vest with one hand. Sit up and grab each side of the front of the vest with each hand (left side with left hand, right side with right hand). Pull the vest straight backward; do not pull down, as it may get hooked on your shoulders. Once it's over the shoulders, pull one hand out of the armhole and bring the vest in front of you. Quickly wad it up and stuff it in your center pocket. You may need to hold the pocket open with your other hand to stuff it down.

Jackets follow the same method as vests, but because of the addition of arms, it is easier to get fabric caught in the drivetrain or rear wheel; there's also more pulling involved in getting the arms out of the sleeves. If you know you'll take it off during the ride and you may not have a chance to stop to take it off, a vest is safer.

Putting arm warmers on isn't too hard; you just have to give a firm pull to get the arm warmer over your gloved hand and be sure to hold your arm forward and pull back toward your body.

Should you be on a ride that isn't stopping much or for long and you need to put on a vest, proceed with caution. Pull the vest out of your pocket and give it a shake to open it. Sit up and bring it in front of you to make sure it isn't tangled—the zipper will sometimes catch on an armhole. Put one arm through an armhole. Reach behind your head and take the collar with both hands, and walk your hands to the edge of the collar opposite the side of the vest you have on. Use your hand to hold the collar out as far as possible and slip your arm through the armhole. Then run your hands down the zipper to the bottom and zip it up.

This is an extremely difficult process, and you should only attempt it if a group won't stop and you feel chilled. Plenty of pros have trouble doing this.

Parkin says not to worry if you can't dress while you're on the bike. "While racing, I couldn't put on a rain jacket or vest to save my life. For that reason, if I felt I might need the thing later, I would just leave it on, opened, letting it just flap in the wind."

In places where temperatures vary widely through the day, you may need to peel off a layer such as a vest.

Practice

Some of these skills can be learned with just one other rider present. Try getting together with a few friends on a grassy field or parking lot to practice. Make sure to wear your sneakers to prevent your feet from being clipped into the pedals in case you need to put a foot down suddenly.

Try riding next to a friend and putting your hand first on his back near the shoulder, then sliding your hand down to the lower back. Just rest your hand there, no real pressure. Try placing your open hand on his hip.

You can practice touching wheels by following another rider and then slapping the rear wheel with your front wheel with a quick flick of the bar. Also, you can try to rub the rear tire with your front tire in tread-to-tread contact.

Bumping another rider in hip-to-hip contact can actually be great fun and is a great education on just how difficult it really is to crash.

Some skills are better learned during a low-key practice session rather than in the middle of a fast ride.

Chapter 5
Challenges for Women

In addition to the concerns that every cyclist faces in road cycling, from buying the right bike to learning to ride in a peloton, women have a set of additional challenges. The good news is that the bike industry has come to appreciate women cyclists, and in many instances does an excellent job of creating products that cater to women's particular needs.

Following, professional cyclist Dotsie Bausch, a four-time national champion and Pan-American Games gold medalist, offers her insight into some of the issues women face as cyclists. As both a racer and coach, Bausch knows what it means to be a serious cyclist.

Geometry and Wheel Size

Had a woman invented the road bike, it probably wouldn't have 700C wheels. Because most women aren't as tall as the average man, they need frame sizes that are, relatively speaking, rather small. The issue here is that as the frame size shrinks the wheelbase shrinks, decreasing the front-center and creating what is called "toe overlap." Sometimes a frame is so small that when clipped into the pedals, a sharp turn of the handlebar can cause the tire to contact the toe of the shoe if the pedal is forward (cranks parallel to the ground).

Toe overlap really isn't the end of the world, but it makes most riders nervous and Consumer Product Safety Commission (CPSC) regulations require a certain minimum front-center distance to prevent it from happening. This issue becomes most acute when designing bicycles for people 5 feet 5 inches and shorter.

Some bikes feature smaller wheels to reflect the more diminutive build of some women.

In fact, under normal riding circumstances, no one ever turns the bar far enough to make toe overlap occur. The only time it ever occurs is during stops and starts, because to turn the bar that far and stay upright (even without experiencing toe overlap) you need to be moving at less than 8 mph. A sharp turn of the bar as you roll out can cause it to happen on occasion, but it is no threat under normal riding circumstances.

One of the solutions to toe overlap has been to build bicycles around smaller wheels. Some bikes have used 24-inch front wheels while other bikes use 650C wheels front and rear. While either of these solutions resolves the issue with toe overlap, they both suffer two liabilities:

❶ Finding high-performance tires and tubes in odd sizes can be as difficult as finding an accountant with a sense of humor. They are out there, but no sooner does one company introduce a new option than another is discontinued due to poor sales. God forbid you should have more flats than you have tubes, as the odds of another rider having your size are poorer than you'll get at a casino.

❷ Bikes with smaller wheels aren't as stable as ones with 700C wheels. The smaller the wheel is, the less centrifugal force it generates. This means these bikes, despite the designer's efforts to offset the effect (usually by increasing trail), lean into turns more suddenly and don't hold a line as well. While the bikes are plenty stable, the difference in handling between a bike with a 24-inch front wheel or 650C wheels and the other bikes in a peloton is noticeable and can unnerve both rider and peloton.

Neither of these is really enough to discount using a bike with smaller wheels; after all, one of the top priorities with any bike purchase should be to find one that fits. What it does mean is that anyone riding a bike with smaller wheels will have to put more work into learning how to hold a line and how to turn with the rest of the pack.

"If you have toe overlap because of your smaller frame, don't stress on its effect in a race or training ride," Bausch says. "You will never turn the wheel far enough in those situations for it to matter. You may just embarrass yourself from time to time when departing the coffee shop."

Bike Fit

While some manufacturers offer special women's bikes, a purpose-built women's bike isn't absolutely necessary to achieve optimal fit. What is most necessary is a fitting by a technician with experience fitting women.

To achieve optimal fit, women frequently need not only a shorter stem but also a smaller handlebar. Women have narrower shoulders relative to men and are usually more comfortable with a correspondingly narrower bar.

Similarly, some bars are made with a short reach to decrease the distance from the bar to the lever. This is a big help to anyone with smaller hands—not just women. And thanks to new designs from SRAM, Campagnolo, and Shimano, brake lever throw is now adjustable to bring the lever closer to the bar, eliminating the difficult reach for many riders.

Finding a bicycle built specifically for a woman's needs has never been easier.

Small vs. Women's-specific

Bicycle comfort is dictated by a number of factors: frame geometry, fit, component selection, and frame stiffness. Of these, frame stiffness doesn't usually reveal itself until you actually ride the bike. Some women face the exact opposite issue that some men face—finding a bicycle that isn't too stiff.

Production bicycles are designed based on averages. Were a road bike manufacturer to make but one frame to fit as many people as possible, it would probably be a 56-centimeter; it's closest to the average of the height distribution. On average, women are shorter, lighter, and less power-generating than men. Even when considered against men of the same height, most women are lighter and generate less power.

The issue is that as bicycle frames get smaller, the shorter tubes make them stiffer, all other factors being equal. Ideally, each frame size should have the same sensation of flex for an appropriately sized rider. With steel, aluminum, and titanium tubing, a frame builder can specify smaller-diameter and thinner-walled tubes to yield a frame of appropriate stiffness for women riders. Similarly, with carbon fiber, engineers can design a frame with smaller-diameter tubes and fewer plies of carbon fiber to result in a frame of appropriate stiffness for women riders.

Of course, this is one occasion when ordering a custom bike can really pay off. Some builders not only offer made-to-measure fitting, but a flex pattern customized to your strength and weight.

Because it can be difficult to judge small changes in tubing diameter, and it's impossible to gauge wall thickness, look for women's-specific components on production bikes, such as saddle and handlebar. And be prepared to ask a lot of questions.

Gearing

As with other new riders, smaller gears are the rule. Because a new male rider simply doesn't have the strength of an experienced racer, and women lack the strength of most men, many women riders (though certainly not all) are faced with a double handicap when they begin riding on the road. Bikes with compact or triple gearing will offer more gears at the low and middle range of gearing to accommodate the needs of the newer rider.

Known for her quick bursts of speed, Bausch suggests, "For quick accelerations, you need to be in an easier gear, so that your turnover rate or cadence is high, which will make it easier for you to jump out of the saddle without much load or lactate buildup. Then you can catch those escapees with a quick jump and hang with them longer because you won't be burning with lactic acid from an explosive move in a big gear."

The low gears of a compact drivetrain can make riding anywhere a pleasure.

Riding in a Group

Women riders new to group riding can have an especially difficult time matching the accelerations of the peloton. The technique of backsliding mentioned in Chapter 3 is particularly useful in trying to limit your losses during a fierce acceleration. Similarly, using other riders to help you move up is a helpful way to conserve energy during slower episodes, courtesy drafting.

Take note of the bigger riders in the group. These riders offer a better than average draft (helpful) and may not be the fastest to respond to accelerations by the group (even more helpful). Following these wheels can keep you in the group when other, more capable, riders are struggling.

"In a group ride, make sure to stay aware of your surroundings always, and use the bigger men and the safer wheels for drafting," Bausch advises. "But always make sure to be looking ahead for what might happen four to five wheels in front of you, and not just staring at the wheel immediately in front of you. Accidents happen this way. It's just like driving. When you are driving a car, you are always scanning the road ahead while simultaneously scanning the activity of the car directly in front of you."

If you're new to a group, trying following a big rider. Image: Patrick Brady

Pushing

On occasion, other riders may offer a push to help you stay in a group if it appears you might be dropped. If a guy offers, chances are, he's not getting fresh. There's no shame in getting a push to stay with the group. Sometimes, if a rider is backsliding through a group especially quickly, another cyclist will give a push simply to minimize the difference in speed for the sake of the group's safety. Pushing is covered in greater detail in Chapter 4.

A push can be a gentle way to help you stay in a fast group. It can be particularly helpful at the top of a hill. Image: Patrick Brady

Clothing

While the basics regarding the different articles of clothing are covered in Chapter 9, women have a few additional considerations. While all men's raglan jerseys will fit with remarkable consistency, as will all jerseys with set-in sleeves, women's jerseys with a princess cut can vary radically in their fit. Some will be cut with more room at the bust for fuller-figured women. Others will be cut for especially slim women. Similarly, the difference in hip and waist dimensions of some shorts may not always match your proportions.

Bausch, a former model, suggests, "Just like shopping for designer clothes, you want to find the cycling clothes that fit you best and work with your unique body type, not against it. Just because it's comfy for one does not make it work for another. Try on various brands and pick what works for you. The same advice goes for saddle selection."

Women's cycling clothing has come a long way over the years; there's more selection in terms of style, fit, and color.

Color

For every woman who prefers feminine colors and feminine-looking clothing, there's another who wants her clothing and equipment to be as close to the guys' stuff as possible. Each company in the industry approaches this differently. Some will stick with decidedly feminine color schemes and designs in bikes, equipment, and clothing, while others simply offer their performance gear in smaller sizes. Be aware that one company's approach won't be another's.

No matter what your taste is, there are manufacturers out there making clothing to suit your style.

Chapter 6
Traffic

Legal Rights and Responsibilities of a Cyclist

No matter what state you live in, you, as a cyclist, have the same right to the road as any car driver. You also have the same responsibilities as drivers to obey the traffic codes in your city and state.

Unfortunately, not all drivers are aware of cyclist's rights, and their lack of understanding can make the roads a dangerous place. Just as defensive driving is a smart strategy for avoiding potential accidents, defensive cycling can help you avoid problems before they happen.

Being Seen
Chances are if a driver sees you, you won't wind up under the car. The occasionally garish clothing for which cycling is (in)famous does have a real-world upside: It's hard to miss anything that painful to the eyes.

Here's where the clothing you select can make a difference. You may have noticed that most fast-food restaurants use red and yellow in their signs. Red, orange, and yellow are the three colors with the longest wavelengths in the visible light spectrum. As a result, your brain can pick these colors out of a mass of visual stimulation more quickly than any other colors. As a driver, if you like to drive fast, avoid red—it gets you noticed. Pick a black car; black is a hole in the visual field—it's the absence of color. As a cyclist, stick to red, orange, and yellow if you are concerned about being noticed. Also, coordinated outfits that repeat the same color in the jersey and shorts create an object with a larger appearance; you'll be noticeable from farther away. Just think: If dog poop were red, no one would ever step in it.

How to Ride on City Streets
If you have a driver's license, you know 99 percent of what's necessary to ride legally. If in doubt, use common sense: Stay to the right, signal your intentions, and make sure you are aware of what other drivers are up to. Beyond that, a little refresher on your state's motor vehicle code never hurts. In some states, there are exceptions to certain laws that can make sense of certain situations. For instance, in some states, it is okay for a cyclist to treat a light triggered by sensors as malfunctioning if it won't change. After waiting through a cycle, it is permissible to cross when safe.

Dealing with Traffic

Unless you live in a small town surrounded by a network of rarely used back roads, you are going to have to deal with traffic, which means you are going to encounter drivers who may not know your rights or may even be hostile to your presence. No matter where you live, you can employ a number of strategies to ride safely.

Where to Ride

Taken in its extreme, you should attempt to ride where cars aren't present. Given that if you and a car try to occupy the same patch of asphalt on the road you will lose, the opposite of that is your goal.

Practically speaking, avoid major thoroughfares if you are on your own, unless they have a wide and well-marked shoulder, or better yet, a bike lane. Residential streets used by local residents won't experience the rush of traffic found elsewhere, except near a school zone.

Some of the best times to ride are before or after rush hour when there is less traffic.

When to Ride

Try to ride when fewer drivers are on the road. The big priorities in your life—job, school, and family—will be the biggest determiners of when you can ride, but within the free time you have, some times of day make for better times to ride than others.

Naturally, no matter where you live, you want to try to avoid the morning and evening rush hours. The reality is, the earlier you can ride, the better. There aren't many cars on the road at sunrise. A road too busy to safely ride at noon can be part of a viable training route early in the morning. For those with a nonstandard schedule, late morning and early afternoon will feature fewer cars on the road, thanks to most folks being at work.

Pre- and post-rush-hour rides can be hampered by a lack of sunlight, especially during the winter months. Having a good light system can add flexibility to your training.

Traffic Flow

Where you position yourself in traffic depends on the distance between lights. Naturally, you are going to be in the rightmost lane, but how you deal with cars depends on the distance between lights, your comfort level, and your fitness. Generally speaking, it is better to stay behind the pack of cars that moves from light to light. Initially, a cyclist may accelerate across an intersection faster than the cars present, but the cars will overtake the rider almost immediately thereafter. If the lane is narrow and there is a long line of cars present, it might be safer to wait behind the cars rather than experience each of them passing you.

In congested urban areas where lights govern each intersection, a strong cyclist is better off taking the lane and sprinting from light to light. This is one situation where having a double-sided clipless pedal that can be rapidly engaged (such as Speedplay or Crank Brothers) can aid your acceleration away from a light.

Parked Cars

Parked cars pose two hazards. First, they have the effect of narrowing the road shoulder, thereby forcing you closer to passing traffic. Rather than weaving in and out of parked cars, it is best to ride to the left of the parked cars so that approaching traffic will be able to see you and (hopefully) will accommodate your presence by moving left slightly. If you suddenly weave back into the flow of traffic from behind a parked car, you may startle a driver who didn't expect to encounter you. Naturally, if the parked cars are few and far between, you should move to the right after passing the car.

The other hazard of parked cars is having a door suddenly opened in your path as you're about to pass. Many drivers fail to check their rearview mirror before opening their car door to exit. Because many cyclists travel within two feet of parked vehicles, a door is a serious threat that can result in a fatal accident. To guard against this, look in the rear window for signs of activity as you approach parked cars. Because you can't tell if the driver is about to exit the car or not, if you see a head on the driver's side, give yourself a little extra room as you pass.

While helmet mirrors are popular with some riders as a way to stay aware of traffic approaching behind, the brain is attuned to notice faces, and turning your head toward nearby drivers may help them notice you. Making eye contact with drivers to let them know you see them can have a powerful impact on your safety.

Looking over your shoulder not only lets you know where the traffic is, it lets drivers know you are aware.

Be sure to be on the lookout for drivers opening doors or walking out from between cars.

Looking Around

The more you know about your immediate surroundings, the safer you are. No matter where you ride, hazards exist. From glass in the road to pedestrians jaywalking to bus drivers rushing to maintain their schedules, the safest rider is the one looking around at all times.

Chapter 7
Crashing

It's going to happen, so be prepared. It's virtually impossible to be a cyclist and not fall. That's the bad news. The good news is that falling doesn't have to be a major crisis. Most injuries you'll experience as a cyclist won't be serious.

You need to keep some items with you as you ride that will aid you in the event of an accident. Also, a well-stocked medicine cabinet at home will allow you to tend to your own wounds. If your accident was as the result of an encounter with a vehicle, you may need to speak with the police or a lawyer.

Items to Carry

Each time you go for a ride, there are a few items unrelated to the bike that you should always carry with you. In the event that you do crash, having the following items can make a significant difference in how quickly you receive assistance.

- Cell phone: They are small enough that you can carry one in a plastic bag in your jersey pocket, and if they have a GPS, they can help with directions, too.

- I.C.E.: Program an "in case of emergency" entry into your cell phone. Emergency responders around the country are being trained to look for such an entry in the event they encounter someone unconscious.

There are a few items you should carry with you on each ride, such as your phone, ID, and insurance card.

47

- Driver's license: Whether you choose to carry your actual driver's license or a photocopy, make sure you have some identification with your address.

- Medical insurance card: In the event you must be transported to the hospital, you will receive care more quickly if you can produce your medical insurance information promptly. This could be on the back of your driver's license photocopy.

- Information on allergies or conditions: If you have any allergies or conditions that could create a life-threatening situation if you're treated while unconscious (such as diabetes or a pharmaceutical allergy), consider wearing an ID bracelet with this information.

Most Common Injuries

- Road rash: Any fall that includes sliding on the ground is going to result in some abrasion. These tend to weep, or drain fluid, in the days following the injury. Most cyclists have the greatest success treating road rash with hydrocolloid bandages—often called "second skin."

- Punctures and lacerations: Even without broken parts, a bicycle's chainring can give a cyclist a puncture wound or laceration. With the prevalence today of carbon fiber parts, the possibility of being cut by a damaged part with a jagged edge has risen dramatically.

- Broken collarbone (clavicle): One of the unfortunate truths of cycling is that the slight build of cyclists makes them vulnerable to broken collarbones in the event of a fall. With the shoulder receiving the bulk of the impact, these breaks are the most common bone breaks for cyclists.

- Wrist and arm injuries: From time to time, a cyclist will fall and extend his or her hand to try to lessen the impact. Unfortunately, broken hands and arms and dislocated shoulders are common outcomes.

- Concussion: Any head injury is serious, but thankfully with the quality of helmets available today both the frequency and severity of head injuries has dropped.

How to Fall

The first rule of falling, of course, is to try not to fall. Practically speaking, that means the longer you can keep the bike rolling, the better your chances are of escaping the situation unharmed. As you learned in Chapter 2, a rolling bicycle is inclined to stay upright thanks to the centrifugal force generated by its spinning wheels.

In the event you are unable to avoid the ground, some general rules can help make things go better:

- Stay with the bike: Most cyclists don't have much experience separating from a bike while in motion; staying with the bike usually results in less damage to both bike and rider.

- Keep your hands on the handlebar: Most hand, wrist, and arm injuries occur when a rider sticks out a hand to break their fall.

- Try to roll: Rolling to avoid impact can mean the difference between some road rash and a broken collarbone. Rolling can also reduce road rash caused by sliding on one body part.

Get as Much Information as Possible

In the unfortunate event you are hit by a car, make your first priority to try to get the license plate number. If the driver stops, get as much information from them as possible, including the license plate, their driver's license number, insurance information, home address, and phone number.

If the driver doesn't stop, at least try to get the license plate number, but if you are only able to get a partial plate number or nothing at all, try to memorize the make, model, and color of the car. Any recourse you have with the driver will begin with the police, and the more information you can provide about the vehicle, the more likely they will be to find the driver.

Try to note other specifics of the incident. Check the time, and note both the location and the direction both you and the car were traveling in. File a report with the appropriate authorities as soon as you can.

Dealing with the Police

In the event you are involved in an accident with a car, you will need to file a police report. As you describe the events to the investigating officer, keep the following in mind:

- Stick to the facts: Report only that of which you are certain.
- Keep your explanation succinct: The longer your story about the event, the more likely the officer will lose the thread of events.
- Describe the events in the order they occurred: To establish causality, the officer needs to know the exact order in which things happened.
- Don't explain the person's motive: If you believe the act was intentional, describe what the person did to make you feel threatened or that led to the crash.

Personal First-Aid Kit

Most crashes don't result in serious injuries that require a trip to the doctor. Keep these items around for immediate home treatment of any injuries you sustain.

- Aloe gel—soothes sunburn
- Adhesive bandages in various sizes—for smaller cuts and scrapes
- Sterile gauze pads—for larger wounds that are actively draining
- Tape

- Scissors
- Self-stick paper bandage wraps—an alternative method for holding gauze pads in place
- Hydrocortisone cream—for minor skin irritation and rashes
- Moleskin—for blisters
- Betadine—to wash the site of a wound and clean it of bacteria
- Tweezers—for removing splinters
- Acetaminophen—for pain relief in the first 24 hours following the injury
- Ibuprofen—for pain relief and reduction of swelling once bleeding has stopped
- Chemical cold packs—to reduce swelling
- Antibiotic ointment—to reduce the chance of infection
- Hydrocolloid bandages—for slightly weepy wounds
- Hydrogel—to keep a wound moist

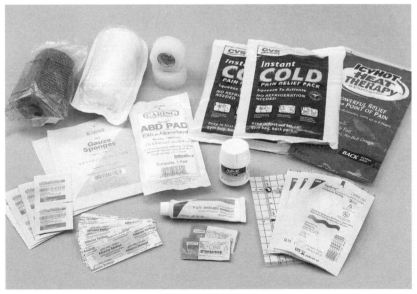

A well-stocked home first aid kit is an absolute necessity.

Replace Your Parts

If ever there was an occasion served by the saying "better safe than sorry," this is it. Have a shop technician inspect your bicycle carefully following any crash, and be prepared to follow the advice you receive.

Components made from steel, titanium, and aluminum are pretty durable, so if they have sustained enough damage to require replacing, it will be fairly apparent. The same holds true for steel frames and forks, as well as titanium frames. Anything that appears bent to the naked eye should be replaced.

Frames and forks made from aluminum should be considered carefully. Because aluminum has an endurance limit—that is, after a finite number of stress cycles, the material will break suddenly—any frame or fork made from aluminum that has gone down in a crash should be inspected carefully by a shop technician. If the frame or fork has sustained a hard enough impact to bend the tubes even slightly, you should replace it.

The proliferation of carbon fiber components has made crashing painful to the body and wallet alike. That's because carbon fiber is anisotropic. As mentioned in Chapter 4, steel, titanium, and aluminum are isotropic—equally strong in any direction—but carbon fiber is strong only in the direction the fibers are oriented, so a hammerlike blow to any frame tube will kill the whole frame. Additionally, carbon fiber structures can sustain damage that is not apparent to the naked eye. Naturally, any obvious damage, such as a visible crack in the fibers themselves, warrants replacing the part. It is possible, however, for a part to sustain trauma-inducing damage in a crash and still appear to be fine. As one company's head of engineering said (off the record, of course), "The frames the top pros are riding are strictly single-use. If you crash it, you should just throw it away."

Give Your Body Time to Heal

When recovering from an injury, let comfort be your guide. Some injuries, such as road rash, cuts, and hematomas, need not keep you off the bike for long. If your injuries required a visit to the doctor, be prepared to follow your physician's advice.

Broken bones will take a number of weeks to heal. At minimum you will need eight weeks, though your doctor may advise even longer, especially if tendons or ligaments were torn; they can require surgery. Head injuries—such as concussions—can take a significant amount of time to heal, and strenuous activity can slow recovery or even reinjure the site. Stay off the bike until you have been cleared to ride by your doctor.

In your first few rides back on the bike, don't worry about going fast. If the injury was to your legs, feet, or back, focus on range of motion and a smooth pedal stroke.

Image: Patrick Brady

Image: Patrick Brady

Chapter 8
Organized Cycling Events

Most cyclists will tell you their favorite way by far to discover the world is from the saddle of a bike. Riding roads in an unfamiliar place gives you a chance to take in more than just the sights of a place. Being outdoors you see more, hear more, and breathe in the smells to give you the richest possible experience.

Organized cycling events are a way to go to someplace new and encounter the local roads in an ideal circumstance. Your entry fee gets you a course planned to the last turn and mile, food and water stops along the way, and generally the best of the local beauty and terrain. Follow it up with the inevitable postride barbecue, and you have a recipe for a great day, especially when you share it with friends.

The stock-in-trade for cycling events is the century—the 100-mile ride. To complete a ride of that length, you need some serious fitness.

Kinds of Events

Organized cycling events can generally be broken into two groups: destination rides and charity rides. The distance of the ride can vary quite a bit, and some events are organized around riding a specific course with a particular set of challenges.

Purpose

Destination rides have no purpose beyond the destination itself, while charity rides are organized to raise money for a charity or other good cause. While the riding itself can be identical, charity rides differ from destination rides by virtue of the fact that to enter you have to meet a pledge goal. Doing the ride is your reward for raising funds for a good cause.

Charity rides combine excellent support, challenging routes, and a terrific sense of purpose in helping others.

Each year charity rides draw thousands of new riders into the sport. Nearly everyone has friends or family who suffer from AIDS, cancer, diabetes, or other diseases. Raising funds to research a cure can be just the impetus many people need to get back into cycling. Many of these events not only help riders meet their pledge goals with sophisticated websites that can help you contact friends and family for pledges, but frequently they help you meet your own fitness goals with clinics, training rides, and expert advice. Charity rides help more than just those who are sick.

Distance

Because not everyone can or wants to ride 100 miles in a day, most events will offer a few different menu items. You will likely see a few different repeatedly. Broadly speaking, you have short rides, medium-distance rides, long rides, and then ultra-distance rides.

Most events will offer three different lengths: one that is 100 miles, another that is 50–62 miles, and a third that is 20–30 miles.
Image: Patrick Brady

When considering events, it is important to note that almost no event is exactly the distance advertised. Most centuries run a few miles long; the point of the ride is the enjoyable course, not a precise distance; try not to be surprised when you hit the 100-mile mark and are still riding by farms.

Short

For newcomers getting their feet wet with their first organized ride, many events will offer an option of between 20 and 30 miles. It's long enough to see some sights, but for cyclists unaccustomed to pedaling for three hours or more, it's still short enough to avoid a day-ruining bonk. If you can average 12 miles per hour while riding, you can finish a 25-mile ride with one stop in 2:30.

Medium

The metric century—100 kilometers—is a 62-mile ride. It's also one of the most popular formats for a ride. A metric century is a great stepping stone toward longer rides for cyclists whose longest excursions haven't exceeded 50 miles. While new riders might require 5 hours to finish a metric century with stops, experienced riders in a peloton can knock one out in under 3 hours.

Long

The century—a 100-mile ride—is the standard-bearer of organized rides. The ability to complete a full century is a confirmation of real fitness. They can range from kitchen-floor flat to Tour de France mountainous with more than 10,000 feet of climbing. As a result, riders might finish one in as few as 4 hours or as long as 12 hours if there's lots of climbing.

Ultra

Double centuries were made for folks who don't like to finish a ride. They come in both double-metric (124 miles) and just plain double (an amazing 200 miles). While a double-metric can be finished with an additional hour or two of riding, a double century requires riders to mount up while dark and frequently finish in the dark as well. Twelve to 14 hours in the saddle isn't for everyone.

Where to Find Events

The Internet has usurped all other resources for finding organized cycling events. There was a time when the best way to find out about an event before it was over was through your local club or bike shop. Notwithstanding the needle-in-a-haystack power of Google, once you join a club, your fellow club members will be one of your best sources of important insight. Let your friends' experiences be your guide.

Many events will have spotty information on course difficulty and rest stops. The more difficult the event, the more likely there will be detailed information regarding the course and location of the rest stops. If you are accustomed to stopping for food and water every 10–15 miles and the event you are considering has stops only every 25 miles, you will need to factor that into your training. Of course, if you don't find that out until mile 25 of the event, it could be a long day.

If any of your friends have done the event, they will be able to tell you how many rest stops there are, what foods and drinks they stock, and how difficult the course is relative to the roads you ride locally. This insight is invaluable, and if an event was particularly well organized or well supported, they will go out of their way to tell you.

Practical Considerations

Any ride that doesn't leave from your front door requires planning and packing. This may seem obvious to the point of redundancy, but showing up to an event with everything except your cycling shoes can wreck your day.

Depending on how far the event is from home, you'll need to decide if you can get up early and drive out the morning of the event or if you'll need to leave the night before and stay in a hotel.

Organized events aren't for late risers. If you are accustomed to riding once the sun is well up or after work, you'll need to train your body to perform early in the day with a few morning rides prior to the event.

The morning of the event, some riders will get partially dressed, putting on their shorts and then putting loose-fitting street clothes on over them. If you're inclined to use chamois cream and/or an embrocation, you need to plan on dressing at the event.

New riders frequently underestimate how difficult it can be to change discreetly both before and after an event. In your car is difficult, but standing next to or behind your car risks giving folks an unwanted show. The long lines for portable toilets generally make them too in-demand to be used as a makeshift changing room. Wrapping a beach towel around your waist is a popular strategy for alfresco changing that avoids offending most sensibilities.

After the event is over, you will likely be too sweaty a mess to get in your car and drive away. Baby wipes or a jug of tap water and a washcloth can help you wipe away the worst of the sweat and road grime—enough to change into street clothes and feel comfortable while you get some lunch.

Sites such as Active.com are a great way to find out about organized events in your area.

Packing

The week of the event:

- Preregister for the event (some events require registration months in advance)
- Tune and clean bike
- Gas up the car
- Check the car's fluids
- Make a motel reservation

Make sure these are in reach in the car:

- Directions to event (many events feature them online)
- Motel-reservation confirmation number
- Directions to motel
- Map of area
- Snacks
- Good tunes (your favorite station only reaches so far)

Pack in your gear bag:

- Shorts
- Jersey
- Base layer
- Socks
- Cycling shoes
- Cycling gloves
- Arm and knee warmers (you never know)
- Vest, windbreaker, or rain cape
- Glasses
- Heart rate monitor (HRM)
- Toilet paper (portable toilets run out of it)
- Basic toiletry kit

- Postride clothes
- Beach towel (for discreet on-site changing)
- Water bottles and/or hydration pack
- Drink mix and/or energy bars/gels
- Sunscreen
- Hand wipes for postevent cleanup
- Safety pins
- Camera
- Alarm clock

Pack with car:

- Bike
- Spare tubes and tire
- Tools
- Floor pump

Packing for an event requires some care and a thorough checklist.

Image: Patrick Brady

Chapter 9
Racing

M any cyclists discover the fun of riding in a peloton and get the itch to pin on a number and race. If you don't happen to have that itch, don't worry; it's not for everyone. If want to pursue the fitness you've gained to its ultimate culmination, however, racing will put your body to the test.

Options for the New Racer

A number of different kinds of races exist within road cycling. No matter what your particular strength or willingness to take risk, there's an event to help you express your competitive side.

Races can generally be broken into two groups: individual events (such as time trials) and mass-start events (such as criteriums and road races). Entry level riders will usually compete in a group of no more than 50 riders. As you rise through the categories, the fields grow in size to sometimes more than 100 riders.

Kinds of races

❶ **Time trials** are the lowest-risk form of racing. Known as the "race of truth," a time trial is an individual-start event where each rider races a set course without taking pace (drafting) off of other riders.

Time trials are the easiest and safest way to try your hand (or legs) at racing.

Courses tend to use one road on an out-and-back basis, or a circuit where the start and finish are close together, if not on the same line. Common lengths for time trials are 10, 12, and 25 miles. Any traditional road bike may be used, but a dedicated time trial bike will offer a notable advantage.

❷ Criteriums are the most common form of racing because the courses are the shortest and therefore easiest to get a city or other government agency to approve; they are at least 800 meters (0.5 miles) in length per lap, but no longer than 5 kilometers (3.1 miles). A criterium is a mass-start event and will have many riders competing in the same pack; riders dropped from this group and deemed out of contention for the win will usually be pulled from the course before the completion of the race. Courses must be a closed loop over which many laps may be raced. A criterium, or "crit," is often composed of a flat, 1-mile course with four 90-degree turns. Paces tend to be high with little slowing. Crits are commonly timed events; entry-level racers may complete 30 minutes plus three additional laps. At the conclusion of 30 minutes, lap cards will count down the final three laps to allow riders to jockey for position before the finish. Because of the high pace and close proximity of riders, crits are the riskiest of all races. Any traditional road bike may be used.

A criterium combines the thrill of riding in a pack with a short but intense effort.

❸ Road races may be conducted either over a circuit of at least 5 kilometers (3.1 miles) for several laps or a point-to-point course. Like criteriums, these are mass-start events with a large pack. Road races for entry-level racers are commonly between 16 and 25 miles, though longer races are possible. Because of the longer distances involved, road races are more likely to feature hills and see a field of new riders broken up. While not without risk, road races generally involve less risk than criteriums. Any traditional road bike may be used.

Road races feature longer and often more challenging courses than criteriums.

❹ **Stage races** are multiday races made up of some combination of road races, criteriums, and time trials. A rider must complete each stage to move onto the next stage. Placings are given for each stage as well as overall classification. Scoring may be decided on points awarded for placings or on cumulative time; the rider with either the highest number of points or lowest cumulative time wins the event. For entry-level riders, stage races will be three to four stages over two to three days. Any traditional road bike may be used.

Track races are especially short and feature high intensity.

A stage race takes the fun of racing and spreads it over several days.

❺ **Track races** take place on a velodrome, and while not every community has a velodrome, many major metropolitan areas have one. There are more than a dozen different kinds of track races, ranging from mass-start events to time trials, and they include a variety of lengths, as well. As with crits, the high pace and close proximity of riders bring with them a fairly high degree of risk. A fixed-gear, brakeless track bike must be used.

❻ **Cyclocross races** mix pavement with off-road terrain. Simply put, cyclocross is the steeplechase of bike racing. A cyclocross race is a mass-start event and requires riders to dismount periodically and pick their bicycles up and carry them over barriers. Because of the lower speeds involved and the low density of riders, cyclocross racing entails fairly low risk. Though a road bike may be used, because of the particular course demands, a cyclocross bike is essential for success.

Cyclocross racing is unusual because it crosses bike racing with a bit of running.

Governing Bodies

Aside from racers, bike races need officials, rules, permits, and insurance. Bike races held on public roads need race permits from the local government. To get a permit, a race must be shown to be sanctioned by a governing body and be insured against injuries and other mishaps.

United States Cycling Federation

USA Cycling's United States Cycling Federation (USCF) is the largest governing body that oversees amateur road, track, and cyclocross racing in the United States. USA Cycling is sanctioned by the Union Cycliste Internationale and the United States Olympic Committee, making it the official governing body for bicycle racing. It offers many athlete-development programs and sanctions the vast majority of all races in the United States. The USCF also administrates collegiate racing through the National Collegiate Cycling Association (NCCC), which is one of the most rapidly growing forms of racing in the country.

Grassroots Bicycle Associations

Several grassroots cycling associations exist in regions to give race promoters an alternative to the USCF. American Bicycle Racing is one such organization; there are several regional associations, including California Bicycle Racing (CBR) and the Oregon Bicycle Racing Association (OBRA).

Licensing, Classes, and Categories

To race, you will need to purchase a license. It is possible to purchase a one-day license when you register for an event, but if you plan to race with some regularity, it quickly becomes more cost-effective to purchase a one-year license.

Racing is divided according to gender and age class, so that a 16-year-old girl isn't forced to race against a 30-year-old man. Broadly speaking the age classes are:

- Junior (18 and under)
- Under-23 (19–22)
- Senior (23–29)
- Master (30 and up)

Many events will feature multiple classes of masters' racing, broken in 10-year increments: 35–44, 45–54, and 55+.

There are five racing categories for men, with Category 5 being entry-level and Category 1 being elite-level amateur. In women's racing there are four categories. While other races can have 100 or more racers competing for the win, Category 5 events for men and Category 4 events for women cap the fields at a maximum of 50 riders because they are meant to be an introduction to racing. To upgrade to Category 4, riders must complete 10 sanctioned races. Further upgrades are gained by points earned through placings at sanctioned races.

The Machine

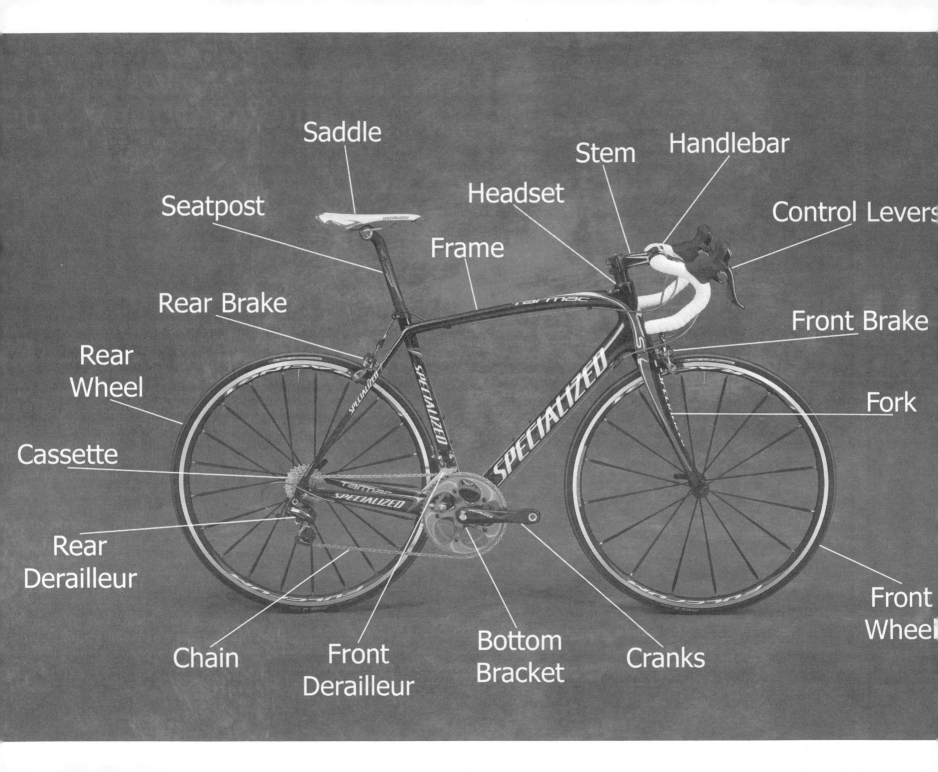

Chapter 10
A Detailed Look at the Road Bike

The road bike is the patriarch of all bicycles. From mountain bikes to beach cruisers, every bicycle on the market today originated as a variation on the first chain-driven bicycles produced in the 19th century. Every bicycle has a standard assortment of equipment; on the road bike, these parts are highly specialized.

Every road bicycle has the following parts:

❶ Frame
❷ Fork
❸ Front brake
❹ Front wheel
❺ Headset
❻ Stem
❼ Handlebar
❽ Control levers
❾ Seatpost
❿ Saddle
⓫ Rear brake
⓬ Bottom bracket
⓭ Cranks
⓮ Chain
⓯ Front derailleur
⓰ Rear derailleur
⓱ Cassette
⓲ Rear wheel

The bicycle frame has the following parts:

❶ Top tube
❷ Head tube
❸ Down tube
❹ Seat tube
❺ Bottom bracket
❻ Chainstays
❼ Seatstays
❽ Fork
❾ Dropouts

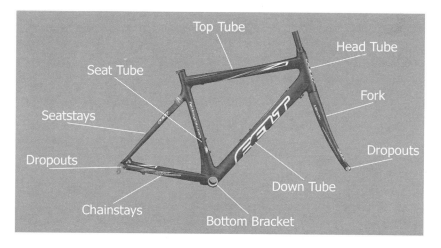

Dimensions

Because the modern road bike was primarily developed in Europe, its parts and dimensions are measured according to the metric system. While many bicycles sold in America are sized in inches, high-quality road bikes use the metric system. Frame sizes are measured in centimeters (cm), while the nuts and bolts used on the bikes are measured in millimeters (mm). For the new rider, this adaptation can be frustrating, but consistent usage of the metric system throughout the bicycle becomes simple over time.

A number of important dimensions dictate the size and handling of a bicycle:

❶ Head tube angle (measured in degrees)

❷ Seat tube angle (measured in degrees)

❸ Fork rake (measured in mm)

❹ Top tube length (measured in cm)

❺ Seat tube length (measured in cm)

❻ Wheelbase (measured in cm)

❼ Bottom bracket height (measured in cm)

❽ Chainstay length (measured in cm)

❾ Trail (measured in cm)

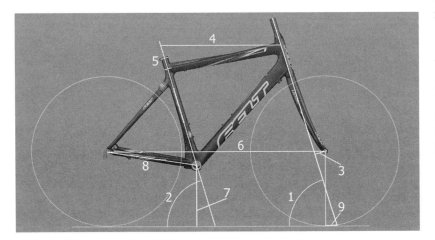

Each of these dimensions is critical to how a bicycle fits and handles. Change any one of these dimensions by a centimeter, and the fit of the bicycle changes as well as the bicycle's handling characteristics. Frame geometry is discussed in greater depth in Chapter 13.

Types of Road Bicycles

Road bikes take many forms. Typically, a road bike is versatile enough to allow a rider to pursue a variety of riding styles, from touring to racing. Each of the bicycles below still qualifies as a road bike; however, they are designed with a special purpose in mind, making them less suitable for other uses.

Competition bicycles are meant for a style of racing called the criterium, which are short and involve frequent turns. Competition bikes turn easily and offer the rider unusually reactive handling in order for the racer to capitalize on lightning-fast changes in race conditions. These constitute the vast majority of all road bike sales.

Competition road bikes feature agile handling for racing.

Touring bicycles are meant for those who want to see the world. They offer stable handling and stout frames that can support the weight of gear carried on the bicycle.

Touring bikes feature relaxed handling and special mounts to carry bags called panniers.

Grand touring bikes are road bikes with geometry derived from the European stage-racing bikes. They are made to handle calmly and offer a comfortable position for riders who enter organized touring events such as centuries (100-mile rides). This category of bike is relatively new and gaining popularity. Grand touring bikes are a perfect starting point for anyone buying a first road bike.

Grand touring bikes combine the relaxed handling of a touring bike with the high-tech performance of a competition bike.

Time trial and triathlon bikes are special-purpose bikes designed for a rider to achieve an especially aerodynamic position on the bicycle. They are best for riders competing against the clock.

Time trial bikes are made specifically for competing against the clock; they aren't well suited to group rides.

Track bicycles are perhaps the purest expression of the road bike. Ironically, they are intended to be ridden exclusively in velodromes and are different from other bicycles in that they have only one gear, no brakes, and no ability to freewheel (coast without pedaling). There are multiple kinds of track bikes, such as models suited to pack riding on the track and models intended for time trials, thus mirroring what we see on the road. Though similar to traditional road bikes, they have evolved as a distinctly different subspe-

Track bikes are the simplest road bikes. They feature only one gear and no brakes.

cies. Riding track bikes—which are often referred to as "fixies" due to the fixed (no freewheel) drivetrain—have really taken off in popularity.

Tandems are road bikes with a twist. They utilize an unusually long frame that allows riders to ride together on the same bicycle. Most tandems utilize much heavier tubing than typical road bikes in order to support the weight of two riders. The long wheelbase makes tandem handling different from typical road bikes.

Tandems are a great way to share riding with another person; nothing else is quite like it.

Cyclocross bicycles are used in a form of racing where racers ride their bikes on the road, on dirt roads, and sometimes on trails during fall and winter. Because race conditions can be wet and muddy, the bicycles use lower gearing and more powerful brakes, plus knobby tires. The frame has to offer more tire clearance to accept the knobby tires. If equipped with standard road tires, only the special brakes would give them away.

A cyclocross bike is essentially a road bike with clearance for fatter tires plus powerful brakes that work in mud.

Image courtesy Cannondale

Chapter 11
Materials and Construction

J ust as it isn't remotely necessary to understand how an internal-combustion engine works in order to drive a car, it isn't necessary to know how a bicycle is made to ride one. That said, knowing a bit about the frame materials used can aid you in selecting the best bicycle for you depending on such factors as price, ride quality, and your dimensions.

The Least You Need to Know

There's a fair amount of technical information in this chapter. Some riders will find this fascinating, but honestly, if you are a new rider, this will make more sense once you've had a chance to ride bicycles made from the different frame materials. When you have a chance to ride a steel bicycle and then one made from carbon fiber, you'll probably become interested in the differences between the various materials.

Four primary materials are used in bicycle frames: steel, aluminum, titanium, and carbon fiber. To one degree or another, all of these materials are used as tubes; different construction methods will determine how these tubes are manufactured and joined together.

Steel was the dominant material for more than 100 years and was used in top-quality racing bikes ridden in the Tour de France as recently as 1995. Aluminum began to be used in the 1970s, as did titanium, though neither gained significant popularity until the 1990s. Carbon fiber was first used as a frame material in the 1980s but has gained its widest and most popular use in the last 10 years. In terms of units sold, it is now the most popular material for high-end racing bicycles.

The materials each offer a different blend of cost, artistry, durability, stiffness, and what is called "road feel," which is a term for the tactile sense you get of the road surface beneath you.

In broad strokes, here are each material's top selling points:

Steel is generally the least expensive of the four materials. It excels at durability and giving artisan frame builders a platform for their artistry. Steel bikes are known for an excellent road feel.

Aluminum is also good for riders on a budget. It combines lower cost with generally less weight than found in steel. Aluminum bikes don't often get high marks for their road feel.

Titanium combines incredible durability with reduced weight, relative to steel. Titanium is appreciated because it won't corrode under normal use, so the frame can be left bare to show a lustrous gray. Titanium bikes are on par with steel bikes for their road feel.

69

Carbon fiber is the material used for today's top bikes. The best carbon fiber bikes are exceedingly expensive, stunningly low in weight, and unfortunately fragile. Carbon fiber gets high marks for its road feel, but it is quite different from the other materials because it isn't metal.

Stiffness is a quality prized because it makes a bicycle more efficient in power transfer from the pedals to the rear wheel, though a bicycle with less stiffness will also afford a rider greater comfort as he pedals. While any of the above materials can be built to make a stiff or flexible bicycle, in current practical application carbon fiber bikes are usually the stiffest. Aluminum bikes tend to be the next most stiff. Steel bikes are usually a little less stiff, while the titanium bikes, though fairly stiff, are the least stiff among contemporary road bikes.

Read on if you find a bicycle's construction interesting or are intrigued by the idea of road feel. Otherwise, skip to the next chapter.

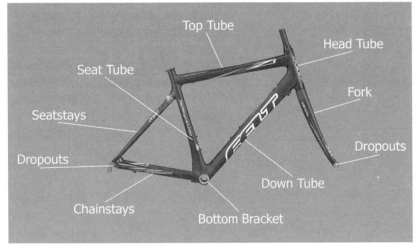

In many cases, a bicycle frame starts out as a collection of tubes that must be cut to length and then joined together.

The Bicycle Frame Defined

A bicycle frame is composed of a number of pieces of tubing. In all but rare cases, a frame will have eight tubes composing the frame and three tubes composing the fork.

The front half of the frame is referred to as the main triangle (as a result of the bicycle's appearance in profile), even though technically it includes four tubes. Those tubes are the top tube, which defines the bicycle's size; the down tube, which defines the ride quality of the bicycle; the seat tube, into which the seatpost clamps (this extendable feature allows one bicycle to fit a number of different riders); and the head tube, into which bearings are inserted and through which the fork passes and allows the bicycle to steer.

The rear half of the frame is referred to as the rear triangle. Four tubes make up this triangle. They are the chainstays and the seatstays. The chainstays and seatstays work in tandem to hold the rear wheel in place.

The fork is composed of three tubes. They are the steerer, which passes through the frame's head tube and headset bearings, and the fork blades, which extend down either side of the front wheel to hold it in place.

The ends of the fork blades and the junction of the chainstays and seatstays feature parts called dropouts. They give the wheels a precisely controlled location into which to be clamped.

Metallurgy for Cyclists

Steel, aluminum, and titanium share many basic properties. What makes each behave differently as a frame material has to do with the following factors:

Density: Density explains a material's relationship to gravity. High density equals high weight. Steel is the densest of the three materials. With a weight of 495 pounds per cubic foot (lbs./cu. ft.), it is nearly twice the density of titanium (280 lbs./cu. ft.) and three times the weight of aluminum (165 lbs./cu. ft.). In an ideal world, the best frame material would have high strength with low density. This would allow the material to be drawn with very thin-walled tubes and yet enjoy great strength against damage.

Diameter: A tube's diameter will vary according to its placement in the frame. The tubes that make up the front half of the bicycle are the largest in diameter. The tubes in the rear half of the bicycle are much smaller in diameter and taper in size as they approach the rear wheel. As a tube increases in diameter or in wall thickness, its stiffness increases. Increasing a tube's wall thickness increases its stiffness at a roughly 1:1 ratio with its weight. Increasing a tube's diameter, however, increases its stiffness at a cubed rate. If you double the diameter of a given tube, the new tube will weigh twice as much but be eight times as stiff as the smaller tube. This is why thin-walled, large-diameter tubing is so popular; it is possible to create an aluminum tube that is both stronger and lighter than those made from steel. As diameter goes up and thickness goes down, the ability to resist dents goes down—so there is a limit to the diameter–thickness ratio.

Elongation: This is a measure of a material's ability to stretch, known as ductility. Chewing gum is ductile. This might not seem helpful to a bicycle, but a material with no elongation will break without ever stretching. Think glass: It has almost no elongation and as a result is brittle. Bicycle tubing needs to bend before failing. Some elongation is helpful. If elongation drops below 10 percent, builders tend to get concerned. Steel is usually 10–15 percent, while titanium is 20–30 percent and aluminum is 6–12 percent.

Fatigue strength: This is the point at which tubing fails after many repeated load cycles; think of a load cycle as anything that causes the bicycle tube to flex. A basketball flexes each time it is bounced; each bounce constitutes a load cycle. The stress of the load is less than the material's ultimate tensile strength (see above right). Both steel and titanium are appreciated for having what is known as an endurance limit; that is, it is possible to apply a load an infinite number of times without the material failing. That is not the case with aluminum. Sooner or later it will break.

Stiffness: Also known as Young's Modulus (E), the modulus of elasticity dictates the stiffness of a given material. Take two tubes drawn to the same dimensions: 35mm in diameter, 60cm long and with a 1mm wall thickness. If one is made from steel and the other from aluminum, they will vary in stiffness. If they are both steel but made from different alloys, they will share the same stiffness.

Ultimate tensile strength (UTS): This is the absolute strength (measured in ksi, or thousands of pounds per square inch) of the tubing—the point at which it breaks. The UTS designates the force required to make a tube break. This determines how thin the wall of the tubing may be drawn. All things being equal, a thinner-walled tube is lighter, and that can make a frame weigh less.

Wall thickness: Steel tubing is made so that the ends of the tubes are thicker than the middle. This is also done with some aluminum tubes, and can be mechanically performed on titanium tubes (by lathe machining). Tubes that are thicker on the ends than in the middle are said to be double-butted. This is done for several reasons. The high heat used to join metal tubes would damage the tubing if it were too thin. Typically, tubes are most stressed at the ends, so reinforcement there increases strength while limiting overall weight. Also, the thin midsection (most of the length of the tube, in fact) dissipates the transmission of vibration through the tube, making the bicycle more comfortable to ride.

Before World War II, tubes were generally straight-gauge, with a 1–2mm wall thickness. Later, when double-butted tubing was introduced, the midsection's wall thickness was reduced to 0.7mm. Butting figures for such a tube are expressed as 1/.7/1, indicating the thickness at each end and the middle. By the mid-1990s, wall thicknesses had been reduced to .7/.4/.7. Today, wall thicknesses on some tubes have been reduced to as little as .5/.38/.5. Aside from the physical difficulty of accurately drawing tubes of very thin walls from such strong materials, there is a reason why bicycle tubing isn't even thinner: the beer-can factor. If a tube's diameter-to-wall thickness rises above a ratio of 60:1, the tube is more likely to buckle under load.

Yield strength: This is the point (measured in ksi) at which a flexed tube prematurely bends, instead of returning to its original position after the load is removed.

Steel

Material Specifics

Steel **is an all-encompassing term for any of a multitude of blends of metals that results in a product that is considered ferrous, that is, magnetic.** While iron and carbon are the base materials in steel tubing, many formulations blend additional materials. The average department-store bike is made from "mild steel" or "1010" (the metallurgical designation for the material). "Chrome-Moly" and "4130" (the metallurgical designation for a type of Chrome-Moly that is often used in tubing specific to bicycles) are common terms for the type of tubing used in many frames from the 1970s to today. They refer to a blend of materials, including carbon, chromium, manganese, molybdenum, phosphorus, silicon, and sulfur. Columbus's Nivacrom is a patented blend that improved strength over conventional Chrome-Moly by more than 30 percent.

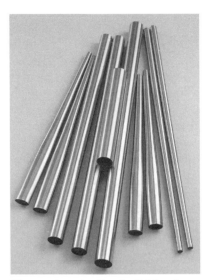

The vast majority of all bicycles made feature steel tubes similar to the ones shown here.

The best-known manufacturers of steel tubing are Columbus, Dedaccaia (pronounced Day-duh-chai), Reynolds, and True Temper. Other producers have included Excel and Tange (pronounced Tahn-gay).

While it is commonly believed that sophisticated alloys are stiffer than 1010, the fact is that all steels share the same density and therefore the same stiffness. What stronger alloys allow a tubing company to do is draw a thinner-walled tube; less material results in a lighter tube. To add stiffness, the tube is drawn to a larger diameter. The increase in material due to the larger diameter results in a tube that is only marginally lighter than its predecessor.

Steel tubing goes through a process of heat treatment in which the tubes are heated to a critical temperature (that depends on the material's composition) and then carefully cooled in order to increase the tubes' strength. The more a tube is heated during frame construction, the greater the loss of this heat treatment. This is why many builders prefer to build frames using lower-temperature silver brazing (low-temperature being roughly 700°F as opposed to the 1,600°F reached in brass brazing). Brazing is a process much like soldering: A thin rod is heated until it melts, and that melted metal essentially glues the tubes together. Brazing is explained in greater depth later in this chapter.

Silver brazing is harder to perform than brass brazing. Joints are more susceptible to separation if the tubes aren't properly prepared, but the tubing isn't heated nearly as much. A more recent innovation in heat treatment is steel that hardens as it cools—gaining strength—following welding or brass brazing. The process overcomes the liability of strength loss due to high heat. Reynolds 853 and True Temper OX-Platinum are examples of this new generation of steels.

Construction

Steel gives a framebuilder more choices in construction method than any other material. There are three major methods of joining steel tubes: lugged construction, fillet brazing, and TIG welding.

For most of the bicycle's history, lugged construction has been used. Lugs are essentially fancy versions of the elbow joints used by plumbers. Many builders will cut and shape them into artful designs.

Fillet brazing is an alternative to lugged construction and involves using brass to solder the tubes together. TIG welding is a recent style of construction for steel. The first frames constructed this way were built in the 1980s. More-specific information on construction methods comes near the end of this chapter.

As a frame material, steel is experiencing something of a renaissance. Most builders working in steel do so to showcase their artistic skills in shaping lugs. Many one-man boutique builders perform exceptional work.

Ride Quality

Double-butted steel tubing is known for its lively ride. Most riders appreciate the way steel offers a balance between road feel, stiffness, and comfort. Double-butted tubing dampens some road vibration while lending a good feel for the road surface below. This quality is what leads many riders to experience the sense that a steel bicycle is an extension of the rider. Because it is impossible to build a steel frame that weighs a single kilogram (2.2 pounds)—as you can with carbon fiber—steel frames are considered a liability on long climbs and during acceleration.

Today's Market

Due to their weight, steel bicycle frames are no longer ridden by top professional cyclists. The last person to ride a steel frame to victory in the Tour de France was Miguel Indurain, whose last win came in 1995.

The majority of steel frames being built today are constructed in one-man frame shops by artisans equally renowned for their fitting skills and artful construction. Generally speaking, most frames will still run on the order of 4 pounds (lbs.), and while that was a reasonable weight in the 1980s, today it is considered heavy by any standard. That is steel's liability—its weight.

Bottom Line (on a scale of 1–5)

VISUAL BEAUTY: 5

STIFFNESS: 4

ROAD FEEL: 5

DURABILITY: 4

WEIGHT: 2

EXPENSE: 3–4

Aluminum

Material Specifics

The most plentiful metallic element in the Earth's crust is aluminum. That should be good news for cyclists, but it's not. The process of refining the metal from bauxite ore into aluminum (the most common varieties used in bicycles are designated 6,000 and 7,000 series) is a nasty, environmentally unfriendly business. Worse yet, bicycle tubing must be made from virgin aluminum; no recycled material can be used.

Aluminum has roughly one-third the density of steel, making it a lightweight material to work with. It also has excellent strength. While not as strong as steel, it has more than 80 percent of the

Aluminum has a dull gray look to it and is thicker than steel tubing. Image courtesy Cannondale

strength of steel in most commonly used alloys. Aluminum, however, does not have an endurance limit. (For reasons I can't explain, the term *endurance limit* is rather counterintuitive. A material with no endurance limit will break easily rather than last nearly forever.) Designing an aluminum frame that will last for more than a few years requires a bit of effort.

Construction

Aluminum bicycle frames have been made by bonding tubes to lugs and by TIG-welding tubes together. Racing frames made from aluminum were introduced in the 1970s. Early aluminum frames were constructed from aluminum tubes bonded to aluminum lugs with an industrial-grade epoxy. The two most popular manufacturers of this frame style were Alan and Guerciotti. The tubes used diameters and wall thicknesses similar to steel frames, resulting in unusually flexible frames frequently referred to as noodles. They remained popular with diminutive women for many years, as no other bikes were available on the market that offered as comfortable a ride in small sizes.

In the 1980s, Klein and Cannondale pioneered large-diameter, thin-walled aluminum tubing. Unlike their predecessors, these frames were TIG-welded (the specifics of construction are covered later in this chapter). The frames had a reputation for being lightweight and stiff. Advances in alloys and heat-treating have helped Cannondale continue to reduce the weight of its frames and balance the efficiency offered by increased stiffness with a rider's need for a modicum of comfort.

Because aluminum frames are susceptible to cracking, precautions must be taken to avoid stresses accumulating in any one part of the frame. Joints where the tubes have been welded together are prone to cracking if there isn't a smooth transition from one tube to another. Vibrations stop anywhere there isn't a smooth transition. Such a location where stresses can collect is called a "stress riser," and it's considered a time bomb in an aluminum frame. In order to cut down on the possibility that the stress riser will encourage a crack to form, the extra material added in welding, called the "bead" of the weld, is typically smoothed by a small, hand-held grinder called a dynafile.

The Italian bike industry embraced aluminum wholeheartedly in the 1990s. Italian tubing manufacturers began offering lightweight aluminum tube sets to builders as typified today by Columbus' Starship tubing. This was the beginning of a radical shift in the Italian bike industry, an upheaval that wouldn't stop for 10 years.

By 1996, aluminum frames had largely supplanted steel as the dominant material for racing frames. There were some pro riders on titanium or carbon fiber frames, but steel had been banished.

Today, aluminum is alloyed with other materials, notably scandium and magnesium, to increase the material's strength. Increased strength means the tubes can be drawn thinner, thereby decreasing their weight. Some manufacturers use a method called hydroforming, whereby hydraulic pressure is used to shape each individual tube.

Ride Quality

Aluminum is usually known for a very stiff ride. While the bonded frames from Alan and Guerciotti were lauded as comfortable on the roughest roads (Sean Kelly twice won Paris–Roubaix while riding an Alan frame), aluminum's more recent history has suffered a public relations challenge. The large-diameter tubes used in aluminum bikes for many years gave the bike a stiff, responsive feel that was great in sprinting, but murder on anything that wasn't glassy-smooth. More recently, manufacturers (led by Cannondale) have decreased the harsh ride of the big-tubed bikes, but in general they are still stiffer than nearly any steel bike. Aluminum tends to be most successful in larger bikes—anything larger than 56cm or so. For tall riders, aluminum is a surefire way to get a stiff frame that won't weigh 4 lbs.

Today's Market

Aluminum was last ridden to victory at the Tour de France in 1998. Aluminum has suffered the very fate it dealt steel—supplanted by carbon fiber as the dominant material used in top racing machines.

Aluminum is offered in some high-end frames, but for the most part it has become a more budget-oriented material for most manufacturers. For example, Trek's aluminum bikes are more affordable than its carbon fiber bikes.

Bottom Line

Visual beauty: 3

Stiffness: 4–5

Road feel: 2

Durability: 3

Weight: 3

Expense: 2–3

Titanium

Material Specifics

Titanium is the marvel of all the metals used for bicycle frames. It is the fourth most plentiful metallic element in Earth's crust, so there is plenty to make into Russian subs and airplane hydraulic lines, not to mention bicycle frames, but the material is even harder to extract from ore than aluminum. Producing titanium tubing is an expensive process because it is labor-intensive and requires large amounts of energy.

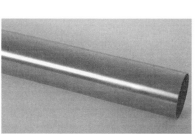

Titanium tubes can be almost indistinguishable from steel before welding; however, it will never rust.
Image courtesy Seven Cycles

Titanium carries half the density of steel and half the stiffness (modulus of elasticity). As a result, it has virtually the same strength-to-weight ratio. What is different is its elongation: how much it can bend before breaking. With roughly double the elongation of steel, on paper titanium looks indestructible. Titanium, like steel, can be built into a stiff or flexible frame, depending on the builder's (or customer's) taste, whereas with aluminum, a stiff frame is virtually required to give the frame a respectable life span.

Titanium is most often found in two alloys referred to by their chemical designation: either 3Al/2.5V (94.5 percent titanium/3 percent aluminum/2.5 percent vanadium) or 6Al/4V (90 percent titanium/6 percent aluminum/4 percent vanadium). The first, 3Al/2.5V, is far more common than 6Al/4V, which is mostly seen in frame fittings such as dropouts and cable guides. Both alloys have high yield strength. Titanium is also available in a "commercial pure" (CP) form with no other metals alloyed. This is the type of tubing that the first titanium builders (led by Teledyne) used; it has also been used by other manufacturers, and almost always to poor results. CP tubing has a reputation for cracking under load.

The challenge to building a top-quality bicycle from titanium comes primarily from its elongation. Though it has great density and modulus numbers, mechanically speaking, the metal is difficult to draw into tubes thin enough to take full advantage of its other properties.

Construction

The only construction method anyone uses in conjunction with titanium is TIG welding. The first frames made from titanium were produced by an American company called Teledyne. The frame tubes were TIG-welded, just as they are today. While a few manufacturers have experimented with bonding titanium tubes into lugs, that construction method has been rare.

TIG welding titanium is unlike welding any other frame material. Titanium is extremely susceptible to contamination by oxygen. When welding titanium, the welder must set up an elaborate argon gas bathing system that prevents oxygen from contaminating a weld as it is made. Due to its incredible elongation, the frame manufacturer must also use special tools when cutting or machining titanium.

Merlin Metalworks, a Boston-based company, was the first company to enjoy commercial success with titanium frames, starting in the mid-1980s. Soon after, the company that is today the largest player in the titanium market, Litespeed, got its start. Eventually, Litespeed's parent company bought Merlin.

While titanium can be painted just like steel or aluminum, most titanium frames are sold unpainted because natural titanium can have a beautiful luster to it. Surface finish varies broadly from one company to another, though, with some imported frames looking more like a firearm than a bicycle. Because titanium demands careful and precise work, a primary indication of a builder's care can be found in the consistency of the weld. Merlin has touted its welders' double-pass weld beads, which look like drops of titanium water lined up shoulder-to-shoulder. Many builders still use this style of weld to this day; great examples can be found on bicycles from Seven Cycles and Moots. This is another reason titanium frames are expensive: The skill required to execute a both beautiful and uncontaminated weld is exceptional, and this workmanship is hard to find.

While the boundaries for titanium seem nearly endless, no builder has been successful in maintaining stiffness while managing to shave weight below 2.5 lbs.

Ride Quality

While it is true that the first titanium frames were all unusually flexible, today it is possible to purchase a titanium bicycle across a broader spectrum of stiffness than you can from any other material. Titanium's greatest selling point—aside from its easy-to-clean finish—is the surprisingly resilient feel the material offers. Most riders who have ridden both titanium and steel say titanium has all of steel's best qualities, and more.

Today's Market

While titanium has been ridden in the Tour de France, it has never enjoyed the widespread success of steel or even aluminum. Today it has been supplanted by carbon fiber at the professional level. Much of this is attributable to a titanium frame's high cost.

Titanium remains attractive because some builders offer exceptional workmanship with the flexibility of custom sizing and even custom geometry. Seven Cycles has taken this range of possibility to its logical conclusion, offering a rider custom sizing, custom geometry, and custom tubing, so that the bike will feature exactly the stiffness the rider wants. And while there are relatively affordable titanium bikes on the market, that silvery luster remains a status statement.

Bottom Line

Visual beauty: 4–5

Stiffness: 2–4

Road feel: 5

Durability: 5

Weight: 4

Expense: 4–5

Carbon Fiber Composite

Material Specifics

Carbon fiber isn't a metal. It is a composite material made up of strands of carbon fiber (or other materials that can include Kevlar and boron) encased in a matrix of resin (also called epoxy). *Matrix* is a fancy engineering term that means that the carbon fibers essentially float within the resin. Strands of fiber are gathered to form what is called a tow. These tows are either woven together or placed side-by-side to form individual plies or layers of carbon fiber. This weave is what you see when you look at a clear-coated carbon fiber frame. Plies are added together to make a laminate (think plywood).

Carbon fiber can be used in a variety of ways to make bicycles. Some designs use traditional round tubes such as this.

Image courtesy Seven Cycles

Most of the rules that apply to steel, aluminum, and titanium do not apply to carbon fiber. The material is so different in application and the variables so numerous that carbon fiber bicycles are, for the most part, the domain of large bicycle manufacturers who can afford to keep composites engineers on staff.

Some of the basic forms of analysis do apply. Carbon fiber has a little more than half the density of aluminum: carbon is around .064 lbs./cu. in., while aluminum is .098 lbs./cu. in. And its tensile strength is higher than steel's. While metals are isotropic, meaning they have uniform tensile strength (you can pull the material in any direction and get the same result), carbon fiber is anisotropic—it is strong in only one direction (along its length) and only when under tension. Under compression, carbon fiber fractures like dry spaghetti noodles. Carbon fiber is little different than rope; it is only useful when pulled upon, so rope can be said to be strong in one direction—anisotropic.

Modulus of elasticity (stiffness) is based on the proportion of fibers to resin (epoxy) and is measured lengthwise, along the axis the fibers run. In this orientation, the modulus numbers are great, better than steel. But as the direction of the measurement changes (say anywhere from 30 to 90 degrees off-axis) the modulus number drops to a fraction of its former heartiness, often as low as 5 percent of its original value. Practically speaking it means that you can experience the stiffness of a frame when pedaling out of the saddle and yet flex the tube wall with your hand by squeezing it—stiff in one direction, but not another.

What carbon fiber absolutely doesn't do is stretch. Elongation is a quality belonging to other materials. While carbon fiber structures can be built to flex, they won't bend . . . ever. What they do instead of bending is break. It's called catastrophic failure and has been the bike industry's great reservation where carbon fiber is concerned. Steel and titanium will generally bend before failing, but carbon fiber snaps like a suddenly angry dog.

Construction

Frames can be made from carbon fiber using several different methods. Plies can be assembled around a round piece of metal called a mandrel. Some manufacturers wind the fiber around the mandrel prior to infusing the fibers with resin. In the case of monocoque (or one-piece) structures, individual plies are grouped together in a specific configuration in a mold to form the laminate. Once "laid-up" (the process of assembling the plies in the mold) around inflatable bladders that press the layers against the mold when inflated, the mold is closed, the bladders inflated, and heat is applied to cure, or harden, the resin.

As mentioned before, carbon fiber's off-axis figures are dismal. To overcome this, engineers will vary the orientation of plies, so that some will be oriented 45 degrees left and right of the original axis. This variation allows the designer to choose in which directions tubes, and ultimately, the bike, will be stiff or flexible.

Ply orientation has also helped engineers solve the catastrophic-failure problem. Traditionally, impacts led to cracks that spread through each layer of fiber, ending with a nasty shearing of the tube. By inserting plies oriented in different directions, cracks are much less likely to occur. Many frames and components are designed in such a way as to direct stress away from certain areas and toward areas that are reinforced, so that if there is a crack, it is much less likely to result in total failure. While a crack means the death of the frame, such engineering can allow the rider to stop safely rather than winding up on the ground.

There are two primary styles of building carbon fiber frames. The first method to emerge (in the 1970s) was to create individual tubes and bond those to lugs. This method is still in use today, though it is losing favor. In 1987, Kestrel debuted the first one-piece frame. With its flowing aerodynamic profile, the bike caused a sensation and became quite arguably the most coveted bike around (at least to the technologically hip—Luddites cried blasphemy).

Each method has its drawbacks. The presence of lugs increases weight. More recently, some companies have assembled frames by wrapping the tubes with carbon fiber, literally lashing them together. Full monocoque structures have sometimes suffered from poor compaction of the layers—unless the layers are fully compressed into a single layer, they lack strength. Manufacturers such as Giant, Kestrel, and Felt mold the front triangle of the frame in a single piece and then bond the seatstays and chainstays later. Manufacturers attempt to differentiate themselves in how they join these sections. Some simply epoxy the pieces together. Others use a process called co-molding, where the joints are wrapped with added layers of epoxy-impregnated carbon fiber in addition to the application of epoxy.

The ability to mold carbon fiber frame components in any shape, configuration, or angle gives the manufacturer much greater control over frame design than is available in working with metals. From being able to place extra material in high-stress areas (such as on the bottom of the down tube where it joins the head tube) to unrestricted geometric choices and even aerodynamic fairings, carbon fiber offers the most limitless palette—and the greatest risk of frame failure if the design has been executed improperly.

One of the new frontiers in carbon fiber technology is a process called "net molding." In this process, carbon fiber is forced under great pressure into precise shapes, shapes that contain hard edges. Due to its anisotropic property, carbon fiber isn't usually suited to making parts with hard edges. The vast majority of carbon fiber bicycles use metal (usually aluminum) inserts at each component interface. The inserts give the manufacturer the opportunity to ensure a secure and properly aligned fit. Net molding was developed by aerospace giant Northrop Grumman as a way to reduce the need to machine composite parts after curing. The process speeds manufacturing and, in the case of bicycles, reduces weight. As of this writing, Trek Bicycles is the only bicycle manufacturer using the technology in bicycles.

The combination of incredible strong new materials, new construction methods, and better design work has caused a carbon fiber revolution in the bicycle industry. Ten years ago, a 3-lb. frame was considered light. Today, some manufacturers offer frames that weigh less than a kilogram (2.2 lbs.)

Ride Quality

If one true thing can be said about the ride of carbon fiber bicycles, it is that the ride quality is as varied as the kinds of music you hear on the radio. Carbon fiber bicycles have ranged in stiffness from sofa cushion to brick wall and in feel from cadaver to swing dancer.

Almost without fail, carbon fiber damps vibration in a way that no metal does. For some riders this smothering of vibration can be rather unsettling, by making it seem as if the bicycle's tires are perpetually underinflated. The best carbon fiber frames balance vibration damping with torsional stiffness and vertical compliance.

Today's Market

Greg LeMond rode carbon fiber to victory at the 1989 and 1990 Tours de France. In 1999, Lance Armstrong initiated a nine-year unbroken streak for the material. Eight of those wins have come aboard Trek Bicycles, the world's largest bicycle company in dollar revenue.

Ten years ago, most manufacturers' top-shelf bicycle was likely titanium or aluminum. Today, almost without fail that bicycle is carbon fiber. Many manufacturers have abandoned steel and titanium entirely, leaving them to custom builders and using aluminum to offer a more affordable alternative.

Custom sizing of carbon fiber frames is offered by an increasing minority of builders, but in each instance the technology used begins with premanufactured tubes bonded together by some method.

Bottom Line

Visual beauty: 4–5

Stiffness: 4–5

Road feel: 4

Durability: 2

Weight: 4–5

Expense: 4–5

Hybrid Designs

Material Specifics

Up until the mid-1980s, bicycle frames had only been built of single materials. Frames were either steel or aluminum or titanium or carbon fiber. Even though on some bicycles carbon fiber tubes might be bonded to titanium lugs, all the tubes were carbon fiber. This changed when Trek introduced a frame that employed three carbon fiber tubes (top, down, and seat tubes) mated to an aluminum head tube and rear triangle. The bikes were fairly light for the day but suffered from poor vibration damping in the rear triangle. Trek all but abandoned this design when it introduced its first full-carbon-fiber bicycle, the OCLV, in the early 1990s.

In 1997, an upstart custom manufacturer, Boston-based Seven Cycles, revolutionized ideas about material usage. By this time, bonding carbon fiber into other materials was largely considered passé. Then Seven introduced a model called the Odonata, which used titanium

Seven Cycles' Odonata led the way in hybrid designs when it was introduced in 1997. Image courtesy Seven Cycles

in every tube except the seat tube and seatstays. Their reasoning was simple: use carbon fiber in the three least-stressed tubes and use titanium in the tubes that most dictate a bicycle's personality and are most vulnerable in a crash. The result was a design that was hailed for its exceptionally comfortable ride. In 1998, many manufacturers introduced models that substituted a carbon fiber wishbone seatstay for aluminum seatstays in their aluminum race models. By 1999, nearly every manufacturer offered a bike with an aluminum, steel, or titanium frame and a carbon fiber rear wishbone. The Odonata is arguably the single most influential road bike design of the last 20 years.

Most hybrids on the market work the theme of incorporating carbon fiber into a frame that would otherwise be made wholly of aluminum or titanium.

Construction Methods

Lugs: The oldest method of joining tubes is lugged construction. Two tubes are inserted into a fitting known as a lug that will hold the tubes at specified angles to each other. The joints are heated with a blowtorch to either roughly 700°F or 1,600°F (depending on if silver or brass is being used to braze the joint) and then a solder (think hot glue) of silver or brass is gently fed into the joint. This form of construction allows the builder

Lugs are often used to join the tubes of a steel frame; they function much like the joints used in plumbing.

considerable opportunity for artistry. The builder may thin, reshape, or cut windows into the points of each lug. Most importantly, this method of construction allows a builder considerable flexibility in designing the frame so that it may be custom sized to a particular rider. While it used to be rare for a steel frame to weigh less than 4 lbs. in a 56cm size, today's steels can enable a builder to create a frame that weighs in the range of 3.5 lbs.

Fillet brazing: In fillet brazing, a builder carefully cuts steel tubes for the frames to exact angles and lengths and then uses layers of brass solder to glue the joint together. When performed by an expert, a fillet will look as if the steel tubes were molded together with smooth, flowing lines leading from one tube to another.

This Steve Rex frame features fillet brazing for seamless transitions between the steel tubes.

TIG welding: TIG stands for "tungsten inert gas." In this form of construction, an electric arc literally fuses the two tubes together. This can be used with steel, aluminum, or titanium. Whereas brazing can be performed with minimal eye protection, welders must wear a darkened mask because the electric arc reaches temperatures upwards of 5,000°F and is as bright as the sun. A filler rod, much like solder, is used to complete the joint, and the welding torch bathes the joint in an inert gas (usually argon) to prevent fusion defects that can be caused by the presence of nitrogen or oxygen. This method is used with nearly all aluminum and titanium frames and a large number of steel frames. In steel frames, this method of construction results in a marginally (a few ounces) lighter frame.

Bonding: A bonded joint is one in which an adhesive is used to literally glue the tube into a lug. This method of construction has been used with aluminum and carbon fiber tubes and occasionally with titanium tubes as well. Today, bonding of this sort is generally only performed with carbon fiber tubes. It's accomplished either by bonding the tubes into carbon fiber lugs or by bonding the tubes into lugged joints in hybrid frames made predominantly of aluminum or titanium, or occasionally steel.

Carbon fiber tubes are frequently glued to steel, titanium, or aluminum tubes; the carbon fiber tube slips inside the other tubes.

TIG welding uses an electric arc to join two pieces of tubing together, one pinpoint zap at a time. Image courtesy Cannondale

Monocoque molding: In monocoque molding, a whole bicycle can be molded as a single piece. This proved to be an inefficient way of working, and the process has been revised some over the past 20 years since it was first applied. Today, sections of a frame are molded in a single piece, rather than as individual tubes, or as one big frame. The most common configurations are the main triangle (top, head, down, and seat tubes, plus the bottom bracket shell), a wishbone seatstay (the two seatstays meet at the point the brake is mounted), and sometimes a wishbone-style chainstay.

Carbon fiber frames that are molded in a few sections and bonded together are called monocoque. Image: Patrick Brady

Chapter 12
The Components of the Modern Road Bike

In other words, everything but the frame.

Since the end of World War II, the bicycle hasn't undergone any radical changes. Its evolution has been a matter of degrees. A bicycle's frame may be its most important ingredient, but it is far from the end of the story. Each part on a bicycle fulfills a specific and necessary role, and has been refined in design and materials to the point that some road bikes can offer a stiff, responsive, and comfortable ride complete with powerful brakes and 20 gears, while weighing less than 15 lbs. With more gears, smoother shifting, handier shift levers, more powerful brakes, more reliable materials, and better engineering, today's technology is to the bikes of the 1970s what the space shuttle is to a hot-air balloon.

While most of a bicycle's dimensions are measured in the metric system and specified in either millimeters or centimeters, some dimensions—for reasons that cannot be easily explained—are measured according to the English system and specified in inches. It is odd and confusing; dimensions are given in the system usually referred to by the industry.

A brief word on value and cost: As with anything in life, performance and quality are directly proportional to cost. With each of the three major manufacturers of components—Campagnolo, Shimano, and SRAM—their top-of-the-line groups are their lightest, best-performing, and most expensive. As it turns out, those seeking the best bang for their buck would do well to purchase midline component groups. When balancing cost against weight, performance, and durability, the best buys have traditionally been Campagnolo's Athena and Centaur, Shimano's Ultegra and 105 and SRAM's Rival and Apex groups.

Components

Fork

The fork is one of the most important parts of a bicycle. It enables the front wheel to turn; without it, a bicycle would only travel in a straight line. Most forks are constructed from carbon fiber and are molded to appear as one seamless piece. In fact, they have four significant elements:

❶ The steerer tube

❷ The crown

❸ The blades

❹ The dropouts

The steerer tube is the portion of the fork the stem clamps to. It passes through the headset bearings and the frame's head tube and joins the crown. The crown is highly reinforced with carbon fiber due to the stresses exerted on it from braking and impacts to things like potholes. The fork blades are the two tubes that run from the crown to the dropouts. The dropouts are usually made from aluminum alloy but are made from carbon fiber on some high-end racing forks.

There are a few dimensions to be aware of with forks; the most important is the diameter of the steerer tube; most are 1⅛ inches, though some top-of-the-line stuff now tapers from 1⅛ inches at the top to 1½ inches at the crown for

The fork turns on bearings hidden in the frame so that you may steer the front wheel.

increased stiffness and strength. The other important dimension of a fork is its rake (covered in more detail in the chapter on geometry). Fork rake is generally 40, 43, 45, or 50mm. This is only important should you need to replace your fork in the event of a crash.

Carbon fiber is used to make most forks because it allows a designer to create a fork that flexes fore–aft, while remaining stiff side-to-side and in twisting. Fore–aft flex makes the ride of the bike more comfortable, while stiffness side-to-side and in twisting makes the bicycle's handling more precise.

Value: While a few forks are available on an aftermarket basis (buying a new fork used to be a popular way to subtract some weight from a bike), frames and forks are usually designed together to give the bike a particular, desired handling.

Weight: A typical carbon fiber fork will weigh a little more than a pound (around 500 grams) while the lightest carbon fiber racing forks can weigh as little as 300g.

Red flags: In the event that you crash, don't be surprised if your fork still looks fine at first glance. Engineers design forks so that in a crash the impact stress will go to the crown. The idea is that should the impact be strong enough to cause a crack, it will occur in the reinforced crown and won't result in catastrophic failure. The upside is that it remains strong enough to allow you to ride home safely. Before riding it again, though, take your bike to your local shop for an inspection. Anything that the technician finds suspicious could result in the suggestion to replace your fork. If they encourage you to replace the fork, take their advice; a fork failure is an ugly event.

Stem

The stem's purpose is to mount the handlebar to the fork and to secure the fork to the frame. The stem clamps onto the fork's steerer tube above the headset, while a removable faceplate clamps the handlebar in place. The stem is a critical component in fitting the bicycle to the rider.

Most stems are manufactured from aluminum or carbon fiber. They are also occasionally made from steel and titanium.

Stems come in a variety of lengths in order to adjust the reach to the handlebar.

Most stems have two Allen bolts clamping the extension of the stem to the fork steerer. The bolts are almost always tightened with a 4 or 5mm hex-key wrench. The inside diameter of the stem's clamp is generally 1⅛ inches, to match the outer diameter of the fork's steerer.

The stem's extension—in combination with the top tube length—dictates a rider's reach (as measured in centimeters) to the handlebar. Stems typically range in length from 80 to 130mm and come in 10mm increments. Occasionally a company will offer stems in 70mm or 140mm extensions, but they are uncommon. The angle of the extension relative to the fork's steerer is called a stem's rise, and it's measured in degrees. An extension cut at a right angle to the quill (90 degrees) is said to have a 0-degree rise. Most stems are reversible so that they can be installed to yield either of two different angles (for example, +/– 6 degrees).

The handlebar clamps to the stem via a removable faceplate that is secured with either two or four bolts. The inner diameter of the clamp corresponds to the outer diameter of the handlebar clamping area, which is generally either 26 or 31.8mm.

Value: Aluminum stems are much more affordable than carbon fiber ones and can reach nearly the same weight. However, the real value in a stem is in its ability to help your bike be fitted to you. Choose a stem first for its fit.

Weight: There's not a lot to a stem, but any stem that weighs less than 150g can be considered fairly lightweight.

Red flags: The aluminum threads found on many stems make them susceptible to overtightening. It's very important that the faceplate and steerer clamp bolts be tightened with a torque wrench. Any snapping sound while tightening a bolt is a bad sign and needs to be followed by a trip to your shop.

Handlebar

The handlebar gives you a place to put your hands while riding, a way to steer the bicycle, plus a secure place to mount the control levers.

Handlebars are manufactured primarily from aluminum and carbon fiber. The prized qualities for handlebars are low weight and stiffness (see a pattern emerging?). Due to the vibration damping offered by carbon fiber, a carbon fiber handlebar is generally more comfortable than an aluminum one.

The drop bar features three different hand positions, which allow a rider to move his hands frequently and avoid discomfort.

Because it is clamped into the stem and levers are clamped to it, a handlebar has no parts other than the single tube that makes up the bar. Despite its simplicity, it has four important dimensions: clamp diameter, width, reach, and drop. The bar's clamp diameter is most often 31.8mm, though 26.0mm, an older standard, is still around. Handlebars generally come in three standard widths: 40, 42, and 44cm, measured center-to-center from each end of the bar. On rare occasions you

may find 38 and 46cm bars, which are handy for women and broad-shouldered men, respectively.

Handlebars also vary in both reach and drop dimensions. Reach is the distance forward of the bar top to which the deepest part of the bend extends, or reaches. Drop is the distance below the bar top that a bar drops; it is not uncommon to hear bars referred to as either shallow- or deep-drop. These variables offer a rider more choices in position and fit.

That's not all; the shape of the drop can vary as well. There are two primary shapes: the traditional round bend, in which the bar curves through a consistent radius, and the anatomic bend, which features a flattened section toward the bottom of the hook that many riders find more comfortable.

Despite the move to carbon fiber for most handlebars, weights have not changed dramatically. In fact, they have generally gone up as broader top sections (often referred to as "wing" bars) have been introduced. Any bar that weighs less than 240g is generally considered lightweight. It is rare to find a bar that weighs less than 200g, though it is becoming more common.

Value: Aluminum offers the best value in a handlebar thanks to its combination of low weight and cost.

Weight: The lightest handlebars on the market are made from carbon fiber and weigh less than 180g.

Red flags: In the event of a crash, if you notice that the bar is bent, feels flexible (which can indicate cracks), or has significant scraping on the handlebar tape revealing the bar beneath, at minimum take your bike to your shop for inspection, and be prepared to replace the bar.

Headset

The headset is the pair of bearings located at the top and bottom of the head tube and through which the fork's steerer tube passes, thereby allowing the fork to turn smoothly. The bearings are situated perpendicular to the steering axis to allow the smoothest possible movement of the fork.

Most headsets use steel ball bearings moving on steel "races" (the path on which the ball bearings travel). Driven onto the fork in a press fit where the crown and steerer tube meet is the crown race, generally made from aluminum. This is the weight-bearing contact point between the frame and fork. Covering the upper bearing is an aluminum cover or cap, followed by spacers (aluminum, carbon fiber, or titanium) when needed in order to match the stem length with the fork length.

The standard diameter of a headset is 1⅛ inches. More and more top-of-the-line bikes feature a tapered fork steerer that uses a larger bottom bearing (usually 1½ inches). The increased diameter has increased fork stiffness, frame stiffness, and bearing life.

Fork length is established at the time a headset and stem are chosen. Generally, fork length is cut to the stack height of the headset (that is, the height that the headset extends above and below the head tube) plus the length of the head tube, plus the height of the stem, plus the height of any spacers used to establish proper fit, minus 3mm.

Value: Higher bearing quality is almost always rewarded with increased bearing life which translates to smooth steering even after years of use.

Weight: Because headsets come in so many styles, it is difficult, if not impossible, to compare weights across brands. As a rule, integrated headsets weigh the least and usually come in at fewer than 100g.

Red flags: An overtightened headset will often develop pits that cause the front wheel to self-center. This is called brinelling and is a sign that your headset should be replaced.

The headset bearings are what enable the fork to turn, giving the bike smooth handling as the bar turns.

Wheels

The wheels on a road bike are clamped in a fork's and frame's dropouts with the help of a device called a quick release. Mounted on the rims are tires and tubes. The rear hub also includes a device called a freehub onto which the set of cogs (called a cassette) is mounted. Most road wheels share the same diameter; hub widths depend on whether the wheel is for front or rear use.

There are two kinds of rims, which correspond to two kinds of tires: clincher and tubular. A clincher rim has sidewalls that the tire inflates against in order to retain shape. Tubular rims have a concave rim profile on which glue is applied, and then the tubular tire is stretched over the rim. Tubular tires and rims offer the highest performance, the most difficult maintenance, and greatest cost. Tubular rims are lighter in weight than comparable clincher rims.

A good set of wheels will run straight (or "true") and feature a smooth, consistent braking surface.

Around clincher rims, a rim tape is stretched to protect the inner tube from the spokes that extend into the rim from the hub. Rims are generally manufactured from aluminum, though more and more, high-performance rims may be made from carbon fiber. Spokes are generally made from stainless steel, though some high-performance wheels use spokes made from aluminum or carbon fiber. The hubs will feature a body made from aluminum or carbon fiber and bearings that are steel, except for some high-performance wheels that use ceramic bearings. The quick-release skewers use parts that may be made from a mix of steel, aluminum, and/or titanium.

On most road bikes, the wheels are sized to a European standard called 700C. The outside diameter is actually 635mm (this can vary by a few millimeters from one manufacturer to the next), so the 700C dimension is essentially meaningless. It dates to a time when an inflated tire on a wheel often measured 700mm. Some decades have passed since that was last the case. Today, a 25mm-wide inflated tire on a rim will typically have a diameter of roughly 680mm.

Each wheel has a hub from which the spokes extend. Hubs are specific to their use, with front hubs being narrower than rear hubs and rear hubs also having a device called a freehub. The freehub is a ratcheting mechanism that allows the rider to coast. It is onto this ratchet that the group of cogs, known as a cassette, is mounted. The cassette will be covered later in this chapter.

On a road bike, front hubs are 100mm wide; rear hubs are 130mm wide. Hubs used on tandem and touring bicycles are frequently 135mm wide.

Most spokes feature a head that prevents the spoke from pulling through the hole in the hub flange, a "J" bend or elbow to orient the spoke on its run from the flange to the rim, and a 1cm threaded section onto which the spoke nipple threads.

The path the spokes travel on their run from hub to rim is called the lacing pattern. While a great many lacing patterns exist, in practice only two are generally used. Radial lacing is the simplest; the spokes run straight from the hub to the rim. This lacing is the lightest because it uses the shortest possible spokes. This lacing pattern is frequently used on front wheels and the nondrive side of rear wheels. The most common lacing pattern over the years is called three-cross, abbreviated as 3x. In this lacing pattern, the spokes are actually woven together like a basket. This process of lacing the spokes together makes for a stronger wheel; it will be less susceptible to lateral forces placed on it.

The number of spokes used in wheels varies widely. Inexpensive, entry-level wheelsets may use 28 spokes for both the front and rear wheels. High-performance front wheels may have only 16 or 20 spokes, and rear wheels may have 20 or 24 spokes.

Rims can also vary in width depending on their use. Rims used for racing are narrowest, while those used on cyclocross, tandems, and touring bikes will be wider.

A smaller rim diameter, 650C, is used with some smaller bicycles built for more diminutive riders. They are most commonly used on bicycles for smaller women.

To be useful, wheels must run true; that is, the rim must not deviate left or right as it spins, or it will rub against the brakes and slow the rider down. Wheels are made true by adjusting the tension of the spokes by turning the nipples that secure the spokes to the rim clockwise or counterclockwise. As wheels decrease in the number of spokes used, the tension required on each spoke to build a strong wheel increases. A wheel with 16 spokes needs roughly double the tension on each spoke (to be strong) of a wheel with 32 spokes.

Some wheels use a new tubeless technology, much like how a car tire and rim work together. While tubeless technology has been used in mountain bikes for a few years, it is by no means a dominant technology; it remains to be seen if it will catch on in the road market.

Except for the frame and fork, no other component has as great an effect on the ride of the bicycle. This is because of a property of physics called rotational mass, which is discussed more in Chapter 13.

Value: Wheels featuring aluminum rims, aluminum hubs and stainless steel spokes offer the best combination of affordability and low weight. Some wheelsets built with these components can weigh less than 1400g.

Weight: Entry-level wheels will likely weigh 1,800–2,000g, while competition wheelsets will weigh between 1,100 and 1,500g, depending on how much carbon fiber is used.

Red flags: Should you notice that a rim is rubbing the brake shoes or even moving noticeably from side to side as the wheel spins, that's a signal to take your wheels to your local shop for truing. If you ever note a crack in a rim, such as one radiating outward from a spoke hole, go see your shop. Ditto for a broken spoke.

Tires and Tubes

Tires and tubes are mounted on the wheels and inflated with air to offer a cushioned ride. There are two kinds of tires, clincher and tubular. Tires have two essential components: a rubber tread and a casing. Clincher tires also have a bead, while tubular tires lack the bead but add a tube and a base tape.

The tread is generally made from synthetic rubber, and this is the surface the bicycle actually rolls on. The tread is quite wide—wider than can be cornered upon. Beyond the tread extends the casing, which is made of several plies of cotton or polyester. As more plies are added, the more puncture-resistant and stiff the tire becomes.

Tubular tires are just that—tubular in cross-section. Though the design is quite old, they are still used today because of their excellent ride characteristics: No other tire offers the rider as much sensitivity or performance in cornering. The tire casing is actually sewn around the tube (why it is sometimes called a sew-up) so the casing encloses the entire tube. A base tape is glued to the tire opposite of the rubber tread, and glue is applied to both the base tape and the rim before stretching the tire onto the rim. The fit is wetsuit-tight.

Tires come in many styles and sizes. Shown here are wire-bead clincher, a Kevlar foldable tire, and a tubular tire.

Clincher tires work a lot like car tires. Air pressure inflates the tube inside the tire, which presses the sidewall of the tire against the sidewall of the rim, and the out-turned edge of the tire, or bead, hooks against the rim, preventing the air pressure from blowing the tire off the rim. Kevlar (yes, the same stuff in bulletproof vests) is used in the majority of all clinchers. The presence of Kevlar allows the tire to be folded for easier mounting and more compact storage.

Tire quality can be judged much the same way bedroom sheets are graded, according to the number of threads per inch (TPI). Just as sheets with a high thread count tend to be softer and more comfortable, a tire with a high thread-count casing will be more supple, offering a more comfortable ride (no one said you'd want to sleep on it). Higher-thread-count tires corner better, are often lighter, and, unfortunately, are usually cut by glass and debris more easily. The finest-quality tires will have a TPI count of 300 or more. Budget tires have fewer than 150 TPI.

The tire may be slick or it may have a bit of tread, but most experts agree that tread on a road bike tire makes little or no difference in the tire's performance, even in wet conditions. The rubber compound used, though, can make a big difference. Softer compounds offer better grip but increase rolling resistance. Tires with a harder compound roll better (lower rolling resistance) and tend to have a longer lifespan, but they don't grip as well in a corner. Many manufacturers offer dual-compound tires. These hybrid tires use a hard compound in the narrow center section of the tire, but on the sidewalls that only touch the ground while cornering, a softer, grippier compound is employed.

Clincher tires offer excellent performance by any measure. They are good enough to be raced and are generally less expensive than tubular tires. The greatest advantage of the clincher tire over the tubular is the ease of changing a flat. With a tubular, the rider must pull the old tire off the rim, overcoming the bond of the tubular cement. With some practice, a cyclist can remove a flatted tube from a clincher, install a new tube, pump it up, and be back on the road in minutes.

Tubes come in a few different varieties. Due to the variation in rim depths, valve stems come in many lengths to make sure the valve stem will extend through the rim so you can pump up the tire.

The valve stem used for tubes appropriate for road bikes is a French design called *presta*. It is quite different from the Schrader valve used on cars and most other types of bikes. It's important to purchase presta valve tubes when you're at the shop, because they have a narrower diameter than Schrader valves, which won't fit in the hole drilled in the rim.

Tubes come in many sizes, but often valve stem length is the more important feature.

Value: The best value in tires is in the midrange of clincher tires, those with a thread count in the range of 150–200. They offer solid performance and reasonable resistance to flats.

Weight: The clincher tire (with tube) is usually a little bit heavier than a tubular tire. As discussed with wheels, rotating mass increases the faster a wheel turns. Lighter tires are easier to accelerate at any speed, and less weight results in superior performance. The benefits of lighter wheels and tires are discussed in greater detail in Chapter 21.

Red flags: Any significant cut in the tread or sidewall of the tire is reason enough to replace it.

Quick-Release Skewers

The quick release is a cam-actuated device that (when operated properly) securely clamps the wheel in the dropout. The quick release has three primary parts: the quick-release head, which includes the cam unit and the lever; the skewer that passes through the hub's hollow axle; and the adjusting nut.

Many quick-release skewers mix materials, using steel-threaded inserts in the adjusting nut, with

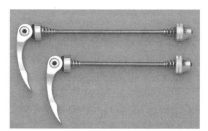

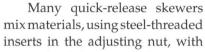

Skewers allow you to remove the wheels with no tools. Very handy for fixing flats on the road.

as much of the rest of the unit made from lightweight materials as possible.

The quick release was invented in 1927 by frustrated racer Tullio Campagnolo. Confounded by a flat tire in cold conditions during a race and unable to loosen the wing nuts holding his wheel to his bicycle, Campagnolo vowed to invent something usable in any circumstance.

The quick release operates by using a lever to operate a cam that tightens the adjusting nut and the quick-release head against the dropout. Serrations on the axle nuts and the ends of the adjusting nut and quick-release head provide a secure grip for the wheel in the dropout. Small springs positioned between the ends of the axle and the head (on one side) and the adjusting nut (on the other) keep the quick release centered relative to the axle for quick installation.

While it is possible to install a wheel with the head and lever on either the left side (nondrive) or right side (drive) of the bike, the standard practice is to position the lever on the left side. Standardized usage became important in racing, where quick wheel changes following a flat meant the difference in getting back to the leaders or not. Also, by placing the levers on the left side of the bike, the drivetrain does not interfere with proper operation of the lever for the rear wheel, which would be more difficult due to the presence of the cogs, chain, and rear derailleur.

Value: The best value in skewers is found in the pair included with almost every wheelset.

Weight: The average set of steel skewers can run upward of 200g, while a pair of titanium skewers can weigh less than 100g.

Red flags: The end of the skewer lever should always point in toward the frame and not out away from it; if the lever points out, it's not tight enough and could come loose.

Bottom Bracket

The bottom bracket is made up of two cups containing bearings that thread into the bottom bracket shell on a frame. The bottom bracket spindle passes through the bearings, and the crank arms mount on the bottom bracket spindle. The bearings allow the cranks to turn.

The bearings, races, and spindle in a bottom bracket are steel, but virtually nothing else is. Aluminum is used for the cups that thread into the bottom bracket shell, and even the bottom bracket shell in the frame (or the insert, if the frame is carbon fiber) is made from aluminum. The bearings feature rubber seals and O-rings to help keep dirt out.

The bottom bracket is composed of two bearings on which the cranks turn.

Increasingly, the spindle is no longer a part of the bottom bracket, but instead an integral part of one or both of the crank arms. It is nothing more than a steel tube that passes through the two bearings.

Value: Again, because the BB is either purchased in conjunction with or as a part of a crank set, riders look at the overall cost of the set.

Weight: Because bottom brackets are integral to the cranks they are made for, no one really worries about their weight; riders will concern themselves with the overall weight of the cranks and BB.

Red Flags: If you notice play in the bearings that allow the crank arms to wiggle side-to-side or grit in the bearings that prevent the cranks from spinning freely, the BB should be replaced.

Cranks

The crankset is composed of the two crank arms (left and right) onto which pedals are mounted. Mounted on the right crank arm are the chainrings. The chain travels over the chainrings to drive the cassette gears on the rear wheel.

The left crank arm has no parts other than the crank arm itself. The right crank arm ordinarily has two chainrings mounted to it, though on some bikes it may have only one or as many as three. Five chainring bolts fix the two chainrings on the "spider" of the crankarm. In the case of a triple crankset (three chainrings instead of two), a second set of five bolts fixes the third ring to the crank arm.

Cranks come in many lengths and chainring combinations. Those made from carbon fiber are noticeably lighter than those made from aluminum.

Many cranksets today incorporate the bottom bracket spindle into one or both crankarms. In the case of Shimano, SRAM, and Full Speed Ahead (FSA), the spindle is part of the right crank arm. In the case of Specialized and Zipp, it is part of the left crank arm. And with Campagnolo, the spindle is a two-piece unit that joins with serrated teeth; each crank arm contains half of the spindle.

Until recently, all crank arms were made from aluminum. Most were constructed through a process called forging (the aluminum is essentially molded under very high pressure). Some manufacturers have used CNC-machined arms as well (a fancy lathe sculpts the crank arm from a big block of aluminum).

Today, almost all the largest manufacturers offer crank arms made from carbon fiber. FSA led the way, followed by Campagnolo, Specialized, and SRAM.

Crank arms come in a variety of lengths to accommodate the varying leg lengths of riders. The most common length is 170mm, but many manufacturers offer cranks ranging from 165 to 180mm in length.

As chainrings increase in diameter, so does the gear development. Small chainrings such as 34-tooth (t) or 39-t are used for slower speeds. Large chainrings such as 50-t or 53-t are used for higher speeds.

Chainring sizes and combinations vary. The most common configuration for many years has been a 53-tooth outer ring paired with a 39-tooth inner ring. This is the pairing the pros use. Recently, the industry (led by FSA) recognized that the average recreational rider does not attain the same speeds as the pros. Lower speeds, combined with the same gears, translate to a lower cadence. To maintain an optimal cadence range of 90–100 rpm, smaller gears are needed. The chainring size is generally 34 teeth for the inner chainring and 50 teeth for the outer chainring. Depending on what cassette is used, this combination gives most riders a great deal more low-end gearing for hill climbing, while maintaining most of the high-end gearing.

A few manufacturers still offer triple cranksets for those riders whose needs are even more low-end. Typically, chainrings of 53 or 52 teeth and either 42 or 39 teeth are paired with a third ring of 30 teeth. This combination can be advantageous for riders who spend a great deal of time in high mountains.

In 1989, Shimano introduced a system of ramps, pins, and chamfers in the cassette cogs and chainrings called Hyperglide. The purpose of Hyperglide is to speed shifting by allowing the chain to be moved more easily and precisely. All the major component manufacturers have adopted the practice of using specially profiled teeth and pins to assist shifting.

Value: Aluminum cranks weigh a bit more than carbon fiber ones, but are more durable and less expensive.

Weight: A pair of carbon fiber crank arms will typically weigh 500–650g. Most aluminum crank arms will weigh at least 700g for the pair, and many weigh much more.

Red flags: Should you ever notice cracks in a crank arm or chainring, the part should be replaced immediately.

Pedals

The two pedals thread into the crank arms and are the point of contact for the cycling shoes. Cleats mounted to the bottom of the cycling shoes clip into the pedals, providing secure attachment for more efficient pedaling.

Pedals have two primary parts, the axle and the pedal body. The axle is made from steel or titanium, or in some cases stainless steel. The pedal body is generally forged from aluminum, though titanium and

Clipless pedals give riders a secure way to fix their shoes to the pedals and yet still release at a moment's notice; there are many different types.

magnesium are also used. The axle will pass through two or three bearings in the pedal body, whose components are steel.

Most clipless pedals work by enabling a cleat mounted on the bottom of a cycling shoe to hook the toe of the cleat in the front of the pedal and then allowing the rear of the cleat to pass a hinged gate at the rear of the pedal. To release the cleat, the rider simply twists a heel out, away from the frame.

Clipless pedals represent an advancement over traditional clips and straps for three reasons:

❶ They do not require use of a rider's hands to operate, and they still hold the shoe securely to the pedal under hard pedaling forces.

❷ They do not cut off circulation in the rider's foot with a strap that wraps around the foot.

❸ They also increase cornering clearance, allowing riders to pedal through corners at higher speeds and correspondingly increased lean angles.

The basic principle behind a clipless pedal was taken from the operation of ski bindings, where the skier inserts the toe of the ski boot in the binding and then steps down to secure the rear of the binding to the back of the boot. Ski-binding manufacturer Look introduced the first clipless pedals in 1984. The Look pedal resonated with cyclists because

it did not require the rider to release the pedal manually; a simple outward twist of the heel disengaged the cleat from the pedal.

Pedals use right-hand threads on the right pedal and left-hand threads on the left pedal to prevent bearing torque from causing the pedal spindle to loosen from the crank arm. Most pedals are secured either with an 8mm Allen wrench inserted in the end of the pedal spindle (through the end of the crank arm) or with a 15mm box wrench on flats near the crank arm.

After 23 years of evolution, pedal manufacturers have yet to agree on a single cleat that can be used for all pedals. At this point, each manufacturer has its own proprietary cleat. The only real point of agreement is the three-hole standard to which most shoes are drilled.

Value: Most pedal manufacturers offer pedals at three price points. In almost every case, the midline pedal gives you the best bang for your buck.

Weight: Because pedal systems vary widely, the weight of pedals is all over the map. A few systems weigh less than 200g, but most weigh between 200 and 350g.

Red flags: Pedals don't often need maintenance, but you should check your cleats every few months for signs of wear.

Derailleurs

The word *derailleur* (pronounced de-RAIL-er) is a French term with enough onomatopoetic oomph that it doesn't need much explanation.

Each bicycle has two derailleurs, front and rear. The front derailleur mounts on the seat tube. The rear derailleur threads into a portion of the frame's right (or drive-side) dropout called the derailleur hanger. Cables that extend from the shifters are fixed to the derailleurs to allow riders to control their movement.

The rear derailleur is responsible for shifting the chain over the cogs of the cassette.

The purpose of the derailleurs is to facilitate gear changes either on the chainrings (front derailleur) or on the cassette (rear derailleur). They accomplish this by guiding the chain through precise movements from one cog or chainring to another.

Most derailleurs on the market are made primarily from aluminum. Both front and rear derailleurs feature springs to assist their movement. The derailleurs move the chain by guiding it through a cage that controls side-to-side movement. The rear derailleur features two "pulley" or "jockey" wheels to guide the chain movement as well as place tension on the chain.

The rear derailleur's spring preload places the derailleur in its rightmost position, behind the smallest cassette cog. All feature a cage with two plates enclosing two pulley wheels. The top pulley is referred to as the guide pulley, while the lower pulley is referred to as the tension pulley. Rear derailleurs will vary depending on their intended use as well. The most common is the short cage, which keeps the pulley wheels close together and uses a design that can accommodate a rear cog as large as 26 or 27 teeth. The long-cage rear derailleur will place the pulleys farther apart than those in a short-cage derailleur so that it can take up the increase in chain length when using a triple crankset, or any time a double crankset is combined with a rear cassette with a large cog of 28 teeth or more.

A rear derailleur features three screws that adjust its function. Behind the derailleur hanger is the B screw, which adjusts how close the upper jockey wheel comes to the largest cog. On the side or rear of the derailleur are the high- and low-limit screws, which set the distance the derailleur can travel.

Precise shifting of the rear derailleur is entirely dependent on proper cable tension. The primary-point cable tension is set at the cable-adjusting bolt, also called the barrel adjustor. The barrel adjustor can be found at the rear of the derailleur; it is the bolt through which the cable passes as it enters the rear derailleur. When proper tension is set, a single shift at the shifter will move the chain from one cog to another.

The front derailleur's spring places the derailleur in its innermost position, over the smallest of the chainrings. The distance inboard and outboard that a front derailleur may travel is called its "stroke." The stroke is set via two screws that limit the travel.

Front derailleurs will vary depending on their intended use. All feature a cage composed of two plates, one inner and one outer; the plates curve to follow the contours of the chainrings in order to guide the chain movement as deliberately as possible.

The front derailleur not only moves the chain from one chainring to the other, it prevents the chain from slipping off the teeth when you hit a bump.

Precise movement of the front derailleur is entirely dependent on proper cable tension. The primary-point cable tension is set at a barrel adjustor. The barrel adjustor is located either at the head tube where the cable housing meets the first cable stop or as part of a device placed in line with the housing shortly after the cable exits the shifter unit. When proper tension is set, a single shift at the shifter will move the chain from one chainring to another.

Value: This goes back to the advice at the beginning of the chapter. Midrange component groups usually offer the best combination of performance, weight and cost. Bear in mind, at the top end of the market, carbon fiber takes the place of a great deal of aluminum. This substitution looks cool, reduces weight, fares poorly in crashes, and costs a bundle.

Weight: Front derailleurs vary widely in weight, though they are, overall, the lightest of all components. Most range between 60 and 100g. Rear derailleurs, due to the higher number of parts, weigh quite a bit more. For rear derailleurs, light is considered less than 200g.

Red flags: The rear derailleur and the derailleur hanger are particularly susceptible to damage in crashes. If you crash, have your shop inspect both for signs of damage; you may need to replace one or both.

Cassette and Freehub

The freehub is the mechanism that allows a rider to coast (or backpedal). An integral portion of the rear hub, it contains a bearing that serves to support the wheel's axle. The cassette is the group of gears that the chain turns in order to drive the rear wheel.

Because the freehub is the point at which pedaling force is translated into wheel motion, it is submitted to incredible stresses. Each freehub part, from the body to the bearings to the springs and pawls that operate the ratchet system, is made from steel, except on Shimano's Dura-Ace freehub body, which is made from aluminum.

The cassette is mounted on the freehub body and is oriented according to a set of splines that prevent the cassette from rotating on the freehub body. It is held in place by a lockring that threads into the freehub body and tightens against the smallest cog of the cassette. Depending on the manufacturer, the cassette may be made of steel (most common), titanium, or aluminum (less common).

In 1991 Shimano introduced its Hyperglide system of cog ramps and tooth contours. The system facilitates smoother shifting by helping the chain transition from one cog to another. Each of the major component manufacturers employs a variation on this system. Riders ultimately benefit, because not only do the cogs and chain wear more slowly due to the smoother movement of the chain across the cogs, but

The freehub holds the mechanism that allows you to coast while riding. Without it, you'd have to pedal all the time.

The number of cogs on the cassette for a bike won't vary, but the sizes of the cogs—the gearing—can vary greatly.

riders may shift under full pedaling pressure, something that was not possible prior to this development.

Today most component groups use a 10-speed cassette. Spacing between the cogs varies a bit from one system to the next, making some systems incompatible with each other. Shimano and SRAM cassettes share the same spacing and are interchangeable. Campagnolo cassettes cannot be used with either Shimano or SRAM.

Value: Steel cassettes offer the best combination of durability and performance.

Weight: Cassettes vary widely in weight. Most weigh less than 300g, but the best-quality racing cassettes weigh less than 200g, with some tipping the scales around 160–175g.

Red flags: Should you ever notice that the chain skips on some cogs, you may need the cassette replaced.

Chain

The chain enables a rider's input to the cranks to be translated into torque on the cassette, which turns the rear wheel. Chains are almost always made from steel. No other material has proven to possess the durability and strength of steel. A few manufacturers have offered titanium chains.

After tubes and tires, the chain is the most consumable component on a bicycle; nothing made of metal wears out more quickly than the chain. The pedaling forces torque the chain enough that it stretches over time. As chains

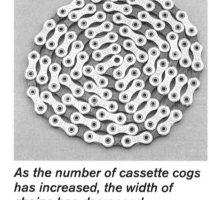

As the number of cassette cogs has increased, the width of chains has decreased.

stretch, the increased distance between pins causes wear on cog teeth. This gradual wearing together of cassette and chain (in extreme cases it can include the chainrings as well) means that eventually both the chain and cassette will have to be replaced. If the chain is replaced frequently enough, however, a rider may avoid replacing the cassette, which can cost four times what a chain does.

Bicycle chains used to be simple to break and reconnect. A chain tool would push a pin through all but two plates, allowing an inner link to be removed from an outer link. Today a variety of special connector pins and master links are used to connect chains. Shimano and Campagnolo both use connector pins that employ a guide or "pilot" to guarantee proper placement of the pin. SRAM and Wippermann use master links that take the place of two outer plates and require no tools to operate.

Value: Stick with steel.

Weight: Chains do not vary in weight much from one manufacturer to another. Most chains weigh 250–275g.

Red flags: If the chain skips over certain cogs on the cassette or has dried out and rusted, it should be replaced.

Brakes

Road bikes have two sets of brakes, one mounted to the front fork and another mounted to the brake bridge in the frame's rear triangle. Each brake functions by a cable that runs to a hand-operated lever.

The majority of a brake's parts are made of aluminum. The bolts holding the brakes to the frame and fork, securing the brake shoes, and centering the brake are usually made of steel, as are some washers, a bearing, and the spring that opens the brake. The brake shoes are made from a hard rubber compound that provides excellent grip but heats up very little even under hard braking.

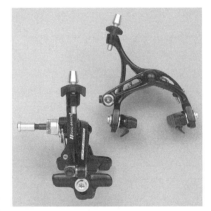

Campagnolo uses a more powerful dual-pivot brake for the front and a less powerful single-pivot brake for the rear to prevent rear-brake lockup.

Most brakes today utilize a dual-pivot design. This reduces caliper flex by shortening the reach of the caliper arms. The low flex of these dual-pivot designs provides greater braking force and more sensitivity in brake application.

Because most tires are wider than the distance between the two brake shoes, brakes also feature a quick release. This release opens the caliper so the tire may pass the brake shoes. Shimano and SRAM brakes feature a small dial adjustor that opens the brake when turned upward. Campagnolo features a two-position retention pin that adjusts at the lever.

Value: Most brakes found in midrange component groups offer a great match of stopping power relative to weight and cost.

Weight: Most calipers weigh in the 250–300g range. Stopping power can be affected by pad selection, and special pads are recommended for use with carbon fiber rims.

Red flags: Should the brake shoes touch the tire, the resulting contact would quickly wear a hole in the sidewall. If you ever notice a loose brake shoe or one that touches a tire, visit your shop.

Control Levers

Road bikes have two control levers that allow a rider to shift gears and brake. The levers are mounted to the hook portion of the handlebar. Two cables run from each lever; one cable runs to a brake, while the other runs to a derailleur. The left control lever controls the front brake and derailleur, while the right lever controls the rear brake and derailleur.

Depending on the manufacturer, the composition of the control levers can vary a bit. The control levers are easily the most mechanically complicated parts on the bicycle; they have a number of small parts, including gears, ratchets, pawls (the "catch" for the ratchet), springs, and levers. The various parts are manufactured

These control levers from Campagnolo feature carbon fiber to reduce weight and two shifter levers hidden behind the brake lever.

from steel, aluminum, plastic, and in the case of the most expensive levers, carbon fiber.

Integrated control levers that allow a rider to both brake and shift with a single unit were first introduced by Shimano in 1991. Campagnolo quickly followed suit. Shimano, Campagnolo, and SRAM have designed systems that operate quite differently. A combination of patent avoidance and innovation has led each company to its own solution.

In Shimano's STI levers, the brake lever doubles as a shift lever. Downshifts for the rear derailleur and upshifts for the front derailleur involve the brake lever as well. By swinging the brake lever inward toward the center plane of the frame, the shift cable is actuated. Upshifts in the rear and downshifts in the front are conducted by a second, smaller lever situated behind the brake lever. This lever also operates by swinging inward. With the rear shifter, downshifts of up to three cogs (depending on the group) may be performed at a time, though upshifts may only be conducted one cog at a time. Both levers can be easily reached whether the hands are placed on the lever hoods or in the drops of the bar.

In Campagnolo's Ergo levers, two different levers independent of the brake lever conduct upshifts and downshifts for the front and rear derailleurs. Downshifts for the rear derailleur and upshifts for the front derailleur are conducted

The right Shimano control lever uses the brake lever to perform downshifts in the rear derailleur. The second paddle performs upshifts in the rear.

The right Campagnolo control lever uses a paddle behind the brake lever to perform downshifts on the rear derailleur. The button on the side of the lever hood executes upshifts in the rear.

by swinging a lever mounted behind the brake lever inward. Upshifts in the rear and downshifts in the front are conducted by a small button situated to the inside of the lever (closer to the center plane of the bicycle). With the rear shifter, downshifts of up to three cogs may be performed at a time, though upshifts aren't restricted at all. Both levers can be easily reached whether the hands are placed on the lever hoods or in the drops of the bar.

In SRAM's DoubleTap levers, a single lever independent of the brake lever conducts both upshifts and downshifts for the front and rear derailleurs. Upshifts in the rear and downshifts in the front are conducted by swinging a lever mounted behind the brake lever inward. Downshifts for the rear derailleur and upshifts for the front derailleur are conducted by swinging the same lever. For the rear shifter, swinging the shifter in only one click conducts an upshift. Swinging the shifter in two clicks conducts a downshift. With the rear shifter, downshifts of up

The right SRAM control lever uses a single paddle to execute all shifts. A single click on the right shifter performs an upshift, while two clicks performs a downshift.

to three cogs may be performed at a time, though upshifts may be conducted only one cog at a time. The lever can be easily reached whether the hands are placed on the lever hoods or in the drops of the bar.

The levers themselves require no adjustment, though the cables should be replaced periodically. Most riders replace the brake and gear cables once each year.

Value: Midrange groups provide the best combination of weight, function and durability.

Weight: Interestingly, control levers are heavier than shift levers and brake levers are separately. Weights have been coming down, but they usually tip the scale in the 300–400g range.

Red flags: It's rare that a crash doesn't result in some damage to a lever. Have your shop check out your levers if you go down.

SECTION II The Machine

Seatpost

The seatpost is the component used to attach the saddle to the frame. It is secured to the frame by a clamp called a seat collar. This system allows a bicycle's saddle height to be adjusted to the proper height for a rider.

Until recently, seatposts were generally made from either steel or aluminum. Carbon fiber has become a favorite material for seatposts due to its incredible strength, low weight, and vibration-damping qualities.

Two diameters of seatposts are found most commonly with road bikes: 27.2mm and 31.8mm. Some manufacturers making frames with aerodynamic tube profiles also use seatposts with an aero profile as well; those posts are generally proprietary.

Seatposts can range 10 centimeters or more adjustment in saddle height and come in a variety of diameters.

The move to compact frame designs has offered an unanticipated benefit to riders. The long seatpost extension (sometimes 100mm or more) offers riders some impact absorption by using a seatpost that flexes some. As bicycle companies have made progressively stiffer frames in the quest to offer superior power transfer, finding a way to reduce shock to the rider has become more difficult. Long seatpost extensions help reincorporate some rider-friendly flex.

Several manufacturers have taken the unusual step of making the seatpost a portion of the frame. Giant led the way on this design and was quickly followed by Time, Ridley, and, more recently, Trek. These integrated seat-mast designs do exactly the opposite of a compact frame with a long seatpost. For riders looking to generate maximum power while in the saddle, riders who need to minimize fore–aft seatpost flex, these frames can offer superior power transfer, if a stiffer ride. Sizing on them can be challenging, though. The integrated seat-mast

designs use a short seat cap on which the saddle is mounted. Most of these seat caps offer 30mm or less of height adjustment, and some actually require cutting away carbon in order to lower the saddle beyond the factory-finished range.

Value: Aluminum offers great strength and durability for relatively little cost.

Weight: Because seatposts are made in two primary diameters and many different lengths, weights vary widely. The lightest posts on the market weigh less than 200g.

Red flags: Seatposts are pretty worry-free, but if your saddle comes loose, you'll want to visit your shop.

Saddle

The saddle is attached to the seatpost and serves as the primary point of contact for a rider because it supports the majority of the cyclist's weight. Saddles come in a variety of shapes, lengths, and widths to accommodate the varied range of human anatomy.

Historically, saddles were hard pieces of leather riveted to steel hardware. Riders would rub these handmade leather saddles with cream to condition them, softening the leather just enough to conform to the rider's specific contours. Unfortunately, if the saddle got wet

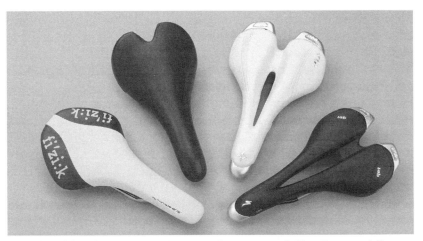

No other bicycle component comes in more varieties than saddles. Despite the fact that they all look pretty triangular, they vary almost infinitely in width, curvature, and length.

for any reason, the leather would soak the water up and then sag. As the saddle dried, it tended to take new shapes, ones usually not to the rider's liking. By the late 1980s, most saddles featured a plastic shell, giving the component its primary shape. Foam padding was glued to the plastic shell and then leather (either real or synthetic) was stretched and glued over that. These saddles were much softer, required no break-in time, and never changed shape.

In 1996, urologist Dr. Irwin Goldstein authored a study concerning erectile dysfunction in cyclists. Telling men that cycling could hurt their ability to perform in bed caused an immediate reaction in the bicycle industry. The two primary responses were either to dismiss Goldstein's findings or to design new products to sell to panicked cyclists.

Goldstein's findings purported to show (this subject is still controversial) that the average saddle compressed the pudendal arteries, which supply blood to the penis. Prolonged interruption of blood flow to the penis is believed to contribute to erectile dysfunction. As it turns out, this is not a strictly male issue. The problem is that cyclists, both male and female, spend most of their time on a racing saddle not on the ischial tuberosities—the "sit bones"—but on the ischiopubic rami, the bone that connects the ischial tuberosities to the pubic bone. This position compresses the Alcock canal, which contains the pudendal arteries as well as nerves, thus decreasing blood flow to and sensation in the genitalia.

The response by many saddle manufacturers has been to make saddles that include a long, narrow cutout in the center of the saddle.

Just as the materials used in other components have evolved, saddle design has incorporated new materials. Saddles often feature rails (the point of contact for the saddle with the seatpost) made from titanium or carbon fiber. The shell may be made from carbon fiber rather than plastic. In some cases, Kevlar may be used in place of part of the shell.

Value: There is little substitute for comfort; most riders concentrate on finding a comfortable saddle, rather than focusing on what it costs.

Weight: Before the advent of the plastic shell and lightweight rails, saddles could weigh upwards of 600g. Today a lightweight saddle will weigh less than 200g.

Red flags: Torn leather is neither comfortable nor good for shorts. If your saddle's leather tears, replace it.

Chapter 13
The Geometry of a Road Bike

When compared with mountain bikes, beach cruisers, three-speeds and other adult bicycles, road bikes handle in a manner that can be characterized as nimble. For anyone switching from another type of adult bicycle—beach cruisers and three-speeds especially—the first mile on a road bike may seem like driving a sports car after exiting a school bus.

Road bikes are meant to turn quickly and capitalize on the agility of an athlete. The idea of "grace under pressure" reflects how a road bike can seem nervous, unstable even, at 8 mph, while at 28 mph the same bicycle seems as relaxed as a napping child. Conversely, anyone who has ridden a beach cruiser down a hill at any real speed is likely to report that the bike seemed unstable and insensitive to rider input. These differences in handling are attributable to the changes in geometry.

Bicycle geometry determines a bicycle's fundamental character. You may have noticed that a sports car handles quite differently than an SUV. While changes in suspension between cars can change ride characteristics, the major changes in handling between one style of car (such as a sports car) and another (such as a minivan) can be defined in terms of geometry.

A sports car has a low center of gravity (CG), a short wheelbase (resulting in a tight turn radius) and, usually, a fairly stiff suspension.

The experience of driving such a car can be vaguely intoxicating and make even a run to the supermarket feel like a trip around the Nürburgring. The SUV, by comparison, has a much higher CG, a longer wheelbase, and a cushier ride. Riding in a big SUV going 85 mph feels like 50 mph due to its calm handling. Quick turns, though, cause them to lean due to the high CG, and the driver's impression of stability fizzles away like a shaken soda. The sports car will never seem as calm and comfortable at freeway speeds, but nothing else gives quite the thrill when driving.

Road bikes are the sports cars of the bicycle world. They are designed to turn with precision and yet maintain composure in a group of cyclists moving at 25 mph. No other bicycle matches straight-line stability with cornering agility so well, which is why no other bicycle is used to ride in that fast-moving group known as a peloton.

The Least You Need to Know

To be perfectly honest, there are scores of pros who don't know much about bike geometry. You really don't need to know anything about geometry to be a cyclist. The vast majority of the information in this chapter is most helpful if you are shopping for a new bike or are reading bike reviews in cycling magazines. If you're curious to know what really differentiates bikes and why some get better reviews than others, read on.

Road Bike Dimensions

A builder determines the dimensions of a road bike according to the anticipated rider's size and the preferred style of riding or racing for which the bike will be used. They are as follows:

Wheel size is the first great determiner of a bike's character. Because the vast majority of all road bikes use 700C wheels (roughly 28 inches in diameter), wheel size is often considered a given. Smaller wheels may be used for some adult women's bikes. While many variables—notably tire and rim weight—can influence a wheel's rotational mass, the wheel diameter has the largest influence on a bicycle's handling. Change the wheel diameter of a bike, and you have essentially changed the nature of the bike.

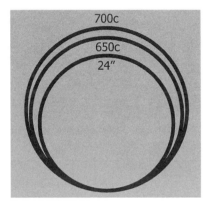

By far, the most common wheel size is 700C, but some women's bikes use a smaller size.

Bottom bracket (BB) height determines a bicycle's center of gravity. Many designers consider this to be a bicycle's most influential dimension when defining a bicycle's handling characteristics. A bicycle with a low center of gravity is generally considered to be more maneuverable, while a bicycle with a higher bottom bracket is considered to have more straight-line stability. Bottom bracket height on an American racing bike is generally 27cm. Until relatively recently, most European road bikes had a lower BB height (ranging from 26 to 26.5cm) due to the need for maneuverability on mountain roads; today almost all carbon fiber bicycle made by European companies have a 27cm-high BB. This height gives the bicycle a CG low enough to be maneuverable yet high enough to allow a rider to pedal through corners without scraping a pedal against the ground. To determine the BB height of a

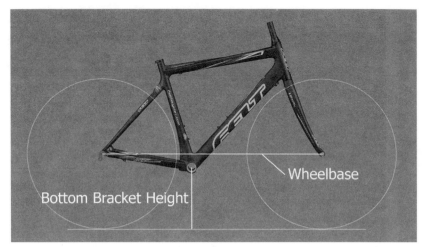

Two of the most important dimensions of a bicycle's geometry are bottom bracket height and wheelbase.

bicycle, hold the bicycle upright and measure along a line perpendicular to the ground that passes through the center of the bottom bracket spindle. BB height is sometimes expressed as BB drop; a height of 27cm generally translates to 7cm of drop. Drop is the measurement builders actually use when designing a bicycle, as they may not know what tires will be used with the bicycle; wider tires are larger in diameter and raise the BB height. BB drop can be determined by measuring BB height and then by measuring the wheel's diameter from the ground to the center of a wheel axle. The difference between these two numbers is the drop. Tire size will affect this dimension—wider tires are larger in diameter and raise the bike's CG.

Wheelbase also influences how a bicycle handles. Just as a car with a short wheelbase can turn tighter corners than a long truck, a racing bicycle with a short wheelbase will carve a tighter corner than a touring bike with a long wheelbase. Bicycles with the shortest wheelbases are designed for racing, especially criteriums. Longer wheelbases will be found on touring bikes and, of course, tandems. To determine a bicycle's wheelbase, simply measure the distance between the center of each dropout, that is, the two wheels' axes. Frame size affects wheelbase; larger frames will have a longer wheelbase. Most road bikes have a wheelbase that falls between 96 and 102cm in length.

Head tube angle (HTA) helps determine how quickly a bicycle steers. It is expressed as an acute angle drawn between the ground and the axis of the head tube. Road bikes typically have a head tube angle between 72 and 75 degrees. A steeper head tube (larger number) results in quicker steering. Touring bikes tend to have slacker HTAs, while racing bikes usually have the steepest HTAs. Frame size affects HTA, with smaller frames typically having a slacker angle and the largest frames having a steeper angle.

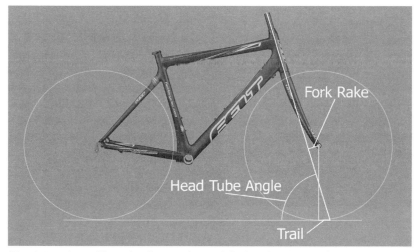

The interplay of head tube angle and fork rake determine a bicycle's trail.

Fork rake is the offset, measured in millimeters, between the axis of the fork's steerer tube and the center of the dropout. More fork rake will make the bicycle steer more quickly; less fork rake slows the bicycle's handling. Road bikes generally use a fork with between 40 and 50mm of rake.

Trail results from the interplay of head tube angle and fork rake. It is the difference between the point where the steering axis meets the ground and the point where a line perpendicular to the front wheel's axis meets the ground. Trail determines how quickly a bicycle steers. Unless you know both head tube angle and fork rake, you will not know the full story of how a bicycle steers (at least on paper). The

contemporary racing bike often has 5.6cm of trail. Smaller frames may have more, while larger frames may have less. As trail increases, a bicycle's slow-speed stability increases, and when trail decreases, a bicycle's high-speed stability increases at the expense of slow-speed stability. After bottom bracket height, trail is the most important aspect of a bicycle's geometry. To find out your bicycle's trail, consult the manufacturer's geometry table for the model or take the known figures for head tube angle and fork rake and plot them in the trail appendix in the back of this book.

Seat tube angle (STA) determines a rider's weight distribution between the front and rear wheels while allowing the designer to accommodate a taller rider's longer femur when increasing frame size for that rider. It is expressed as an acute angle drawn between the ground and the axis of the seat tube. Taller riders need slacker seat tube angles while more diminutive riders need steeper ones. This relationship is explained in more depth in Chapter 16.

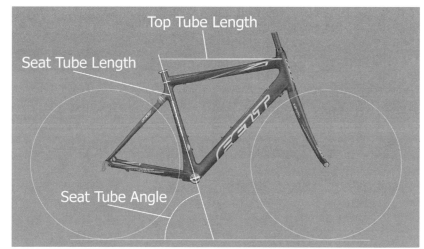

Seat tube angle and top tube length are the two most important dimensions when determining what size bicycle to purchase.

Seat tube length is how frame size used to be determined. For more than 100 years, road bikes were built with a top tube that was horizontal, that is, parallel to the ground. Measured in centimeters, seat tube length was determined by a rider's standover clearance above the top tube. Optimal clearance between the top tube and a rider's crotch was 2–3cm. The advent of sloping top tubes, which have increased frame stiffness while decreasing frame weight, have made this measurement nearly irrelevant. While a designer still needs to select a particular length, the number has no relation to determining who will fit on the given bicycle.

Top tube length is the real determiner for which bicycle fits which rider. Measured in centimeters, top tube length is measured on the horizontal from the axis of the head tube to the axis of the seat tube. The actual length of a sloping top tube will be different, but it's that measurement taken horizontally that is what's important. That number gives the bicycle-fit technician an easy-to-digest figure that can be correlated to a person's reach. This relationship is explained in more depth in Chapter 16.

Chainstay length is the distance from the axis of the bottom bracket to the center of the frame's dropouts, measured in centimeters. Most road bikes have chainstays in the range of 40–41cm. Touring bikes can have chainstays as much as 6cm longer than this to allow clearance between the rider's heels and the bags on the rear rack. Bicycle designers tend to increase chainstay length on large frames in order to properly distribute a rider's weight between the front and rear wheels. The

Front center and chainstay length determine the weight distribution between the front and rear wheels.

corresponding measurement to chainstay length that allows a designer to determine weight distribution is called front center.

Front center is the distance from the center of the bottom bracket to the center of the fork dropouts. The distance, measured in centimeters, helps a builder to distribute weight proportionally between the front and rear wheels. Typically, weight should be distributed so that 40 percent of a rider's weight is on the front wheel while 60 percent of a rider's weight should rest on the rear wheel.

Road Bike Evolution Post-1945

At first glance, today's road bike looks much the same as the road bikes that were sold after World War II. On closer inspection, while they have all the same tubes, the dimensions used have evolved quite a bit.

In broad strokes, today's bikes have a higher bottom bracket, a shorter wheelbase, and less trail. Why have these dimensions changed? In short, the nature of bicycle racing has changed. Because racing has driven most of the innovation in road bikes (touring bikes are a definite exception to this rule), as racing has changed, bicycles have changed to reflect this. Indeed, racing has changed in part due to evolutions in the bicycle itself.

Postwar bicycles were long on stability and shy on aggressive maneuverability. It was easy to keep them pointed straight, but due to the low bottom bracket height, it was fairly easy to get them to lean over in a turn. No one pedaled through corners back then, so pedal clearance wasn't an issue. The bikes had more trail because the highest speeds they reached were low by today's standards.

Fast-forward 60 years, and racing bikes are very different. The BB has risen dramatically because racers will pedal through corners in part due to the advent of low-profile clipless pedals. The wheelbase is noticeably shorter because racers carve much tighter turns in races. Trail has decreased to allow bicycles to be steered into tight turns as racers respond to lightning-quick changes in circumstances. These bikes enjoy their greatest stability at speeds above 20 mph. Indeed, today's road bike has evolved to such a point that manufacturers offer many subspecies of the road bike.

Road Bike Subspecies

The following eight bicycles are the most common variations of the road bike. Included are the differences between the bikes as expressed in geometry. It used to be that anything that wasn't a touring, track, or cyclocross bike was a "road" bike. Today, many manufacturers have begun to distinguish between road bikes meant for racing and road bikes meant for purely recreational riding.

Sport road bikes are designed specifically for the most aggressive riders and riding conditions. They are meant to handle much better at 28 mph than they are at 14 mph. They usually feature little trail (shorter than 5.6cm), a high bottom bracket (higher than 27cm) and a short wheelbase (only the largest size will exceed 100cm). The handlebar is often 8–10cm lower than the saddle, giving the rider an aerodynamic position. The bikes are great fun for a one-hour race, but on a six-hour century (a 100-mile ride) are nervous enough in their handling to weary some riders. Popular examples include the Specialized Tarmac, Trek Madone, Giant TCR, Cannondale Super Six, and Felt F series.

Sport road bikes offer the agility necessary for racing in close corners.

Touring bicycles are the 18-wheelers of the pedaling world. They use heavy-gauge tubing and come equipped with brazeons that allow racks to be mounted that carry panniers—the luggage of the touring set. A loaded touring bike can weigh 100 lbs. or more. As a result, they use strong cantilever brakes and a drivetrain that features a triple chainring crankset. A well-designed touring bike will have a low bottom bracket (around 26cm) and an exceedingly long wheelbase to allow clearance between the rider's heels and the rack-mounted panniers. Head and seat tube angles are traditionally very slack. The slack angles tend to transmit less rider shock; also, a slack seat tube angle allows the rider to sit more upright. A touring bike's saddle position encourages a pedaling style that recruits the larger muscle mass of the hip flexors to head off fatigue over the long days. The handlebar is generally positioned nearly level with the saddle. Touring bicycles are heavier than your average road bike because of the heavier tubing used to carry both the rider and his bags.

Touring bikes allow you to travel backpack-style with your bike. They offer calm handling for long days in the saddle.

Grand touring road bikes split the difference between the low-weight and high-performance components of the competition bike with the calmer demeanor (thanks to a longer wheelbase and more trail) of a touring bike for riders who aren't racing much or at all. Endurance road bikes are made with a longer head tube to give the rider a more upright riding position than found with competition bikes. The BB will typically be around 27cm high, have a wheelbase of between 96 and 102cm, and feature 5.6cm of trail. The long wheelbase helps contribute to vibration damping, leaving the rider fresher at the end of a long ride. The cyclist riding organized centuries and charity rides benefits from the calmer handling that these bikes exhibit over the five to seven hours an event may last. Popular examples include the Specialized Roubaix, Trek Pilot, Giant Defy, Cannondale Synapse, and Felt Z series.

Grand touring bikes combine the high-performance features of a sport bike with the calmer handling of touring bikes.

Time trial bikes are used in the race *contre le montre,* against the clock, as the French say—the race of truth. They feature special bars that give the rider a choice between a higher position with more steering control for cornering and braking and a forward-reaching but exceedingly low and aerodynamic position for going as fast as possible. Usually the BB height, wheelbase length, and frame angles won't deviate that much from a traditional road bike, though the fork may feature a little less rake. The shape of the frame itself will emphasize aerodynamics to increase a rider's advantage over the wind. Time trial bikes intended for triathlon use may have a steeper seat tube angle (sometimes ranging from 75–78 degrees) or a forward-swept seatpost to adapt a traditional time trial frame to the needs of a triathlete.

Time trial bikes evolved for racing against the clock; they offer exceptional aerodynamics.

Track bicycles are built solely for velodrome riding, perhaps the most specialized form of bicycle riding. These bikes feature one gear and no brakes. Unlike a BMX bike (which has but one gear but also freewheels, thus allowing the rider to coast), a track bike uses a fixed gear, which means that as long as the bike is moving, the pedals are turning. These bikes have a high BB (often higher than 29cm), an exceedingly short wheelbase (even the largest sizes won't exceed 100cm) and combine a steep HTA with little fork rake for more trail than the average road bike. While they are made specifically for riding on a track, they have gained popularity for use on the road.

Track bikes are the essence of a bicycle with little more than a frame, wheels, handlebar pedals, and chain.

Tandem bicycles are built for two riders and bear little in common with other road bikes. A tandem's wheelbase is nearly double that of a standard road bike (170–185cm), has a higher BB (27.5–28cm is common), and little trail (5cm or less). There is, however, much less agreement between manufacturers on what constitutes acceptable geometry for tandems than there is for road bikes.

Tandems are great fun for sharing the riding experience with another cyclist. It's a different and intimate take on cycling.

Cyclocross bicycles are built for a form of racing gaining in popularity in the United States. Cyclocross is a form of off-season racing in which riding takes place both off- and on-road. Riders encounter barriers periodically intended to force the racers to dismount the bike and carry it over the barrier. In ideal conditions, the brief run warms the feet, allowing the rider to continue racing. Conditions in cyclocross races are typically cold, often muddy, and sometimes quite slick. The cyclocross bike is similar to a standard road bike but features a great deal more tire clearance to allow for knobby tires (sometimes as wide as 40mm) plus sticky mud; a high bottom bracket (28cm is considered low); and powerful cantilever brakes such as might be found on a touring bike. Due to the off-road conditions, cyclocross riding speeds are lower than typically experienced with a road bike. As a result, smaller chainrings are used (a combination of 46 and 39 t chainrings is common) and a larger cassette (such as a 12–27) to give riders the low gear combinations necessary to ride through the variable conditions.

Cyclocross bikes are purpose-built for cyclocross racing. They feature more clearance for wide, knobby tires, lower gears, and a slightly shorter reach.

Changes to an Existing Bike

The way a bike handles isn't static. The geometry chart tells only part of the story. What ultimately determines how your bike handles is weight distribution; where your weight is situated relative to the front wheel and bottom bracket will make a big difference in how your bike handles. A number of factors influence how your weight is distributed. They are:

Stem length: As stem length increases, handling slows (by increasing weight on the front wheel), making the bike feel more calm and stable. Conversely, as stem length decreases (by decreasing weight on the front wheel), handling quickens, making the bike feel more responsive. Any change in stem length of 1cm provides a minor, but noticeable, change in handling.

Bar height: As bar height increases (due to stem angle or spacers used), handling quickens (by decreasing weight on the front wheel), making the bike feel more responsive. Conversely, as bar height decreases, handling slows (by increasing weight on the front wheel), making the bike feel more calm and stable.

Saddle height: As saddle height increases, handling slows (by raising the rider's center of gravity), making the bike feel more calm. Conversely, as saddle height decreases, handling quickens (by reducing the center of gravity), making the bike feel more maneuverable.

Saddle setback: As the saddle moves forward, handling slows (by increasing weight on the front wheel), making the bike feel more responsive. Conversely, as the saddle moves backward, handling quickens (by decreasing weight on the front wheel), making the bike feel more calm and stable.

How It All Adds Up

Now that you've got the basics of road bike geometry, you're asking yourself, "What's it all mean?" It can be difficult to corroborate geometry charts with real-world experience if you've only ridden one bike. Despite the subtle differences in their design, road bikes can offer a rich variety in ride, like different colors of a rose. Whenever you have the opportunity to ride another bike, give it a try; who knows, you might find something you like even better.

No one detail is particularly important. Some European bike companies used to keep their head tube angle measurements secret, which is silly because all road bike head tube angles fall in a tiny range; this is not unique like the formula for Coca-Cola. The most important factors are top tube length (for fit), trail (steering geometry), and BB height and wheelbase length (for overall handling). Smaller riders must also consider the effect that wheels smaller than 700C will have on overall handling.

Chapter 14
Purchasing the Right Bicycle

We will assume that because you are reading this book you have discovered an interest in road bikes and find them preferable to beach cruisers or skateboards. The most important question you must answer before purchasing a bicycle is how you'll use it. Understanding how the different bike designs affect the riding experience is imperative if you want to have fun. Imagine your shock if you were to purchase a Mini Cooper only to learn you couldn't transport your daughter's Brownie troop to the park.

There are many rules of thumb in cycling, but when purchasing a bike, there is one the purchaser must keep in mind: As performance increases, so does the cost of a bicycle. Similarly, the more specialized the bicycle, the more expensive it tends to be.

Which Bike Is Right?

As you learned in Chapter 13, there are a number of types of road bikes. The bike you choose should reflect your current and anticipated needs.

Sport road bikes are rather specialized bikes. They are made to excel in the tight quarters found in bike races. Due to their quick handling and low-slung position, these racing bikes are good but not ideal for centuries. If your idea of fun is lining up for a bike race, this is the bike for you.

Touring bikes are designed for riders who want to see the world turtle-style. They are best suited to riders who wish to blend backpacking with cycling. So if sleeping under the stars and cooking your own meals sounds like romance itself, this is your bike.

Grand touring road bikes (sometimes called century bikes) are the first real alternative to racing bikes that recreational riders have been offered in decades. Grand touring bikes can make any long ride (50 miles or longer) more enjoyable yet still offer handling sharp enough to allow you to dip your foot into the racing world as well.

Time trial bikes are primarily purchased by triathletes. Road racers usually only participate in a few time trials each year, unless they consider themselves specialists. Time trial bikes are special-purpose bikes and not well suited to century or group rides. They aren't allowed in road races and criteriums. If your day isn't complete without a swim, a ride, and a run, this is your bike.

Track bikes have gained popularity among many urban riders but are intended for one use—the velodrome. If you frequent a track and are planning to race on it, having your own properly fitted track bike will benefit your performance. On the road, these bikes are referred to as "fixies" and score big style points, but without the benefit of brakes, their use on the road is not without hazard, rather like attempting to tame a grizzly bear.

Tandem bikes are most popular with couples who both ride. They can be a fun alternative within road riding. For couples, the captain (rider in front) is most often the man, who is usually the larger and stronger rider, while the stoker (rider in rear) is usually the woman. Riding tandem tends to be most successful and enjoyable when both riders are experienced cyclists.

Cyclocross bikes are made for those racers who experience existential ennui when the road-racing season ends; they take up cyclocross racing in the fall and winter in order to satisfy their racing jones. Even if you don't plan to race cyclocross, a 'cross bike can be the right answer for you if the roads near home are largely gravel or unusually rough.

Price Point

You have probably noticed that with most consumer goods, manufacturers tend to offer fairly similar-quality goods within a given price range. Price competition has forced manufacturers to offer similar (if not identical) features at a given price. If we look at the example of cars, it means that all $30,000 sedans are going to offer roughly the same gas mileage, horsepower, and amenities, from the stereo to ABS and airbags.

In bicycles, price point can be determined by a few factors, but the primary one is componentry. The three largest bicycle-component manufacturers—Shimano, Campagnolo, and SRAM—each offer a variety of component groups to reach consumers on different budgets. Shimano offers seven different component groups covering the broadest price spectrum; Campagnolo offers six groups, and SRAM three. Many of these component groups are offered in multiple crank configurations, including standard doubles, triples, and compacts.

Bicycles equipped with a given component group tend to fall within a several-hundred-dollar price range. Faced with three bicycles made from the same frame material and same component group, price variation can usually be attributed to the other parts included on the bike; higher-quality parts will ordinarily result in a reduced weight for the bike, as well as an increased price. Conversely, a lower cost for the bicycle will usually result in an increased weight due to the component choice.

Following are some basic guidelines to the various price points. Bear in mind that they overlap some and many riders (and their habits) cannot be defined in a single sentence—not all racing bikes get raced, and not every racer has an $8,000 bike.

Entry-level

PRICE RANGE: $1,000–$1,500

RIDER: New to the sport

MILEAGE: 50 or fewer per week

Typically, entry-level bikes are those intended for riders new to the sport and likely to restrict their riding to weekends. These bikes are vastly better than the 10-speeds most people first rode as children. Shimano's Sora and Tiagra and Campagnolo's Xenon and Mirage parts groups were designed for this price range and user. Bikes in this price range are relatively lightweight (some will weigh less than 20 lbs.) and offer integrated control levers and an 8-, 9-, or 10-speed drivetrain combined with a compact crank or a triple. They offer good performance for the weekend user.

Recreational

PRICE RANGE: $1,800–$2,500

RIDER: Fit and committed to the sport in season

MILEAGE: 50–75 per week

Recreational bikes are meant for the cyclist who rides every weekend during the season and may even make it out some during the week. Shimano's 105, Campagnolo's Veloce, and SRAM's Rival components were designed to serve this price range and user. These bikes will be lightweight (they will weigh less than 20 lbs.) and will include integrated control levers and a 10-speed drivetrain mated with a triple or a compact crank. They will offer solid performance for the consistent rider.

Enthusiast

PRICE RANGE: $3,000–$5,000

RIDER: Cycling is their favorite sport

MILEAGE: 75–150 per week

The enthusiast bicycle is generally intended for the rider who is riding three or four days per week so long as the weather is good. Shimano's Ultegra, Campagnolo's Centaur, and SRAM's Force groups were all intended for this market. Bikes in this range are lightweight (they will weigh less than 17 lbs.), and they include integrated control levers and a 10-speed drivetrain mated to a standard double or compact crank. These bikes offer performance barely distinguishable from that of the best racing bikes.

Racing

PRICE RANGE: $5,000 or more

RIDER: Lives to ride

MILEAGE: 150 or more per week

The vast majority of all bicycles costing more than $5,000 will never be raced. One of the oddities of cycling is that because riders are more likely to crash in a race than on a group ride, many cyclists will have a less expensive bike to race and save their best bicycle for group rides with friends, where the risk is lower. Riders who spend more than $5,000 on a bike generally consider themselves cyclists first and foremost. These bikes offer the lowest weight (often less than 15 lbs.) and greatest performance and comfort.

Fitting

While fitting is covered in Chapter 16 in some detail, getting properly fitted at the time you purchase a bicycle is imperative. Unless an experienced bicycle fitter takes the time to size the bicycle to you, you cannot be certain you have the proper size bicycle. Some shops include a basic fitting with the cost of the bicycle. If you plan to ride the bicycle two days or more per week, a thorough fitting is a good investment. Plan to spend at least $100 on a fitting that will last roughly 2 hours.

Production vs. Boutique

It used to be that high-quality bicycles could not be made production-style in large batches. The care required to reliably join the best steel tubes necessitated that builders create each bicycle essentially one at a time. This approach gave builders the opportunity to build bicycles for each individual customer, thereby helping to ensure an ideal fit for the customer.

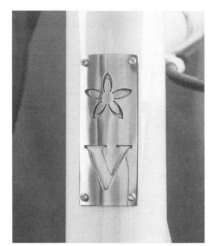

Most custom builders include a head tube badge on the front of the bike. Think of it as the status symbol of the cycling set.

Production methods have improved dramatically in the last 30 years. Indeed, the most sophisticated carbon fiber bicycles are made using production methods. Because quality is not a concern, the question is really whether a production bike will fit you and your wallet. Only you can decide which bike fits your budget. Anatomically speaking, a professional bicycle fitter can make a production bicycle fit nearly anyone. Unless you are very tall or very short, or have an anatomic issue that requires specially tailored clothes, it is unlikely that you will have difficulty finding a production bicycle to fit you.

Custom-sized bicycles produced by small boutique builders still represent the pinnacle of the bicycle-buying experience. Many cyclists report greater satisfaction with the buying experience due to the extra service, and greater satisfaction with the final product due to the increased range of choices—including everything from color to how stiff you want the bike to be and how you want it to handle. For many, the custom experience gives the rider the opportunity to combine the handling of an old favorite with low weight and the stiffness of more recent material innovations. Think of a custom bike as a buffet with all of your favorite foods present.

Handbuilt bikes, such as this Speedvagan by Vanilla Cycles, offer the customer the opportunity to interact with the builder.

Image: Patrick Brady

Chapter 15
The Bicycle and Rider Combination

The fastest cyclist is one who is both comfortable and efficient. Even if you have no interest in racing a bicycle, your experience will be more enjoyable if you ride a bicycle that has been fitted to you. A properly fitted bicycle will allow you to go farther with less effort, enabling you to return home with energy to spare.

How you interact with your bicycle determines your comfort, control, and efficiency. Comfort can be defined as your ability to continue pedaling in the given riding position—a position that allows you to ride for 4-5 hours is definitely comfortable. Control is your ability to propel the bicycle, both in terms of driving the bicycle forward and controlling its direction of travel. Efficiency means that you're optimizing your power, comfort, and aerodynamic drag. These components operate somewhat independently of each other. Consider it this way: A cruiser offers a comfortable posture but isn't efficient for cycling due to the upright stance and poor use of the rider's muscles. Conversely, the most aerodynamically efficient position is the time trial position, in which a rider rests the upper-body on her elbows with the hands outstretched in a downhill-ski-like tuck and positions her legs in such a way that optimal use of the pedaling muscles is guaranteed. The position slices through the wind, but the restrictive position sacrifices maneuverability. A road bike blends efficient pedaling, good aerodynamic positioning, great comfort, and maneuverability—all in one bike.

Points of Contact

As with other types of bicycles, a rider has three points of contact with the bicycle: the seat, the handlebar, and the pedals. Governing your comfort and efficiency at these points of contact are the pedal type, cleat position, and shoes; the saddle height, type of saddle, and cycling shorts; and the handlebar reach, type of bar, and handlebar tape and gloves. A change in any one of these parameters can dramatically affect your comfort and ability to generate power.

The equipment used at these three points of contact also dictates your comfort. Your choice of clothing and how well you're insulated from shock and vibration help determine how long you can ride comfortably. The more shock and vibration that reach you, the quicker you'll become fatigued and even experience pain or numbness.

Let's look at how variations in each of these components can affect your control and comfort:

Pedals

The pedals are a rider's most important point of contact with a bicycle. You use them to propel the bicycle, but they also allow you to distribute your weight, and so control the bike's direction of travel. While a bicycle may be steered by turning the handlebar (which

The pedals do more than just allow you to propel the bicycle forward; they help you to shift your weight from left to right, aiding your control over the bicycle's direction.

A good shoe must strike a balance in many regards. It must have a stiff sole, but not too stiff. It must also have a snug, form-following fit, but cannot be too tight.

controls the direction of the front wheel), you primarily control it by shifting your weight between the pedals and at the hips. Doubt this? Try executing a turn with your feet off the pedals.

Clipless pedals—pedals that secure the foot via a shoe-mounted cleat that locks into the pedal and releases by twisting the heel away from the bicycle—are the industry standard on all but the least-expensive road bikes. The cleats are meant to give the rider secure contact with the pedals, not only allowing the rider to apply power through a broad range of the pedal stroke but also giving the rider superior control over weight distribution.

Shoes
Shoes are the other half of the equation in the shoe–pedal combination. A good cycling shoe will feature a stiff sole made of carbon fiber, fiberglass, or another strong, thin material. The thinner the sole, the closer the cleat will be to the foot, which ultimately will minimize the distance between the foot and the pedal axle. A short distance between the bottom of the foot and the pedal axle increases muscular efficiency, which decreases fatigue over the course of the day.

A good shoe will have a strong upper to secure the foot without stretching and will be secured with between two and four straps; three seems to be most common. Closures for the shoes vary but generally can be classified as either hook-and-loop or ratcheting systems. A good

shoe also needs proper arch support to keep the arch from collapsing during the pedal stroke.

The Saddle
The saddle supports the majority of a cyclist's weight. As a result, a rider's comfort on the bike begins with finding a comfortable saddle. Despite its rather simple triangular shape, bicycle saddles come in a seemingly infinite number of contours. A cyclist's concerns can be boiled down into three general categories:

Finding the right saddle is no easy task; many riders may try a half-dozen or more before settling on the saddle best suited to them.

Saddle width. A saddle's width should reflect the width of the rider's *ischial tuberosities*, better known as the "sit bones." Generally speaking, men have fairly narrowly spaced sit bones while women have more widely spaced sit bones. The difference in men's and women's saddles reflect this. A saddle should be wide enough to accommodate the sit bones on the highest contours at the rear of the saddle. This will relieve pressure on the soft tissues forward of the sit bones.

Determining the width of the sit bones can be accomplished with the aid of the rather comically named "Assometer" available at Specialized Bicycle Dealers. The Assometer uses memory foam to record an impression of the cyclist's posterior, which leaves two sunken spots in the foam. The distance between these two dents will correspond to the width of the supportive contours of a saddle.

Foam density. While many folks think that softer is better, superior support comes from denser foam. Dense foams reduce soft-tissue irritation by cutting down on the amount of pressure put on more delicate areas. Some saddles use two densities of foam: a firmer density where support is needed at the ischial tuberosities and softer foam to relieve pressure on more sensitive tissue.

The Specialized "Assometer" helps riders determine just how wide a saddle must be to support their sit bones.

Contours and cutouts. For most of the history of cycling, saddles used on road bikes have tended to show a rather arched contour from left to right. That began to change a little more than a decade ago, when Dr. Irwin Goldstein published the first report regarding impotence among cyclists related to tissue damage caused by the saddle. Since that time, saddle manufacturers have offered saddles with a cutout in the center of the saddle to reduce soft tissue, arterial, and nerve

pressure. Another solution was to reduce the foam density in that area. The central idea? It's better to support as much of the cyclist's weight as possible on the sit bones.

Cycling Shorts
Cycling shorts contain a pad to help cushion the rider from the saddle and to reduce chafing of the sensitive skin at the point of contact with the saddle. The general idea is that placing the pad against the body, the rider is better protected—and it works. Shorts are covered in greater depth in Chapter 18.

The advantage cycling shorts offer is in placing padding exactly where it is needed while reducing it where it is unnecessary.

Handlebar
The contemporary road bike's handlebar offers three hand positions. These positions allow you to move your hands for reasons of aerodynamics, power, and comfort. Let's consider each of the positions and their uses:

Bar top: This position allows the rider the most upright posture on the bicycle. It is useful for easy riding when aerodynamic efficiency isn't a consideration, and during climbing, when getting air to the lungs and generating high, sustained power is important. This position offers

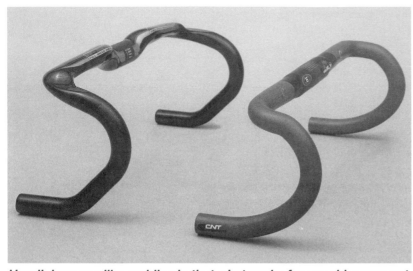

Handlebars are like saddles in that what works for one rider may not work for another.

you the best visibility of your surroundings. With less weight on the front wheel and no access to the brakes, this position isn't appropriate for descending, sprinting, or other out-of-the-saddle efforts, or riding in tight quarters when sudden braking might be necessary.

The hoods: The hoods of the control levers are the most favored hand position of professional cyclists. From this position, you have complete control over the bike, with the ability to shift or brake. While your hands are not as high or as near the upper-body as with the bar tops, they are close enough and high enough to offer good visibility. The position is high enough to remain comfortable for long periods, and out-of-the-saddle efforts—either sprinting or climbing—work well. Descending also works well in this position.

The drops: From the drops you have complete control over the bicycle for shifting and braking, but the drops offer a notable advantage over riding on the hoods: They offer you the most aerodynamic position available on a road bike. This is a racer's preferred position for the hardest efforts, especially when sprinting. More important than aerodynamics is the fact that riding in the drops lowers your center of gravity, which inspires confidence—the feeling of increased control is remarkable.

There are three dimensions that determine how a handlebar will fit a rider. They are width, reach (essentially the forward-reaching length of the bar), and drop (the depth of the bar). Often, handlebars are sold on the basis of the width of the bar alone; it can be difficult to find out the reach and depth of the bar. Sometimes manufacturers will call a bar a "deep drop" or a "shallow drop" without actually quantifying the exact measurement. How these dimensions affect fit was explained in Chapter 12.

Gloves

Gloves are meant to pad the rider's hands from shock and offer protection in the event of a fall. The practice of wearing gloves while cycling began back when the handlebar was made from steel tubing and was wrapped with cellophane tape or, occasionally, leather, in order to give the rider better grip. The gloves had padding sewn into the palm to cushion the rider's hands from bumps and vibration.

A well-designed glove can reduce pressure on the nerve that causes carpal tunnel syndrome as well as insulate your hand from road shock, not to mention give you a convenient way to wipe your face.

Today's gloves are made of superior shock-absorbing materials. The padding is placed more strategically to avoid compressing sensitive nerves at the base of the hand. They also help to increase a rider's control of the bike by offering superior grip to sweaty hands.

Gloves offer an added benefit in protecting the rider's hands in the event of a crash. They can take the brunt of the friction in a slide, protecting the rider's palms from the ravages of road rash, which is what cyclists call the abrasions that occur when they crash.

Handlebar Tape

Handlebar tape used to be made from cellophane and was essentially a decorative element for most bicycles. Today it is seen as key to minimizing the vibration and shock transmitted to a rider's hands, shoulders, and neck—the three upper-body locations where riders are most likely to experience discomfort while riding.

Most handlebar tapes today are made from artificial cork or foam and offer great comfort even on long rides. With this kind of tape, grip is also improved, and when combined with gloves, a rider will feel great confidence

Handlebar tape provides excellent padding to insulate a rider's hands from road shock.

while gripping the bar, even when soaked in sweat. For riders whose hands or upper-body are especially sensitive to shock and vibration, some companies make gel-infused tape or gel inserts (such as those from Specialized and Fi'zi:k) over which the handlebar tape is wrapped for even greater vibration damping.

Chapter 16
Fitting the Bike to the Rider

The goal in fitting a bike to a rider is to optimize the rider's comfort and efficiency. Because cycling is an activity based on constant repetition of motion, your ability to pedal for extended periods of time will be compromised if you are not comfortable or if you are expending more energy than is necessary. A proper fitting by a trained professional will enable you to realize more energy at the rear wheel with less effort.

A road bike is like dress clothing: You can buy something off the rack that fits you fairly well, but some alterations will need to be made to perfect the fit. Of course, if you have the spare change, you can go for the fully tailored treatment and buy custom. A proper fitting with a trained technician can take 2 hours to complete and will reveal things about your body that might even surprise you. Once you have been fitted by a certified technician, you'll find that you generate more power from a more comfortable position; you will be able to ride longer, faster, and with greater comfort.

Bicycle Sizing

In broad strokes, bikes come in two flavors of sizes: production and custom. If you walk into a bike shop and purchase something off the showroom floor, it will feature production sizing. The alternative is to order a custom bicycle made specifically to your measurements.

Production Sizing

Production bicycles are designed around a set number of sizes. For most companies, a model will be offered in 5 or 6 sizes, though sometimes women's-specific sizing will bring that number to 8 or even 10 sizes. Each size reflects the anatomic differences that exist among people of varying height. As a person's height increases, so does reach.

Be aware that sizing varies from manufacturer to manufacturer. One company's medium may not fit the same as another company's.

For the vast majority of people, production bikes can yield an excellent fit following a fitting session. If you're in good health and have no known physical anomalies that require custom-made clothing (such as a very short torso and really long arms), chances are you'll be able to achieve an ideal fit with a production bike.

One of the great advantages to buying a production bike is that you may have the opportunity to ride the bike in your size before buying it. A test ride will reveal much of the bike's character, and the more time the shop takes to size you properly for your test ride (all shops will take time to set the saddle height, but some will also swap out a stem for a better fit), the better the feel you will have for a bike.

Custom Sizing

Purchasing a custom bike is an opportunity to achieve an unparalleled degree of excellence in fit. Riders who have developed particular tastes in bike handling or fit may choose a custom builder to find the perfect bike to suit their tastes. Part of the attraction of buying a custom bike is dealing directly with the builder to create a bike that reflects your taste in appearance, handling, and fit. It's a level of service that rises above what some shops can achieve. For those riders who want their bike to reinforce their sense of individuality, nothing says one-of-a-kind the way a custom bike does.

Most bikes are like off-the-rack clothing; they come in a select number of sizes. One of the production sizes will fit the vast majority of all riders.

For those riders who have unusual proportions, some manufacturers offer custom sizing, though you don't have to have unusual needs to enjoy the benefits that come with a custom bike.

Body Dimensions for Fit

Naturally, how big or small you are determines what size bike you need. The goal is to provide you with a bike that allows for optimal leg extension through the pedal stroke and a comfortable reach to the handlebar.

Ultimately, your height is a symptom, an indicator of what size bike you need, but it will not determine your fit. The specific dimensions that influence fit are:

❶ **Upper-body reach:** This is the combination of the length of your torso and the reach of your arms, and it will help to determine top tube and stem length. A properly sized bicycle will allow you to ride with your hands in each of the three bar positions comfortably.

❷ **Leg length:** The full length of your leg will help to determine your saddle height.

❸ **Femur length:** The length of your upper leg influences the saddle height and setback.

❹ **Foot size:** The size of your feet will affect both saddle height and saddle setback.

❺ **Shoulder width:** The width of your shoulders will affect how wide the handlebar should be.

❻ **Hand size:** Your hand size will influence what handlebar

Your bike's dimensions should be based exclusively on your personal dimensions. Your inseam, flexibility, and reach will determine the size that is best for you.

Hands on tops

shape feels most comfortable, which lever shape is most comfortable, and more importantly, the reach to the levers.

Flexibility

How the bicycle is fit to the rider has changed as knowledge of our musculoskeletal structure has increased. While bike builders have been aware of the relationship of a rider's height (and therefore leg length and reach) to the bike's size, only in the last 10–15 years have builders and fit technicians become aware of the role flexibility plays in a bike's fit.

It was once believed that your style of riding dictated your position. If you were a racer, you adapted to a low handlebar position to achieve a flat back reflecting the racer's aggressive posture. If you were a tourist, you rode with a high handlebar position reflecting an emphasis on comfort for long miles in the saddle rather than a need for aerodynamic efficiency.

Today, fitters trained by the Specialized Bicycle Component University, Serotta Cycling Institute, Fit Kit Systems, and others understand that while your personal dimensions will determine your bike's size, your flexibility and range of motion will determine your position on the bike.

Hands on hoods

Hands on drops

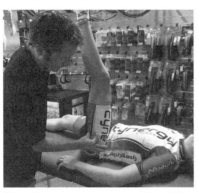
Whether you are upper-lip stiff or as flexible as a yogi will greatly influence your fit.

Adjusting the bicycle

Buying a correctly sized bicycle is only the first step to riding a bicycle that fits. A properly fit bicycle will increase the rider's comfort, allowing a ride without pain. It also makes for a more efficient ride because the rider can generate more power with each pedal stroke.

For a cyclist to be both comfortable and efficient, a number of adjustments must be made to the bicycle. These distances are measured in centimeters. They are:

❶ *Saddle height: This is the distance from the pedals to the top of the saddle. Saddle height determines leg extension.*
Image: Patrick Brady

❷ *Saddle setback: This determines the relationship of the knee to the pedal spindle. It is measured by dropping a plumb bob (a weight at the end of a string) from the kneecap. Ideally, the knee should be positioned directly over the pedal spindle.* Image: Patrick Brady

❸ *Handlebar reach: This is the distance from the nose of the saddle to the center of the handlebar. It determines how far forward a rider must reach to the handlebar.*
Image: Patrick Brady

❹ *Handlebar drop: This is the distance from the midpoint of the saddle to the top of the handlebar. It determines how far down a rider must bend to reach the handlebar.*

Bar Drop

❺ *Lever reach: This is the distance from the handlebar to the levers. All of the major component manufacturers now offer levers with adjustable reach.*

Ideally, each of these dimensions will reflect the anatomy of the rider of that bicycle. And, generally, each of these dimensions will increase in proportion as the size of the rider increases. Consequently, a tall rider who needs a high saddle position will usually need more significant saddle setback than a more diminutive rider. Additionally, a tall rider will need a substantial reach to the handlebar and can accommodate more handlebar drop.

Determining these dimensions of fit is a process best performed by a professional fitter. For many years, racers and coaches believed that many of these dimensions were a matter of personal preference or were ideals to which a dedicated rider could eventually adapt. On the contrary, the most knowledgeable sources in bicycle fitting all concur that a properly fitted bicycle will reflect the individual physiology of the rider.

Elements of a Good Fit

While each bicycle's dimensions will reflect the physiology of its rider, the elements that determine proper fit are amazingly consistent. That's because they are based on the rider's skeletal structure and flexibility.

In addition to each of the factors of body dimension mentioned previously, during a fitting a technician will examine some other aspects of a rider's physiology. These include the following:

❶ **History:** A fitter will ask if you have any previous injuries that might affect your fit.

❷ **Experience:** Your degree of cycling experience will affect your fit; experienced riders tend to exhibit more flexibility on the bike.

❸ **Flexibility:** Your flexibility in your back, neck, shoulders, legs, hips, and ankles will all affect your fit on the bike.

❹ **Knee angle:** Proper saddle height results in a roughly 30-degree bend at the knee. A larger bend means the saddle is too low, while a smaller bend indicates the saddle is too high.

Your history as a rider and overall activity level will come into play in the fitting experience. Old "war wounds" can have a surprising influence on your fit.
Image: Patrick Brady

❺ **Asymmetry:** If you show inequalities between your left and right sides, such as a leg-length discrepancy, tilted pelvis, curved spine, or other issue, this will affect your fit.

Component Choices that Affect Fit

In seeking your perfect fit, you'll discover as many variations in component dimensions as there are paparazzi following Hollywood starlets. Depending on your personal dimensions, flexibility, and riding style, you'll have a few choices to help you achieve pedaling Nirvana.

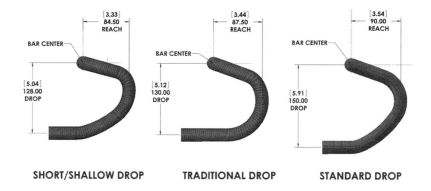

SHORT/SHALLOW DROP	TRADITIONAL DROP	STANDARD DROP

- *Seatposts: These vary in both length and setback to allow you to achieve proper saddle height and saddle setback.*

- *Saddle: The most common fit issue with saddles is width. Saddle width should reflect the width of your Ischial tuberosilies—your sit bones. Not all women need a wide saddle, and not all men can tolerate a narrow saddle. Rail length on saddles can vary by several centimeters; this can affect saddle setback, since the longer the rails are, the greater the adjustability.*

- *Stem: To help you achieve proper bar height and reach, stems generally come in seven lengths (80–140mm in 10mm increments) and a variety of angles for various amounts of rise. Because stems can be mounted in one of two ways (an "up" angle and a "down" angle), each stem offers two different handlebar heights. Some stems now come with shims that allow the angle of rise or drop to be tuned plus or minus 2 degrees.*

- *Handlebar: The dimensions that determine a handlebar's fit are numerous. Bars vary in width (measured center of drop to center of drop): 40cm, 42cm, and 44cm most often, though some bars are available in 38cm and 46cm widths. Bars also vary in reach and depth from one model to another. Compact bars are relatively new on the scene and have a short reach and a short drop; they are great for riders who have limited flexibility. The shape of the bend also varies; some riders prefer a traditional round bend, while others prefer the flattened grip of an anatomic bend.*

- *Crank: Most fit experts agree that as leg length increases, so should crank length. Most manufacturers offer crank arms in three lengths: 170, 172.5, and 175mm, though some offer additional lengths of 165, 167.5, 177.5, and 180mm.*

Chapter 17
Helmets: Or Why Your Noggin Is Worth More Than $30

For all our resilience, human beings do have vulnerabilities. Despite our ability to bounce back from double-knit polyester pants and the travails of Britney Spears, a knock to the head can have lasting consequences. Bumps, scrapes, and cuts accumulated in a crash are unpleasant, but they don't have the ability to affect the quality of your life the way a brain injury can. A helmet can mean the difference between a headache and a funeral.

How a Helmet Works

The principle behind a bicycle helmet's protection is pretty simple—it's a sophisticated pad. Any pad used to protect something—from packing foam to football pads—is intended to slow an approaching object. You may recall from physics class that speed equals energy. The lower the object's energy at impact, the smaller the chance of it causing damage or injury. Naturally, no one wants to be hit by a speeding semi truck, but if it's been slowed to turtle-at-dead-run, you probably won't be hurt.

In a crash, you have little hope of controlling what's moving and how fast it's moving. The helmet gives you a chance to slow your head before an impact.

While it may seem like a helmet won't slow the speed of impact should you crash, it does have a remarkable effect on the velocity of your head—and therefore your brain—as it slows to a stop during a crash. The foam in the helmet is designed to absorb the impact energy by collapsing, much like a car's crumple zones. Rather than stop you immediately, the helmet is like the hand you put out to break your fall. As the foam collapses, your head slows, but it doesn't come to an immediate stop; those few inches of foam can make the difference between a concussion and a bump.

Helmets through History

The earliest bicycle helmets were better in theory than in practice. Frankly, they offered nearly as much protection as a $100 car insurance policy.

Referred to as "leather hairnets," they were made from leather sewn around foam padding. A central band encircled the head with three additional bands running lengthwise from front to rear, with several smaller bands attached crosswise. Two bands curled around the ears and a chinstrap held the contraption on.

At best, it looked a bit like a cross between a spiderweb and a sandal. Unfortunately, the foam padding was too thin and soft to provide real protection. Yet for all its drawbacks, the leather hairnet did at least get the idea started.

Bell, a manufacturer of helmets for motorcycles and motorsports, made the next step forward with a hard shell that encased an inner foam layer; a chinstrap held the helmet in place, more or less.

While the Bell Biker offered improved protection over the leather hairnet, it suffered from great weight and straps that could not keep the helmet from tipping—either forward or backward.

The first great advancement in helmet technology came in 1986, when Jim Gentes invented the Giro ProLight. This was the first helmet made from expanded polystyrene and contained most of the features found in today's top helmets. It covered the head from forehead to occipital lobe and ear to ear, was made from a lightweight foam to absorb impact energy, had vent holes to allow air to pass over the rider's head, and included straps with a releasable buckle to hold the helmet in place.

Since the introduction of the Giro ProLight, advancements in weight and ventilation have been a matter of degrees. Two major advancements, though, have made helmets noticeably safer. Internal roll-cage technology acts as rebar to hold the helmet's structure intact better in the event of a crash, while occipital lobe devices prevent the helmet from sliding backward or forward and exposing the forehead or the base of the skull.

The Giro ProLight was the first attempt to combine great protection, good ventilation, and reasonable fit in a package that didn't look completely dorky. Not bad for 1986.

Features of the Modern Helmet

Today's helmet may seem more air than helmet. With many helmets featuring two dozen vents, it is reasonable to wonder just how a modern helmet can protect someone's head, especially if you can still see much of it.

The starting point for today's helmet is invisible to the naked eye. Within the foam is a roll cage, just like a racing car. The roll cage offers structural support to the foam to help keep the helmet intact during impact. Early helmets often broke up during impact, failing to provide full protection during a crash.

Straps are integrated into the roll cage to make sure the helmet stays in place. Because the foam is fairly fragile, it isn't a good place to anchor the straps. By anchoring the straps to the roll cage, the manufacturer ensures the foam remains where it will offer the best protection.

The two straps are connected by a simple chin strap with a quick-release buckle, which eliminates the need to adjust the chin strap every time the helmet is worn.

In addition to the straps, an occipital device wraps around the back of the occipital lobe (that bump at the back of your head) to prevent the helmet from tipping forward or sliding back on your head.

Foam is molded over the roll cage with the straps and occipital device already in place. The helmet's shape is created by a group of designers and engineers who determine how much of the head should be covered, how many vents the helmet will have, where the straps are positioned, and, interestingly, how air will flow through the helmet.

Because helmets have struggled to gain acceptance with riders, helmet companies have worked hard to improve their ventilation. Today's top-of-the-line helmets have been designed around flow dynamics that use the frontal vents as air intakes and the rear vents as exhaust ports; air is channeled through the helmet and over the head in such a way that more air is pushed across the head than if the rider went bare-headed.

As the helmet is formed, an external shell is co-molded with the foam. This thin Mylar shell serves several purposes. Like the roll cage, it helps maintain the helmet's integrity in the early stages of a crash. Day-to-day durability increases thanks to the shell. It also provides a slick surface to help the helmet slide rather than grab the ground. And finally, it gives the manufacturer a bold way to decorate the helmet with sharp graphics to accent the rest of a rider's kit.

Inside the helmet, a small set of pads gives the rider more comfort. Most are attached with Velcro and can be removed to rinse perspiration out.

Sizing the Helmet

Most helmets are available in three sizes. When you try helmets on, if there is fore-to-aft or side-to-side movement in the helmet, you may need to try a different brand. Each brand has a slightly different internal shape. Some are more round while others are more oblong.

Once you have determined the proper size and brand of helmet for your best fit, you will need to adjust the occipital device at the back of the helmet. The idea with this band is to make it snug enough to reduce the helmet's movement if you shake your head back and forth. If it is

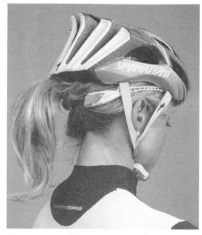

Every good helmet on the market has an occipital-retention device at the back of the helmet. It can be credited with preventing the helmet from dropping over your eyes or slipping back like a trucker's cap.

Your helmet should be comfortable, and making sure the straps avoid your ears is an important part of that.

too snug, it can cut off circulation to the small blood vessels at the back of the head, creating numbness, or give you a headache by placing too much pressure on the forehead.

The straps extending from the helmet should run clear of (or in front of and behind) the ears and meet at a point below the earlobe. If a strap passes over the ear, it can impair hearing and cause discomfort for the rider.

The chinstrap should wrap below the jaw. It is not meant to run over the chin like an English Beefeater soldier's headgear. It should be snug enough to keep the helmet in place but should not be so tight as to restrict movement of the jaw. In general, if you can't speak or take a drink from your bottle, the strap is too tight.

Replacing the Helmet

Though they are considerably more expensive, a bicycle helmet is like a packet of ketchup—strictly single-serve. Helmets for motorcycles and motorsports are designed to take multiple impacts. Bicycles helmets, due to the type of foam used—which is necessitated by the need for low weight—are meant to take but one impact before being replaced.

Even a single, light impact has the ability to compromise the integrity of the helmet by reducing its ability to absorb impact energy and thus increasing the force of the impact to the head.

Ultraviolet light takes a toll on helmet foam. Repeated exposure to sunlight causes the foam to break down. Most helmet manufacturers report that the helmet's integrity degrades after roughly three years of regular use, with regular use defined as several rides per week.

And while it may seem an unwarranted expense to replace a helmet that has yet to be crashed, helmet manufacturers continue to increase ventilation, comfort, and fit so that last year's helmet won't be as advanced as next year's.

Chapter 18
Bicycle-Specific Clothing

Cycling clothing is often derided for its bright colors, man-made fibers, and snug fit. To the uninitiated, it does look funny; the last time men dressed in clothes that tight, Studio 54 was still in business. There are good reasons why cycling clothing is styled the way it is, though.

Every piece of cycling clothing has a role to fulfill. Properly designed clothing will encourage free movement, place padding where it is needed most, wick perspiration from the body, create a smooth airflow over the body, and alert drivers to the presence of a cyclist.

Every traditional practice in road cycling has developed for a reason, and the design and use of cycling clothing is no different. The first thing to understand about cycling clothing is that it works best if it is used *instead of* street clothing, not *in addition to* it. That is, leave the cotton at home. From the T-shirt to the shorts and underwear, cotton holds moisture and will cause problems if worn beneath cycling clothing. It's not uncommon to see a new cyclist wearing underwear beneath cycling shorts. Wearing underwear can cause chafing around the leg holes, and the wet fabric can cause a rash. Not fun.

The watershed events in cycling clothing came in the 1970s and '80s. Up to this point, all cycling clothing was made from merino wool. Lycra was used for the first time to make cycling shorts in the mid-1970s. Manufacturers moved to polyester for jersey construction in the '80s. The introduction of the color-sublimation process changed sponsors' ability to put their name and logo on cycling clothing. Prior to this, loop stitching was used to embroider sponsor names on jerseys. Color choices and design complexity were limited by the colors the wool and thread were dyed. Sublimation is a process whereby dyes are heat-transferred to the polyester or Lycra, permanently fixing the colors in the material. Sublimation allows manufacturers to use complex designs and multiple colors in bright hues. Frankly, it has made cycling a brighter, more visually appealing sport.

Materials

Merino wool: Merino wool is made from some of the finest wool fibers available. As a result, merino is soft enough to wear against the

Wool jerseys have made a comeback; the material is comfortable in both the hot and cold, and old-school designs such as this have the classic appeal of, say, a '68 Mustang.

skin without causing irritation. Merino was used as the basis of shorts and jerseys for more than 80 years. Wool has been praised by cyclists for its ability to hold heat on cool days while staying cool under the hot sun. Today, wool is making a comeback for a variety of reasons: People like the retro look, the fact that it is a natural fiber, and its great qualities for heat retention and dissipation.

Lycra: This DuPont fabric stretches like a superhero and returns to its original shape. This quality makes it perfect for garments that need to be especially form-fitting. Cycling shorts are made from Lycra, as are skinsuits, tights, knickers, and arm, leg, and knee warmers. Lycra comes in several weights. Lycra in 8-oz. weight comes in solid colors and is used as the basis for shorts due

Polyester dominates the market in cycling clothing. Most jerseys are made mostly, if not exclusively, from this material. It comes in a variety of weights and weaves; some are surprisingly thin and breathable while others pack a surprising amount of warmth.

Nothing is as aerodynamic—or as revealing—as a skinsuit. It's perfectly suited to time trials.

to its durability. Six-ounce Lycra is available in white so that it may be sublimated, but it isn't as durable as the 8-oz. weight. There is also a heavier version of Lycra with a brushed finish inside for added warmth; this is called Roubaix Lycra in honor of the Spring Classic race in Northern France, which, due to its early April date, is often run in cold conditions.

Polyester: This man-made fabric is the material of choice for jerseys. Jerseys don't need to conform to a body's contours to the same degree as shorts. Form-fitting is enough. Among polyester's selling points is its ability to wick moisture away from the body and push it to the surface of the fabric so that it can evaporate. It can also be sublimated in any color and with any design, even the "Mona Lisa."

Garments

Shorts

Cycling shorts are the single most important piece of cycling clothing you will wear. Originally, cycling shorts were fashioned from merino wool and contained a pad cut from chamois leather. Unfortunately, wool can stretch out of shape and shrink, and it smells like a lot like a wet dog when it gets damp. Once Lycra was used for the first time in a cycling short, the rest, as they say, was history.

Construction: Shorts are generally made from either six or eight panels of Lycra. As the number of panels increases, the better the shorts fit. Occasionally, inexpensive shorts will be cut from four panels. Avoid these; they aren't worth the money. Shorts will also contain a pad made from synthetic materials to protect the rider's bottom from the saddle. Unlike the old-style chamois, the synthetic chamois will dry quickly and even wick moisture away from the rider's body. Men's shorts also feature an absorptive synthetic terrylike material in front of the pad. Good

It's rare that a single garment can be held responsible for either a great day or a lousy one, but a great pair of shorts can make all the difference in the world.

shorts will also include gripper elastic at the end of each leg to prevent the shorts from riding up the leg, and a drawstring or gripper elastic at the waist to keep them from drooping during the ride. Top-quality shorts include bibs, essentially suspender straps incorporated into the short that go over the shoulders to hold the shorts up.

Shorts come in three basic cuts: men's, women's, and bib. Men's and women's shorts are essentially the same, featuring six or eight panels, a pad, gripper elastic at the legs, and gripper elastic or a drawstring at the waist. The difference is in the cut: men's shorts are cut with little waist, while women's shorts are cut with more room in the hips, a broader pad, and a smaller waist. Bib shorts are cut for men, eliminate the waist by adding the two suspender straps, and are preferred by riders who log more saddle time. Bibs make it a little harder to answer the call of nature, but their pluses are numerous. The shorts stay up better, keeping the pad in place better; the higher waist doesn't cut into the belly; and the bibs have a slimming effect, making nearly anyone who wears them look more trim.

Bib shorts are to regular shorts what HDTV is to regular TV. Though the advantage bibs offer is somewhat male-specific, anyone can appreciate how keeping your shorts in position will give you greater comfort.

Fit: A good pair of shorts will conform to the body and allow unrestricted movement through the pedaling motion. To do that, the shorts must be tight enough to follow the contours and curves of the body without being too tight. If, when trying on a pair of shorts, the material bunches up or remains loose, try the next size down.

The shorts will contain a pad to insulate you from the saddle. The idea is to place the most helpful padding in the shorts so it can't chafe you as you slide on the saddle. Originally the pad was made from chamois and it is often still called this. Today the pad is made from synthetics that allow it to breathe more and to move more harmoniously with your body.

Pricing: Expect to spend upwards of $80 on a good pair of shorts. The best bib shorts run more than $200. That may seem a princely sum, but the additional money always translates to added comfort.

Jerseys

A jersey is a surprisingly technical garment. Like early shorts, jerseys were made from merino wool. Early on, pockets were sewn in at the breast, but they caused the jersey to sag, which is why jersey pockets are placed along the lumbar now. The move to polyester had a major economic impact on cycling. The advent of sublimation allowed jersey designers to include additional sponsor names on the jersey, thereby increasing a team's income. In the early 1990s, some of the Italian teams really overdid it and their jerseys looked like the notebook of a sticker-mad teenage girl. Fortunately, jersey designs are a little smarter these days.

Construction: Jerseys come in both long- and short-sleeve designs. Generally speaking, they are composed of front and rear panels, a collar, two side panels, plus two sleeves. The inclusion of the side panels allows the jersey to conform closely to the contours of the torso. Jerseys have a front zipper that determines ventilation. Originally, zippers were quite short, often just four inches—just enough to get your head through the opening. Today, many jerseys are sold with either a ¾-length zipper or a full zipper to completely open the jersey up on a hot day.

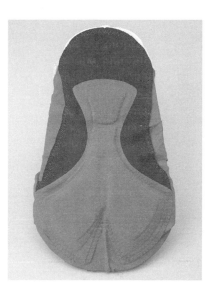

The chamois has come a long way from the days when it was literally cut from chamois leather. Today's pads use multiple densities of foam and channels to relieve pressure on sensitive tissues.

Fit: Sleeve design determines how a jersey will fit. Sleeves come in two different styles: set-in and raglan. A set-in sleeve is cut the same as a sleeve on a T-shirt. A raglan sleeve tapers into the jersey itself, ending at the collar. Set-in sleeves are good for riders with broad, muscular shoulders. Raglan sleeves tend to be preferred by those with a more classic cyclist's physique, which is to say, kind of skinny. The raglan cut tends to eliminate billowing in the upper part of the chest, which can happen when a slender cyclist wears a jersey with a set-in sleeve. A jersey should conform to the rider's shoulders, and a short sleeve should extend midway down the bicep. The pockets should ride right at the lumbar—the jersey should not be so long as to droop over the butt. The sleeves of a long-sleeve jersey should extend all the way to the wrist when the arms are stretched forward. Some manufacturers have begun offering jerseys cut with more room through the chest and waist for more casual riders.

A jersey is a pretty technical piece of clothing. From its breathable material to the pockets in back and long zipper, it is designed around the needs and comfort of the rider.

Many women's jerseys are designed around the princess cut. The princess cut adds two panels to the front of the torso to help taper the jersey from the flare at the hips through the waist and the opening up at the bust. Finding a jersey that fits can be a little more difficult for women than for men. Jerseys must conform to the shoulders, open up enough at the bust, and taper sufficiently at the waist before flaring again at the hips.

The number of jersey pockets increased from two to three when they were moved from the chest to the back; some designs feature an extra zippered pocket for keys or change. A few women's designs aimed at more petite riders include only two pockets.

Pricing: Good jerseys can be found for as little as $50. Jerseys made from better materials or that bear the design of a pro cycling team may run double that, while premium pieces may run several times that.

Base Layer

Dry skin is happy skin. A base layer can serve several purposes, but its main one is to keep you dry. It can help wick sweat away from your torso, pushing it to the jersey to keep you drier and reduce chafing. On hot days this can help keep you cooler, while on cold days this will keep you warmer.

Construction: Base layers are made from polyester blends as well as merino wool and come in a variety of weights.

Fit: Base layers come in sleeveless, short-sleeve, and long-sleeve varieties. They are meant to be worn under your bibs and should be form-fitting to keep the material from bunching up and staying wet.

Pricing: Base layers start at around $30 and go up from there.

A lightweight mesh base layer will help transport perspiration away from the skin to keep you dry and comfortable on both hot and cold days.

Jackets

Staying warm in challenging conditions can be difficult. Wind breakers are the lightest in weight and are really only meant to keep the wind out; they need to be as lightweight as possible to fit in a jersey pocket. Winter jackets feature a lining that can keep you warm to temperatures well below freezing, depending on how you layer; some are waterproof and windproof. Winter jackets are bulky and meant for cold days where you'll need the insulation to stay warm for the whole of the ride. Rain jackets are meant to keep you dry but provide no additional insulation.

Construction: Windbreakers are made from a tight polyester weave to make them windproof. Winter jackets will feature an outer polyester shell combined with a polyester lining. Manufacturers have a variety of fancy names for their materials based on special knits, fabric treatments, or other factors. Rain jackets may be made from polyester and simply have waterproofing, or they may be made from polyvinylchloride (plastic sheeting, essentially) to keep them waterproof, light, and easy to stuff in a pocket.

Fit: As with long-sleeve jerseys, jackets need long sleeves that extend to your wrists, but the tail

There are many different kinds of jackets, from lightweight windbreakers to heavy, insulated winter jackets.

Most rain jackets aren't known for great breathability, but they can be valuable in keeping your torso somewhat dry.

of winter and rain jackets should extend down over your butt to protect you from road spray coming up off your rear wheel. Windbreakers and rain jackets need to have a snug fit to prevent them from flapping in the wind like a flag. The roomier they are, the noisier they are, and the more drag they create. Winter jackets should also have a fairly snug fit, but need a bit more room to allow for layers beneath. Because of their heavier weight, they don't tend to flap as much in the wind.

Pricing: Windbreakers and rain jackets start at around $70 and go up. Winter jackets are more costly: Inexpensive ones start close to $150.

Tights and Knickers

In cold conditions, tights or knickers can keep your legs warm to extend your riding earlier in the spring and later in the fall; in some places, you may be able to ride through the winter. Some knickers and tights come with a pad, making them a substitute for shorts, while others feature no pad; you wear them over your shorts, giving you an extra layer of insulation. Bibs are helpful with both tights and knickers to keep the Lycra from sliding down; this is especially problematic when you wear tights over shorts, as the Lycra tights slide over the shorts quite easily.

Tights and knickers come in many varieties: with pad and without, lightweight and thermal, plus regular and bib.

Construction: Most tights and knickers are made from Lycra, though some tights will feature heavier materials in the front, such as Windstopper, to keep out the cold and wind.

Fit: Both tights and knickers should be form-fitting and snug throughout. Most knickers will only extend to the bottom of the knee, though a few makers offer knickers that extend to the calf.

Pricing: Inexpensive tights can be found for as little as $50, but expect the good stuff to run more than $100. Pads and bibs will raise the price significantly.

Vests

A vest may be the single most versatile piece in a cyclist's arsenal. It's light enough to fit easily in a pocket, easy to take off, easy to put back on, and can make a huge difference on a descent or when riding into the teeth of a chilly wind.

Construction: Most vests are made from the same tight polyester knit used in windbreakers, but some will feature heavier construction, including a fleecy liner. The more robust versions will often include pockets as well.

Fit: A vest should be snug in fit, just large enough to fit over your jersey.

Pricing: Great vests can be purchased for as little as $35.

Arm, Knee, and Leg Warmers

Arm, leg, and knee warmers are extremely versatile pieces of clothing that can help you adapt to changing conditions through the course of the day. Arm warmers are the most important of these pieces, as they can be pushed down to your wrists if you heat up and pulled back up whenever you need; they are easy to take off if you don't anticipate needing them again. Knee and leg warmers are great alternatives to tights and knickers as they can be combined with your existing shorts for cold-weather riding.

Often, the difference between feeling comfortable and frozen can be as simple as keeping your torso warm. A vest, despite its small size works wonders on a cold day.

If you ride in a place where temperatures can vary widely through the day, arm, leg, and knee warmers can add incredible versatility to your wardrobe and help you stay comfortable any time of day.

They don't need to be washed after every single ride, unlike shorts. Leg and knee warmers can be difficult to take off during a ride, but unlike tights, they will fit in your jersey pockets.

Construction: Most arm, leg, and knee warmers are made from Roubaix Lycra. This is a heavier-weight Lycra that sports a brushed, fleecelike finish on the inside for added warmth and windproofing.

Fit: Warmers need to be snug to do their job. If the fit isn't tight, they are apt to slide down.

Pricing: Inexpensive warmers start around $25 and go up.

The secret to cold-weather gear is Roubaix Lycra, which features a brushed finish near the skin and gripper elastic to keep it from sliding down as you ride.

Gloves

It used to be that all cyclists wore gloves, the way all men wore hats. The advent of padded handlebar tape has contributed to the fall-off in their use. They do provide a few practical purposes. First, they increase

A good pair of cycling gloves will reduce pressure on the nerve the causes carpal tunnel syndrome while improving grip and giving you a handy place to wipe your face.

your grip on the bar on hot days when you sweat profusely. Strategically positioned pads in the palm can also reduce pressure on the median nerve, which is the nerve that causes carpal tunnel syndrome when compressed. Most gloves also include some sort of absorbent material (such as terry cloth) on which you can wipe your nose or mouth. And in the event of a fall, gloves can protect your hands from the asphalt. Some gloves feature special materials to further cushion the hands from shock and vibration.

Construction: Most gloves pair an artificial leather in the palm with a Lycra or similarly stretchy material in the back to give them a form fit. Most have something like terry cloth to absorb moisture and will feature a Velcro closure at the wrist.

Fit: Gloves should have a snug fit but shouldn't be so tight they cut off circulation.

Pricing: Basic gloves start at $20, though some with real leather or vibration-damping gel inserts can be more than double that.

Socks

Socks are an essential, if small, item in a cyclist's wardrobe. They are crucial in helping to wick moisture away from the feet, keeping them drier and cooler than they would otherwise. They are also crucial in cushioning the feet just enough to prevent blisters from forming.

Construction: Most cycling socks are made from a lightweight knit of polyester. Some manufacturers offer merino wool socks, which offer the added benefit of keeping the feet warm in cool weather and cool in hot weather. The typical cycling sock has a short (3-inch) cuff to keep the majority of the leg exposed.

Like every other garment a cyclist wears, a good pair of socks needs to wick moisture away from the feet in order to keep them dry and you happy.

Fit: A good sock should feature a snug fit but shouldn't bind or constrict the feet.

Pricing: Socks can be found for as little as $4 per pair, but better quality socks will typically range from $6 to $10.

Toe Covers and Booties

Booties and toe covers are designed to keep your feet warm on cold days without trying to stuff a thick sock into an already snug cycling shoe. Toe warmers will provide adequate protection on cool days, but for the coldest days or wet days, booties offer superior protection.

Construction: Neoprene, the stuff from which wetsuits are made, is the most popular material as it can keep you warm even when it's wet.

Fit: Toe warmers fit over the front half of the shoe and feature a cutout for the cleat; a strap of material passing behind the cleat holds them in place. They are great for riders with really big or wide feet. If you have a high instep or really wide or long foot, booties that fit can be difficult to find. Neoprene offers more stretch than other versions.

Pricing: Toe covers will start around $20, but good booties will be considerably more. Expect to spend $40 or more for a decent pair.

Booties are overshoes for the cycling set. They have a small hole to allow the cycling shoe's cleat to engage the pedal but add great insulation to keep your feet warm on cold days.

Weather-Appropriate Dressing

There are no firm rules about how to dress for cooler weather. Above 70°F, the only question is whether you include a base layer or not, but for colder weather, staying comfortable can involve a variety of strategies, not to mention personal preference. The simple fact is, cold to a San Diego native is merely breezy to a resident of Chicago, and each rider will wear entirely different outfits in 55°F weather due to their experience with the cold.

With pros, the basic rule is once the temperature drops below 70°F, they start covering up. Of course, some supermodels look well fed compared to the average pro, but their caution is worth considering. A chilled body consumes more calories, and chilled muscles don't fire as well, so anything you can do to operate more efficiently is in your best interest.

Pieces such as arm and knee warmers and a vest will give you flexibility—and comfort—on days where conditions can change by as much as 20°F.

Dressing in Layers

Unless you live in a place where temperatures remain static for the whole of the ride, what you wear at the beginning of the ride may not be what you need at the end of the ride. The longer you are out, the more likely conditions are to change, especially if you head out in the morning or afternoon. Bear in mind what you need to stay warm at the beginning of a ride before you have warmed up is more than you'll need once you begin making hard effort.

If temperatures are likely to rise or drop over the course of your ride, stick with pieces that can be added or removed easily. When added to a pair of bibs and a jersey, a pair of arm warmers and

On truly cold days, it is better to dress with several thin layers than one really heavy layer. Thin layers will help your body's own heat transport moisture away from you.

In cold weather, long-finger gloves are a necessity. The good ones will feature a windproof material on the back of the hands.

a vest can increase your comfort range by 15°F or more. Add to that a pair of knee warmers, and you can ride comfortably in even cooler temps.

If conditions are unlikely to change much through the day, consider using heavier, long-sleeve pieces that you won't need to strip off. Keep in mind that the heaviest jackets don't breathe too well, and if you are doing hard riding in gear with a wind-stopping material, you'll wind up feeling like you're wearing a sponge.

As temps drop, long-finger gloves, cycling caps, and skullcaps can help keep you warm while riding. Cycling caps and skullcaps are thin enough to fit beneath a helmet, allowing you to be both safe and warm.

Chapter 19
Accessories

There's more to the sport of road cycling than just having a bike. Of course, the bicycle is the first, most important, and most expensive piece of equipment, but it is hardly the last word on necessary equipment. There are a few accessories that every cyclist needs to ride safely, plus a number of additional tools that can aid a cyclist in riding longer and tracking his or her fitness.

Necessary Accessories

In addition to having the basics to fix a flat as detailed in Chapter 20, you need to have the following to look after yourself if you plan to ride for an hour or more at a time.

Water Bottles

Cyclists perspire at a high rate. High heat, humidity, and altitude can drive that rate even higher. Fortunately, air running over the body causes convective cooling, which is a fancy way to say wind-powered air-conditioning. Evaporating sweat cools the body, and the body can remain surprisingly dry thanks to modern cycling clothing. Carry at least one 20-oz. bottle on any ride lasting an hour, and if you ride more than an hour you will want a second bottle. Typically, bottles come in 20- and 24-oz. sizes.

Water-Bottle Cages

Water-bottle cages give you a secure place on the frame to keep the water bottles, making them easy to reach and put away. Unless you purchase an unusual cage for a specific type of bottle, they are one-size-fits-all. Weight is vaguely proportional to strength, as is durability.

Eyewear

You need to be able to see clearly on your rides. Wind, even without the addition of dust, can cause your eyes to tear. Add dust to the equation, and a simple blink won't clear your vision. Good

If you plan to ride for more than a half hour, you'll need to hydrate during your ride.

Water-bottle cages give you a convenient place to put your bottles.

141

Good eyewear protects your eyes not only from the sun's UV rays but also from bugs and dirt.

eyewear will offer a wide field of vision with a distortion-free lens. Most companies offer a variety of lens tints for different light conditions. Some lenses increase contrast, while others are polarized to reduce glare.

Blinking Light

For those who ride before or after work, it's not uncommon to run into low-light conditions. In order to maintain maximum visibility to other traffic, a blinking red light facing rear and a blinking white light facing forward can help alert motorists to your presence.

Cyclocomputer

A cyclocomputer may seem a luxury and not entirely necessary, but for riders trying new routes or interested in increasing their endurance and strength, a cyclocomputer is a must-have. While knowing your current speed is handy, the computer's greatest use is in tracking your time and mileage.

Blinking lights will increase your visibility dramatically in low-light conditions.

Your body has no idea how many miles you ride at a time, but it does understand how long you've been pedaling. Each minute pedaled is a few more calories burned. Tracking your time on the bike will help you to know if you are drinking enough and when it's time to eat. Tracking your average speed over a known course is a great benchmark for judging your fitness. The typical cyclocomputer will include the following features:

A cyclocomputer helps you to know how much work you have done. This is key for postride refueling, understanding fatigue, and, often, getting home on time.

- Current speed
- Maximum speed
- Average speed
- Trip distance
- Total odometer
- Elapsed time
- Clock

Higher-end computers may also include the following:

- Cadence
- Current elevation
- Total elevation gain
- Total elevation drop
- Rate of ascent
- Current gradient
- Maximum gradient
- Temperature
- Estimated calories burned
- Wireless transmitter for lower weight and easier installation

Optional Accessories

If you are a fair-weather or daylight-only recreational rider, you may not need these items, but if you are bitten by the cycling bug (generally not contagious to family members), these items can increase safety, enjoyment, and your training's effectiveness.

Fenders

The presence of fenders on a bike can make any wet ride bearable. Depending on where you live, rain might only be an occasional hazard, or it might be a nearly daily occurrence. Fenders can make riding in the rain tolerable by keeping road spray from soaking you. Older bikes will tend to have clearance for traditional fenders, while a new style of clamp-on fender can be mounted on any bike, regardless of its design.

Headlight

If you know you'll be riding before sunrise or past dusk on a regular basis, you should consider purchasing a headlight. Be aware that the amount of power a headlight needs to aid visibility is inversely proportional to how dark it is. The darker it is, the less actual power you need; in darkness your eyes adjust, and a relatively low-power light offers fairly adequate

Rain doesn't need to ruin or even interrupt your riding. A great set of fenders will keep you dry and happy.

If you ride late at night or early in the morning, a headlight can guide your way.

lighting. Conversely, at dusk a headlight needs more power to overcome the ambient light and increase the level of perceived illumination. Also, the faster you ride, the brighter the light necessary to avoid outrunning the illuminated field of vision.

Heart Rate Monitor

Knowing just how hard you are exerting yourself is the next step along the data road. Portable heart rate monitors appropriate for exercise have been around since 1977, when the first one was introduced by Polar Electro for cross-country skiers. Because speed is relative (25 mph on a flat is much different from 25 mph downhill), a cyclocomputer offers only a rough approximation of the work you are doing. A heart rate monitor (HRM) will use a chest-strap sensor to wirelessly transmit data to the display, which will also record the data for downloading to a computer for analysis. A heart rate monitor can teach you how to differentiate your efforts, called training zones, putting firm numbers to hard, medium, and easy. HRMs will usually include the following features:

- Current heart rate
- Maximum heart rate
- Average heart rate
- Time in training zone
- Time above training zone
- Time below training zone
- Total training time

Heart rate monitors can be a good way to gauge your effort during rides.

Wattage-Measuring Devices

The final word on data capture is the wattage device. First introduced by SRM (Schoberer Rad Messtechnik—Schoberer Wheel Measuring) in 1986, the wattage device measures the actual workload put out by the cyclist in watts.

The vast majority of all pros make wattage a keystone of their training. Lance Armstrong helped to popularize its use on his way to winning the Tour de France seven times.

A wattage device measures the power a rider puts out via strain gauges that are incorporated into the bottom bracket, the rear hub, the crank arm, or the pedals. Where these gauges are located will depend on the manufacturer. The signal is sent to the computer, which then translates that information into wattage figures.

When combined with a heart rate monitor, a wattage device can indicate if you are achieving your training goals or if you are tired and have not yet fully recovered from the last hard workout. Wattage devices have the added benefit of being able to tell you just how much energy you burned as measured in kilojoules. Knowing how much energy you burned helps you to pinpoint your caloric needs during the ride as well as at home. The typical wattage device will usually include all the features found in a high-end cyclocomputer and heart-rate monitor, plus the following features:

- Current wattage
- Average wattage
- Peak wattage
- Time in, above, and below training zone
- Multiple training zones
- Software for your computer to download data

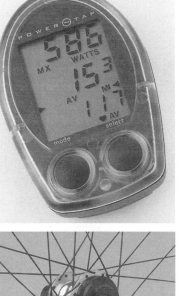

Wattage is the single most telling piece of training information you can track. Unfortunately, wattage devices aren't cheap.

GPS

If you want to know more about where you rode in addition to how well you rode, the GPS device offers a marvelous mix of features. With their large displays, GPS devices have the ability to give you large amounts of data at a glance. Some, such as the Garmin Edge units, allow you to select just how many and which functions you see on the screen. A complete list of the features available in a GPS unit could fill a book, but for cyclists, these are the most relevant:

- Current speed
- Maximum speed
- Average speed
- Trip distance
- Total odometer
- Elapsed time
- Clock
- Current elevation
- Total elevation gain
- Total elevation drop
- Rate of ascent

A GPS unit combines all the great features of a typical cyclocomputer with the power of a navigation device. You'll never be lost with a GPS unit.

Some of the Garmin units come with external sensors to aid in the accuracy of the recorded speed/distance and offer cadence functionality. Some also integrate heart rate functions into the unit via a wireless chest strap. Having more functions integrated into a single handlebar-mounted unit makes for a cleaner appearance on the handlebar and reduces weight. It also allows more data to be downloaded to your computer, making analysis simpler and more complete.

The communications protocol ANT+ allows Garmin Edge GPS units to receive data from PowerTap power-measuring hubs. This communication standard allows the Edge units to incorporate an incredible amount of information into a single device. This enables riders to download information on speed, distance, ascent, heart rate, power generated, and energy expended. It is as complete a record of performance as is currently available.

Analysis Software

Products from Polar, SRM, PowerTap, and Garmin all come with software that will allow you to download data from each workout. In addition to these, there are several other third-party applications (most notably, TrainingPeaks) that help users analyze their workouts for maximum effectiveness. You can think of them as a coach in a box. They help the rider analyze the stresses of individual workouts in detail while also incorporating them into a broader picture of training cycles where a period of intense training is followed by one of rest.

Several Web-based interfaces also allow users to download GPS data that will not only track ride stats such as speed, time, altitude gain and loss, and heart rate, but will also overlay the route on a map to show each road ridden and turn made, as well as create an elevation profile based on the data. Map My Ride (**mapmyride.com**) and Garmin Connect (**connect.garmin.com**) are the two leading sites. Users can upload rides and view rides by other members of the community. Some GPS units allow users to download data so that they may re-create those rides turn-by-turn. They are, effectively, electronic route sheets, guiding the rider turn-by-turn through the ride.

What accessories are right for you? Do you need a wattage device? A headlight? Full fenders? Only you can know how much, when and where you will ride. Many riders have as much interest in riding in wet conditions as they do intestinal distress. The same goes for night riding.

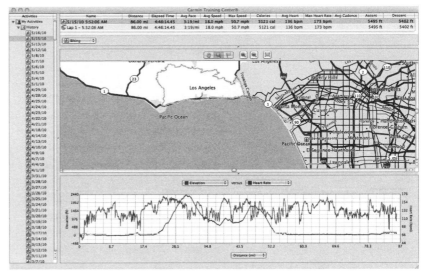

If you want to get stronger, you'll need to track your training by some method, even if you just do it with a notebook.

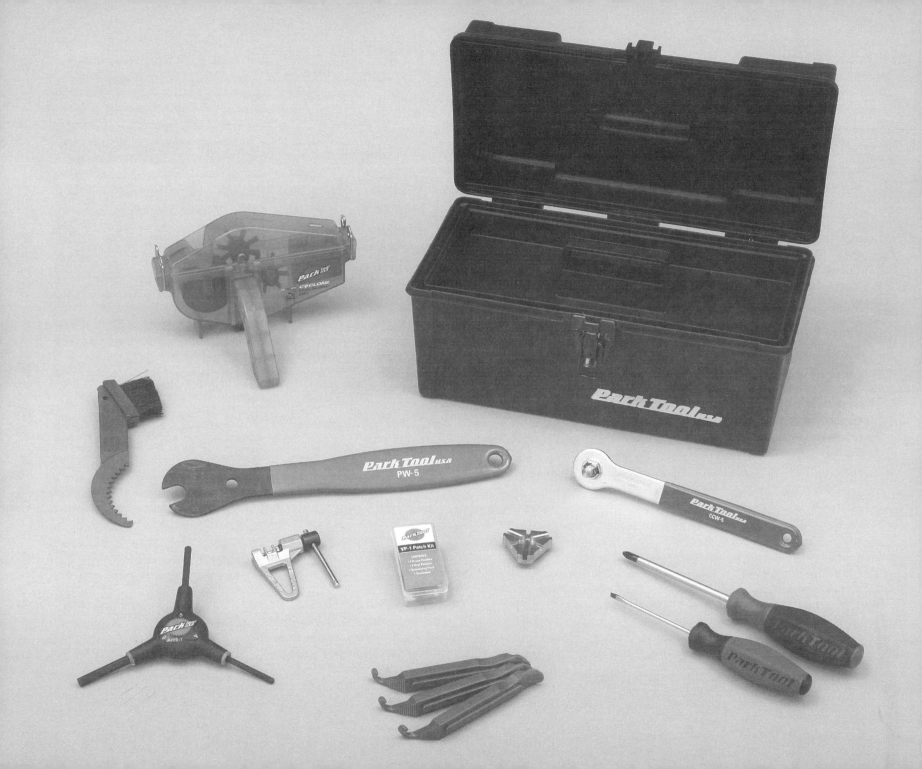

Chapter 20
Tools and Maintenance

Today's road bike is a highly technical piece of machinery. For it to operate properly at all times, it requires regular maintenance. Some of this maintenance can and should be provided by the rider; other maintenance is best provided by an experienced mechanic working for a bicycle retailer.

Each cyclist needs a basic collection of tools in order to be able to ride from home without assistance. The most elemental duties include maintaining tire pressure, lubricating the chain, and cleaning the bicycle. You should have the tools necessary to make minor adjustments to the bicycle. Beyond this, if you feel more ambitious, it can be helpful to have the tools necessary to perform a full tune-up.

The Necessities

If you plan to ride from your front door, then you will need to have some necessities to make sure you can get home should you experience a flat.

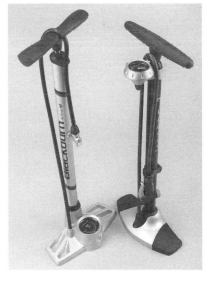

- **Floor pump:** A floor pump with a pressure gauge will allow you to pump the bike's tires to the same pressure before each ride, ensuring a consistent ride quality. Beware of models with large barrels (the "pump" portion of the pump). A large-diameter barrel can be difficult to pump because it requires greater force to push. Narrow-diameter barrels require more strokes to reach full pressure but much less strength to push the plunger.

- **Chain lube:** A rusty chain wastes energy; keep a lightweight lubricant around to keep the chain running smooth and silent.

- **Tubes:** Keep some on hand; you don't want to have to run to the bike shop after every flat.
- **Tire levers:** Ditto.
- **Frame pump or CO$_2$ cartridges:** Frame pumps offer reliability and are less expensive than CO$_2$ cartridges over the long run. Using a frame pump to pump your tire up to 120 psi is a laborious process, and many riders quit well before they hit full pressure. A 12-gram CO$_2$ cartridge can take a tire to 100 psi quicker than now, a handy shortcut for anyone riding with impatient friends.

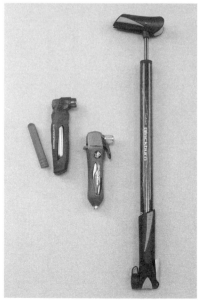

- **Patch kit:** Most riders don't ride with a second or third tube, so having a way to fix that occasional additional flat during a ride is imperative.
- **Seat bag:** Your bicycle needs a small seat bag so you can carry the aforementioned replacement tube, patch kit, and tire levers.

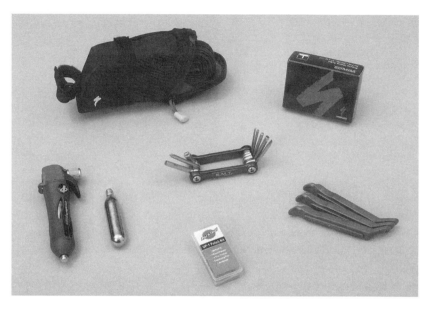

- **Multitool:** You won't often need to adjust anything on your bike during a ride, but a multitool can be handy following a crash or other unexpected event. Typically, it has 3, 4, 5, 6, and 8mm Allen wrenches, standard and Phillips-head screwdrivers, and sometimes a spoke wrench and/or a chain tool.

Basic Tool Kit

Once you have the necessities for any cyclist, it's a good idea to pick up a selection of tools to allow you to perform the most basic maintenance on your bike. A small degree of self-sufficiency can help you in two ways:

❶ By knowing more about how your bike works, you can perform minor maintenance, which can cut down on the amount of time your bike is at the shop. This will save you time (in visiting the shop as well as lost riding time) and money (in gas and labor). Why miss a ride just because your bike needs a bit of work?

❷ Once you know more about how your bike functions when you do take your bike in for service, you are better able to describe what the bike is or isn't doing. For a mechanic, there's a big difference between "the gears don't work" and "it won't downshift properly." The better the information you give, the quicker the mechanic can solve the problem.

Basic Tools

- **Allen wrenches:** 2, 3, 4, 5, 6, and 8mm. Allen bolts are used to attach most components to the bike.
- **15-millimeter pedal wrench.**
- **Chain-wear indicator:** Even if you never plan to change a chain yourself, you can avoid wearing out your cassette by checking the chain's wear every month.
- **Crescent wrench:** In order to change out a cassette, you will need a large crescent wrench, a cassette tool, and a chain whip.
- **Cassette tool:** These are specific to the component makers Shimano, SRAM, and Campagnolo.
- **Chain whip:** This is a wrench with a length of chain that is used to hold the cassette in place, while the cassette lockring tool loosens the lockring.

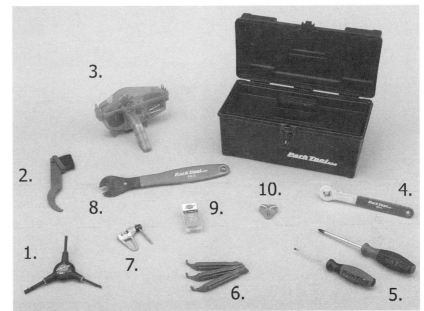

Legend: 1) 4, 5, and 6mm Y-wrench. 2) Cassette and chainring scraper/brush. 3) Chain scrubber. 4) 8mm crank wrench. 5) Phillips-head and standard screwdrivers. 6) Tire levers. 7) Chain tool. 8) 15mm pedal wrench. 9) Patch kit. 10) Spoke wrench.

Basic Supplies

- **Lubricant:** Your bike will need the chain lubed from time to time to keep it running smoothly.
- **Cleaner:** Heavy cleaners are not necessary. Generally, a mild soap with a degreasing agent (such as Dawn or Simple Green) will do the trick.
- **Sponge, brushes, and rags:** You need to be able to clean your bike periodically and wipe off excess chain lube and grease. Natural-fiber brushes and sponges are preferable because they don't hold grease and lubricants.

- **Tires:** It's a good idea to have one or two spare tires. You never know when you'll run over a piece of glass that will open the tire like a garage door.

- **Handlebar tape:** Rewrapping your own handlebar tape isn't difficult to learn and can be a great way to make your bike look fresh after a wash.

- **Cables:** Brake and gear cables don't break too often, but replacing your own cables will save you downtime. Fresh cables can be a great way to improve shifting response.

- **Chain:** Most riders need to replace their chain at least twice per season. Chains stretch and should be replaced before they stretch enough to wear the teeth on the cassette, which will force you to replace both the chain and the cassette together.

- **Cassette:** Many riders will have more than one cassette so they can choose gearing appropriate for the terrain they will be riding.

Advanced Tools

As you become more comfortable working on your bike, there are a few tools you may want to add to your arsenal. These will give you a bit more independence from your shop as well as teach you a bit about how to be a savvy customer.

- **Repair stand:** Working on your bicycle is much easier if you have a work stand to hold it. A work stand will not only hold your bicycle securely as you work on it, it will position the bicycle up off the ground, making it easier to see the parts you are working on (especially the drivetrain) and allow you to adjust your bike's shifting without having to ride it to find out if your adjustment was correct.

- **Tape measure:** A metric tape measure is a must-have if you adjust your saddle position up, down, back, or forth. Before making a change, measure the saddle height (center of the bottom bracket to the

top of the saddle, measured along the seat tube) and reach (distance from the nose of the saddle to the center of the stem clamp).

- **Torque wrench:** The bolts that tighten the stem to the fork, the handlebar to the stem, and the seatpost in the frame usually have specific torque specs indicating how tight the bolt should be. Tighten them much more and either the bolt will break or the component can be crushed.

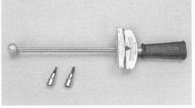

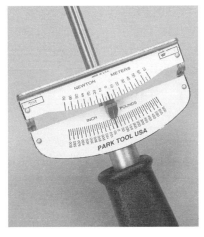

Basic Maintenance

How to Use a Brake Quick Release

A brake quick release opens the brake caliper to allow you to remove the rear wheel once the quick-release lever has been opened. The brake quick release allows brake adjustment to be set so that the brake pads are closer to the rim than the diameter of the tire. Were this not the case, you would always have to inflate a tire after installing the wheel and deflate a tire before removing the wheel.

Some riders will use the brake quick release to adjust the lever throw. This isn't the best way to make this adjustment, as it will limit the brakes' ability to open to allow you to remove the wheel.

- On Shimano and SRAM brakes, turn the dial lever upward, toward the barrel adjuster.
- On Campagnolo brakes, squeeze the brake lever slightly, and then depress the brake lever retention pin.

How to Use a Wheel Quick Release

When Tullio Campagnolo invented the quick-release skewer in 1927, he revolutionized not only bicycle racing but the bicycle itself. The quick release uses a cam-actuated lever that enables someone of even modest hand strength to secure a wheel to a bicycle.

It is standard practice to place the quick-release lever on the nondrive (left) side of the bicycle. This is an established practice from racing, but it is helpful to riders by keeping the rear quick-release lever away from the rear derailleur and chain. Knowing that both levers are on the nondrive side will speed flat changes on your own or in a race.

A quick-release lever of any design isn't fully closed until the lever is turned in toward the center plane of the wheel. If the lever is either parallel to the bicycle or points out, it isn't sufficiently closed to secure the wheel.

❶ Screw the quick-release nut until light finger pressure closes the quick release 90 degrees.

❷ Place the heel of your hand over the quick-release lever and press it closed until the lever points inward, toward the wheel. Some riders use the spokes or chainstay to assist their hand.

❸ Simply open the quick release to remove the wheel. Many forks have tabs on the dropouts to prevent a wheel from accidentally dropping off. Removing the wheel completely usually requires unscrewing the quick-release nut two full turns.

Step ❶

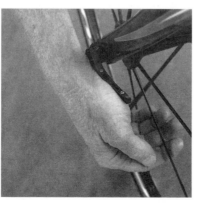

Step ❷

How to Lubricate a Chain

A bicycle chain must be lubricated to pedal smoothly and shift properly. A rusty chain will actually make the bicycle harder to pedal, slowing most riders. Periodic chain lubrication will keep your bike quiet and efficient.

To lubricate the chain, secure the bicycle in a repair stand.

❶ Shift the bicycle into the smallest cog; applying lubricant is easier if the chain is as far from the spokes as possible.

❷ Begin backpedaling the bicycle with your hand.

❸ Apply the lubricant to the chain as it passes over the cog. You can use the cable housing to steady your hand.

❹ Use only a drop per link.

❺ Let the bicycle sit overnight so the lubricant may penetrate the links fully.

❻ Wipe the excess lube from the chain with a rag in the morning.

How to Fix a Flat

Flat tires are an inevitable part of cycling. Changing a flat quickly can make the difference between thinking of the event as a minor frustration and a major ordeal. With some practice, most riders can change a flat in five minutes or less.

Front

❶ Open the brake release.

❷ Open the quick release.

❸ Remove the wheel.

❹ Lay the bike down, drive-side up.

⑤ Hook one tire lever under the tire bead.

⑥ Quickly run the lever around the wheel.

⑦ Remove the old tube.

⑧ Inspect the tire for cuts, glass, tacks, etc. Be sure to run your fingers inside the tire casing. Captain Obvious says remove anything you find.

⑨ Take out a new tube and put enough air in the tube to glve It shape (just a few psi).

⑩ Insert the valve stem into the valve hole.

⑪ Gradually work the rest of the tube into the tire and rim.

⑫ Make sure the tube sits on the rim and not to the side.

⑬ Starting at the valve stem, push the tire bead back into the rim.

⑭ Use your thumbs to push the final section of the bead over the edge of the rim. Do not use the tire lever!

⑮ Inflate the tire to pressure. Generally, it's wise to pump a small amount of air into the tire and check it to make sure the bead is properly seated before taking the tire to full pressure.

⑯ Reinsert the wheel into the dropouts.

⑰ Close the quick-release lever.

⑱ Close the brake release.

Step ⑤

Step ⑥

Step ⑦

Step ⑧

Step ⑨

Step ⑪

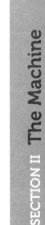

Step ⑬

Step ⑭

Step ⑮

Rear

➊ Shift the chain into the smallest cog. You may need to hold the bike up and pedal with your hand.

➋ Open the brake release.

➌ Open the quick release.

➍ Remove the wheel by holding the bike upright and giving the rear wheel a firm downward push.

➎ Tilt the wheel to the left to bring the quick-release nut around the chain.

➏ Lay the bike down, drive-side up.

➐ Hook one tire lever under the tire bead, and quickly run the lever around the wheel.

➑ Remove the old tube.

➒ Inspect the tire for cuts, glass, tacks, etc. Be sure to run your fingers inside the tire casing. Captain Obvious says remove anything you find.

➓ Take out a new tube and put enough air in the tube to give it shape (just a few psi).

⓫ Insert the valve stem into the valve hole.

⓬ Gradually work the rest of the tube into the tire and rim.

⓭ Make sure the tube sits on the rim and not to the side.

⓮ Starting at the valve stem, push the tire bead back into the rim.

⓯ Use your thumbs to push the final section of the bead over the edge of the rim. Do not use the tire lever!

⓰ Inflate the tire to pressure.

⓱ Place the wheel in the rear triangle.

⓲ Hook the chain on the smallest cog.

⓳ Pull back and up and the wheel will slide into the dropouts.

⓴ Close the quick-release lever.

㉑ Close the brake release.

㉒ Step over the bike and clip one foot in a pedal.

㉓ Grab the front brake and push the bike forward so the rear wheel rises.

㉔ Give a couple of quick pedal strokes and downshift three or four cogs to make starting easier.

How to Wash Your Bicycle

Your bicycle needs to be cleaned periodically to remove dirt, grease, and grime that have built up on the frame and components. Once your bike is clean you can inspect it to see if it needs more serious maintenance.

➊ Spray the bike down with a hose. Be careful to avoid spraying water directly at the bearings located in the headset, bottom bracket, and hubs.

Step ➊

Step ➋

Step ➌

Step ➍

❷ Sponge the bike down with the cleaning solution. Use small brushes to get in the hard-to-reach places. Pay particular attention to the chain, cassette, derailleurs, and chainrings.

❸ Spray the bike off.

❹ Wipe the bike down with a rag. As you go, inspect the frame and other components for cracks or other signs of wear. If you find something out of the ordinary, take your bike to your local retailer.

How to Adjust Indexed Shifting

Indexed shifting requires cables be set to a particular level of tension so that each shift causes the derailleur to move the exact distance required to execute a shift. If the cable isn't tight enough, the derailleur will undershift and have difficulty downshifting from one cog to the next. If the cable is too tight, the derailleur will overshift, and tend to jump more than one cog at a time.

Barrel adjusters are used to set the cable tension for the front and rear derailleurs. A barrel adjuster can be found at the rear derailleur where the cable enters the derailleur. Two more barrel adjusters can usually be found on the frame near the junction of the head tube and down tube.

To adjust the derailleurs, secure the bicycle in a repair stand.

Tools needed: Phillips-head screwdriver and 5mm Allen wrench.

Front derailleur

❶ Begin with the chain on the small chainring.

❷ Check that the inner plate of the front derailleur has a maximum 3mm gap to the chain.

❸ If the inner plate is too far away, turn the derailleur's low set screw clockwise. If the inner plate is too close, turn the derailleur's low set screw counterclockwise. When adjusting a set screw, turn the screw a half turn and then check the alignment.

❹ Check the tension of the front derailleur cable with your finger; there should be slight tension on the cable.

❺ If the cable is slack, loosen the front derailleur cable-fixing bolt and pull the cable taught, then tighten the bolt again.

Step ❶

Step ❷

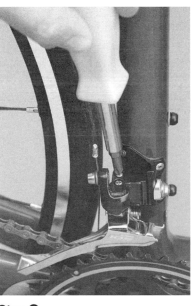
Step ❸

Step ❺

6 Begin pedaling the bicycle with your left hand.

7 With your right hand, give the front derailleur shift lever a firm shift to the big chainring. If the cable is properly adjusted, the derailleur will shift the chain smoothly from the small chainring to the big chainring.

8 If the cable isn't tight enough, the chain will hesitate before shifting up or it won't shift up at all. Shift the chain back to the small chainring. To increase tension on the cable and speed shifting, turn the front derailleur barrel adjuster (usually found on the frame near the head tube–down tube junction) counterclockwise; turn the barrel adjuster in half-turn increments. Repeat this process until the chain shifts smoothly up to the big chainring.

9 If the front derailleur set screw is adjusted in too far, it will not permit the front derailleur to move far enough to shift the chain onto the large chainring. Turn the high set screw counterclockwise to allow the derailleur to move farther out. The front derailleur's outer plate should have a maximum gap of 3mm to the chain.

10 If the derailleur's high set screw is improperly adjusted and allows the derailleur to shift too far out, the derailleur will push the chain beyond the big chain ring and throw the chain off.

11 Place the chain back on the large chainring manually. With the shifter still in the high gear position, begin turning the set screw clockwise.

12 Once the chain moves smoothly from the small chainring to the large chainring with a single, swift movement of the shift lever without shifting beyond the chainring, check to make sure that shifting back to the small chainring occurs with a firm release of the shift lever.

Step **7**

Step **8**

Step **9**

Step **9** *(continued)*

Step ⑩

Step ⑪

Step ❶

Rear

❶ Begin with the chain in the smallest cog (usually an 11- or 12-t cog).

❷ Check to make sure the high set screw is adjusted so that the rear derailleur is in line with the smallest cog. Turn the set screw clockwise if the derailleur is to the right of the cog, counterclockwise if it is to the left.

Step ⑫

Step ❷

③ Check the tension of the rear derailleur cable with your finger; there should be slight tension on the cable.

④ If the cable is slack, loosen the rear derailleur cable fixing bolt and pull the cable taut, then tighten the bolt again.

⑤ Begin pedaling the bicycle with your right hand.

⑥ Downshift the derailleur one cog. If there is sufficient tension on the cable, the chain will move smoothly to the next largest cog.

⑦ If the cable isn't tight enough, the chain will hesitate before shifting up to the next cog or it won't shift at all. Shift the chain back to the small cog. To increase tension on the cable and speed shifting, turn the rear derailleur barrel adjuster (found at the rear of the rear derailleur) counterclockwise; turn the barrel adjuster in half-turn increments and check shifting performance again. Repeat this process until the chain shifts smoothly up one cog.

⑧ Once the derailleur shifts the chain smoothly up one cog, shift the chain up to each successively larger cog. The derailleur should perform each shift smoothly; if not, continue to increase the cable tension until each shift up is smooth.

⑨ Shift the chain into the largest cog. Check that the low gear set screw is properly adjusted by pushing the shift lever while pedaling to see if the derailleur can push the chain beyond the cog and into the spokes. A properly adjusted set screw will not allow the derailleur to move beyond the largest cog.

⑩ If the derailleur can push the chain beyond the cog, turn the low gear set screw clockwise until the derailleur moves no farther than the largest cog when the shift lever is pushed.

Step ③

Step ④

Step ⑥

Step ⑦

Step ❽

Step ❾

Step ❾ *(continued)*

How to Use a Brake Barrel Adjuster

As brake pads wear, the distance the brake calipers must travel increases. Accordingly, lever throw increases, meaning a rider must squeeze the lever more to achieve necessary stopping power. To restore the throw, the barrel adjuster can be used to decrease the lever throw.

❶ Squeeze the brake pads lightly with your hand; this will reduce the pressure on the brake cable, making the barrel adjuster easier to turn.

❷ Turn the cable adjuster counterclockwise to decrease lever throw.

❸ Squeeze both the front and rear brake levers at the same time to make sure their throw is equal and adjust accordingly. A difference in throw can result in one brake being applied sooner or with more force than the other, which can result in a loss of control.

Step ❶

Step ❷

How to Wrap Bar Tape

If you can wrap your own bar tape, you can give your bike a fresh look any time you want.

❶ Insert 1 inch of tape into the end of the bar.

❷ Viewed from the end of the bar, wrap the left side counterclockwise, the right side clockwise.

❸ Pull the tape tight and overlap ½ inch of tape. Check the underside of the bar to make sure the tape doesn't pucker.

❹ Wrap the tape in a figure-8 around the lever. With Campagnolo levers, be sure to tuck the edge of the tape under the edge of the lever mount so as not to interfere with the action of the Ergo shifters.

❺ Continue wrapping to the bulge of the bar. If the bar is a carbon fiber model with a large, flat palm surface, many riders only wrap to the 90-degree bend.

❻ Trim a 2-inch section of tape at an angle to finish the wrap without a big bulge.

❼ Wrap electrical tape over the end of the tape with three full wraps.

❽ Gather the edge of the tape and insert the bar end plug with a firm push.

Step ❶

Step ❷

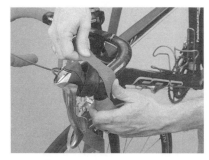

Step ❸

Step ❹

Step ❺

Step ❻

Step ❼

Step ❽

Step ❽ *(continued)*

Image: Patrick Brady

Tools and Maintenance   161

Chapter 21
Upgrades for Your Bicycle

Bicycling is a pretty straightforward endeavor. If you train, you'll gain fitness and be more efficient. Efficiency can be expressed as increased speed, but it can also be expressed as reduced effort. So while some riders may always be looking for more speed, there are plenty of riders who may be satisfied with their pace, but increased efficiency can mean longer rides with little or no increase in fatigue.

Your hard work, expressed either as time in the saddle or dollars spent at a bike shop, can result in more efficiency and a better experience. With bicycles—as with most things—quality pays. As equipment improves in quality, myriad benefits can be realized. You can purchase equipment for your bicycle with more benefits than an auto club membership. Among the ways you can improve your bicycle are:

- Lightweight equipment to help you accelerate more quickly and go up hills faster
- Vibration-damping equipment to reduce fatigue
- Aerodynamic equipment to reduce wind resistance
- Stiffer components to make power transmission more efficient
- Better-quality tires to improve traction or puncture resistance

Here are some of the upgrades you can make, beginning with the most helpful:

Wheels

Easily the biggest improvement you can make to your bicycle comes from purchasing a set of high-quality wheels. The benefits of a set of racing wheels can be reduced weight, greater aerodynamics, or, if you are willing to spend enough, both. It used to be that a high-quality wheel set was built by a veteran mechanic at your local shop. Today, that isn't as common; most wheels come prebuilt from the factory. Find the shop in your area with an experienced wheel builder, because any time you need your wheels serviced, his experience will be helpful.

A new set of wheels can make you feel like you have a new, faster bike.

Climbing wheels: If you live in an area with hills or mountains, the local climbers will all have lightweight wheels. For less than $1,000 you can purchase a lightweight set of wheels that will be easier to accelerate due to their reduced rotating mass, which will help you on climbs. Aluminum rims are still king in the sub-$1,000 market; they are easier to service and don't require new brake shoes. Low weight for a set of aftermarket wheels is 1,500g for the wheel set (no skewers, cassette, tires, or tubes).

Lightweight wheels can be helpful if you have hills or mountains where you live.

Aerodynamic wheels: While reduced weight is immediately apparent upon picking up a bike, most engineers are saying that aerodynamics trumps weight. A deep-section rim (generally defined as any rim with a profile of 30mm or greater) does increase weight, but it will more than offset that increase in weight by increasing the wheels' aerodynamic efficiency; though heavier, the wheel is faster. A pair of deep-section aluminum rim wheels is the most cost-effective method to make your bike faster other than adding aero bars (discussed later in this chapter), and they can be used safely on group rides and centuries, unlike aero bars.

Tubulars vs. clinchers: Bar none, the finest riding wheels and tires out there are tubulars. Tubular tires, also known as sew-ups, actually sew the tire casing into a tubular shape around the inner tube. These tires are then glued onto special tubular-specific rims.

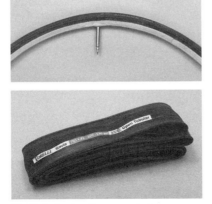

Both tubular tires and rims are different in construction from clincher tires and rims.

The combination of special tire and special tube can cut noticeable weight from a set of wheels. Because the tires retain a circular profile with only minimal distortion at the contact patch where the tire meets the ground, they corner exceedingly well. They are, however, difficult to glue on and even more difficult to change in the event of a flat. Most riders who do use them only use them on wheels reserved for racing.

Carbon fiber rims: In the quest to reduce weight on the bicycle, carbon fiber has been used to make rims, hubs, and, in some cases, even spokes. Carbon fiber rims are available in both tubular and clincher designs, and can shave 200g from an already lightweight set of wheels while offering a deep-section rim profile. The combination gives riders a set of wheels with superior aerodynamics with a weight appealing to climbers: the best of both worlds, as it were. This powerful combination comes at a price, though. Carbon fiber rims require special brake pads, crack easily (a cracked rim can fail suddenly, resulting in a crash for the rider), and don't dissipate heat as well as aluminum rims. This makes braking on long descents more hazardous, because it is possible to heat the air in the tube to the point that it expands and blows the tire off the rim. A carbon fiber rim can melt from the heat generated by braking on a long (more than 2-mile) descent. And finally, wheels built with carbon fiber rims are expensive; in most cases, expect to spend $2,000 or more.

To purchase a set of wheels, you will need to specify the type of freehub you need, which is based on the components on your bicycle. The two types are made by Campagnolo and Shimano; SRAM-made wheels use a Shimano-style freehub.

Tubular tires require care during installation but offer an incredible ride.

Tires

With both clincher and tubular tires, the market is dominated by relatively inexpensive training tires. Upgrading from these will offer you a choice based on your priorities. You can either go for a tire with a reinforced casing for more puncture resistance, or you can select a tire with a more supple casing and grippier tread for higher performance.

Puncture-resistant casings are reinforced with any of a variety of man-made fibers; Kevlar is a frequent ingredient. The upside is that you could ride your bike through a minefield without getting a flat. The downside is that the tires weigh as much as iron ore and are just as stiff. They also don't corner as well, and they rattle the rider like a washboard due to the stiff casing.

High-quality tires can improve your riding experience by increasing sensitivity and cornering grip.

High-performance racing tires are popular because their supple casing and soft rubber tread offer the rider a high degree of sensitivity to the road surface and the tires' grip; think surgical, not winter, glove. While most riders can't tell you exactly what they feel, they will report feeling more confident when riding a better set of tires. High-performance tires feature a casing with a high thread count, just like your favorite sheets; the maximum you'll find is 290 threads per inch (tpi), but occasionally you'll even see 320 tpi. Cotton is king. The top-of-the-line clinchers combine a tubular casing with the flexible bead (the part of the tire that hooks on the sidewall of the clincher rim) of a folding clincher; they are called "open tubulars." Many high-performance tires will feature two different rubber compounds in the tread; the center section that meets the asphalt when you ride in a straight line will be harder for reduced wear and rolling resistance, while the sides will feature a softer compound for better grip when cornering.

To purchase a new set of tires, you will need to specify the tire's dimensions. All but the smallest riders use bicycles with 700C wheels; some women's bikes use wheels with 650C wheels front and rear or occasionally with a 24-in. wheel on the front paired with a 700C wheel in the rear. The most common tire widths are 23 and 25mm, but beware that one company's 23mm tire may be another company's 25mm; how tire width is measured varies somewhat.

Saddle

Saddle selection is highly personal, and what works for one rider may not work for another. It is up to the rider to try to find a saddle that works with his or her body. A high-quality saddle will offer greater comfort and reduced weight.

Many saddles offer a central perineal channel or cutout to relieve pressure on a group of blood vessels and nerves that run beneath the rider's pelvis. Cutting off blood flow here results in numbness and discomfort for both men and women, and saddle companies have invested millions of dollars designing new saddles in an attempt to keep blood flow constant while riders are seated.

Finding the right saddle can require a fair amount of trial and error, but options abound.

To reduce saddle weight, most manufacturers offer saddles with the rails made from titanium or even carbon fiber. Carbon fiber, while light, has the added benefit of reducing vibration that will fatigue the rider.

Carbon Fiber Handlebar

Carbon fiber has revolutionized handlebar design. Engineers now have unprecedented freedom in bringing new handlebar shapes to market. The most notable change has been the flattening of the bar top to give riders a more comfortable location to rest their palms when climbing, reducing pressure on the hands. And because carbon

Carbon fiber handlebars can improve your comfort in many ways.

fiber reduces the vibration that travels through the bicycle to the rider, it cuts muscle fatigue, allowing a rider to ride longer or with greater strength later in the ride.

One of the more popular trends in handlebar shapes is the compact design. With a compact bar, both the handlebar's reach and drop are reduced. While this results in less variation in body position among the three hand positions (bar tops, lever hoods, and bar drops), this design is an excellent alternative for riders who don't have the flexibility of an octopus. Compared with other bars, the compact bar effectively brings the hoods closer and the drops up, making the reach easier for anyone with a fussy back.

So while a carbon fiber handlebar can result in increased comfort for the rider, it will almost certainly cut the bicycle's weight, as well. There are several bars on the market that weigh fewer than 200g, a weight no aluminum bar has achieved.

While a carbon fiber stem is not required to use a carbon fiber handlebar, many riders choose to purchase a matching set from the component maker responsible for the bar. While some aluminum stems rival carbon fiber in weight, the additional vibration damping can increase a rider's comfort perceptibly.

It used to be that if you crashed with a carbon fiber component, it would break rather visibly, something called catastrophic failure. Today, manufacturers will design parts with layers of carbon that prevent a crack from causing a part to completely fail. It may feel unusually flexible, or in some cases the part may even feel okay under light loads. It is important, however, to replace a handlebar following a crash. It's just not worth the risk.

To purchase a handlebar, you will need to specify the handlebar clamp diameter (31.8mm is the new standard, though 26.0mm and 26.2mm are still out there) and width (usually 40cm, 42cm, or 44cm measured center-to-center). To order a stem you will also need to know the handlebar clamp diameter, the length (80–130mm in 10mm increments), the bore diameter (1⅛ in. is most common) and the rise (or angle: 0, 6, 8, and 12 degrees are most common). Rise is the change in angle from the fork's steerer tube; 90 degrees is the starting point, 0 degrees. A plus angle means the stem points up, and a minus angle means the stem points down.

Aero Bars

Aside from wheels, one of the easiest ways to purchase speed is by adding a set of "aero" (short for aerodynamic) handlebars to your bicycle. Time trial bikes will use a specialized "base" bar along with aerodynamic extension bars to allow you to ride in a downhill-skier-like tuck. For greater versatility, you can opt to add a set of "clip-on" bars that mount on your existing drop handlebar. These clip-ons act as the extensions to

Aerodynamic bars are the perfect answer to gaining more speed when you ride alone.

give you the low aerodynamic tuck so helpful for time trials. They are an inexpensive alternative to purchasing a dedicated bike, and while they do add weight, the aerodynamic savings, as measured in time, more than offsets the additional weight. One word of caution: This is not a piece of equipment to be used on group rides; these are most appropriate for time trials and other individual rides.

Carbon Fiber Seatpost

Switching from an aluminum to a carbon fiber seatpost is a relatively inexpensive upgrade, and it can result in more comfort at the saddle, as well, while cutting weight slightly. The real advantage to adding a carbon fiber seatpost is for riders who have a bicycle with an aluminum frame; a carbon fiber seatpost can noticeably cut vibration transmitted to the saddle.

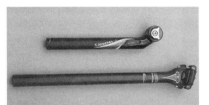

A different seatpost can increase your comfort and even improve your fit.

To purchase a seatpost you will need to specify the seatpost diameter (27.2mm is most common) and length (300mm and 350mm are most common). Setback is the distance in millimeters behind the axis of the seat tube that the seatpost clamp lies; this distance varies from manufacturer to manufacturer, though 20mm is fairly common. Some manufacturers offer seatposts with varying amounts of setback, ranging from as little as none to as much as 35mm.

Aftermarket Cranksets

Cranksets made from carbon fiber have become quite popular. Under the right circumstances, a carbon fiber crankset has the potential to be lighter than an aluminum crankset, as well as stiffer and stronger. Achieving this has been another matter. Shimano continues to make its top-of-the-line Dura-Ace crankset from aluminum because the company has not been entirely satisfied with the results from its testing of carbon fiber cranks.

A new crankset can allow you to select more appropriate gearing and drop weight from your bike.

Most riders purchasing carbon fiber cranks are doing so for reasons of weight loss. The fact is, most carbon fiber cranksets are only marginally lighter than their top-of-the-line aluminum counterparts, while the aluminum cranksets are usually stiffer, as well.

Carbon Fiber Fork

It used to be that upgrading a bicycle's fork to carbon was a popular way to gain some comfort and reduce weight. Most road bikes today are designed with a specific fork in mind that's meant to ensure a harmonious appearance and optimal handling. Replacing your bicycle's fork with a new aftermarket fork can cut weight while increasing upper-body comfort, thanks to vibration damping. Any change should be undertaken with some caution.

Changing a fork for one with less fork rake will slow the bicycle's handling, making it more resistant to turning. Conversely, changing to a fork with more fork rake will speed the bicycle's handling, making it more responsive to steering input. Also, different forks will have a different axle-to-crown distance. If that distance is reduced, the bicycle's head tube rotates down (relative to the rear axle), thereby increasing

the head tube angle and making the bike handle more quickly. A longer axle-to-crown distance will decrease the head-tube angle and make the bike more resistant to turning.

To purchase a fork you will need to specify the steerer diameter (1⅛ in. is most common) and the rake (usually 40, 43, or 45mm).

Lightweight carbon fiber forks can cut vibration that fatigues your upper-body.

Chapter 22
Gearing for Your Bicycle

Twenty gears gives you a great many options for finding the right cadence when you're riding. Depending on where you live, though, you may want to purchase gearing more appropriate to your local terrain.

Inside, we all imagine that we're as flexible as yogis, both in brain and bone. The fact is, human beings suffer a pretty narrow operating range. Most of us refrain from hanging around in our skivvies when the temp drops below 60°F, and run for the ice cream parlor when the mercury hits triple digits. Similarly, as cyclists, most of us operate best at a cadence of between 80 and 120 rpm and a heart rate between 60 and 90 percent of maximum. It's a tight fit, a little like trying to get dressed in your car. This is where a bike's multiple gears come in handy.

Adaptation

The purpose of gearing is to allow you to pedal at a consistent cadence over a variety of terrain. This is accomplished by adapting the bicycle's gearing to the terrain present. Ideally, your bicycle's lowest gear should be low enough to get you over the biggest hill you ride regularly, and the highest gear no bigger than you can turn at your highest cadence.

There's little point to having 20 gears on a bike if you only use 10 of them. Chainrings and cassettes are available aftermarket so that you can match your bike's gearing to the terrain you ride.

Many road bicycles are sold with gearing either too broad or too narrow for where the bicycle will be ridden. It's like climbing a mountain in ballet slippers or showing up to a ball in ski boots. The bike manufacturers, for their part, do what they can to offer bikes that will appeal to the masses. The unfortunate reality is when they create a bike perfect for people living in the Rocky, Green, or Santa Monica mountains, it will have gears too low to be of any use to someone living in Florida or Nebraska. Similarly, if they gear the bike for the flats, anyone who rides in the mountains will think someone is trying to torture them.

So the average road bike comes equipped with 39-t and 53-t chainrings and a 12- to 23-t cassette. This gearing is appropriate for a rider strong enough to hang on to group rides in hilly (though not mountainous) terrain. The same rider, living in flat terrain, would find a 12- to 21-t cassette more appropriate and may only need a 42-t small chainring. And that same rider living in mountainous terrain would likely prefer an 11- to 25-t cassette combined with a compact crankset with 34-t and 50-t chainrings to give a broad gearing.

A Brief History of Gearing

As mentioned in Chapter 1, the earliest chain-driven bicycles were fixed-gear. Riders could not coast, and racers had to be careful how they chose gears. Even with the advent of a flip-flop hub that put a cog on each side of the rear hub (thereby giving the rider the opportunity to remove the wheel and "flip" it around to use a different gear), because the process was time-consuming, riders needed to be selective about when they stopped to change gears. Frequently riders would have one gear for the flats and downhills and another for the climbs.

One of the earliest shifters, the Campagnolo Cambio Corsa, involved lever-operated changers that required the rider to reach back to the seatstay for rear changes and under the leg to the seat tube for chainring changes. They were called "suicide shifters" because of the precarious placement of the levers near the rear wheel; a finger or hand caught in a wheel was an unfortunate Technicolor affair.

The rear derailleur as we know it was invented in 1951 by Campagnolo. The Gran Sport rear derailleur was the first to feature a return spring, meaning it could be operated by a single lever-actuated cable. The Gran Sport front derailleur received a return spring operated by a lever and cable as well.

Since that time, refinements to derailleurs have done four things:

❶ Increase the range of gearing

❷ Reduce weight

❸ Ease operation

❹ Reduce friction and noise

From the 1950s to the 1980s, the average rear derailleur had a maximum gear span of 14 teeth, while the average front derailleur could accommodate a span of 10 teeth. Led by Shimano, a series of innovations to both front and rear derailleurs began increasing gear spans, making it comfortable to pedal through an increasing variety of terrain.

In the 1980s, front derailleurs and cranks were designed to accept a 14-t range, replacing the standard 42- and 52-t chainrings with 39- and 53-t chainrings. The only way to increase gearing range was to add a third chainring. Unfortunately, the 20-t difference between the largest and smallest chainrings necessitated a new rear derailleur to keep the chain properly tensioned. The long-cage rear derailleur was invented,

but it rarely shifted with the crisp precision of its short-cage brethren—and it was heavier as well.

In the 1990s, new rear derailleur designs increased the gear span to 15 t. Today both Shimano and SRAM offer rear derailleurs that can accommodate an 11- to 28-t cassette—an impressive 17 teeth.

Cranks evolved as well. Component manufacturers found it difficult to decrease the size of the inner chainring further, due to the bolt circle diameter of the crank arm "spider." In 2003, FSA introduced a new style of crank called a compact. It features a smaller bolt circle diameter that allows smaller chainrings to be mounted. The average compact uses a 34-t small ring and a 50-t large ring. Today, thanks to the advent of the compact and new rear derailleur designs, a bike with two chainrings can cover as much gearing range as many triples used to cover—more than 80 gear inches from the smallest gear to the largest gear, an increase of nearly 10 gear inches on average.

Gear Development

Because gearing is not a constant, but relative to wheel size, it is described in inches. Gear development is how gears are compared; it is equivalent to the wheel diameter if the wheel were on a direct-drive bicycle (think antique high wheel). To figure the gear inches for a given gear combination, the equation goes like this:

Number of chainring teeth / Number of cog teeth x wheel diameter = gear inches

The gear development for a road bike geared with 39-t and 53-t chainrings and a 12–23 cassette looks like this:

	# OF CHAINRING TEETH	
	39	53
23	45.8	62.2
21	50.1	68.1
19	55.4	75.3
18	58.5	79.5
17	61.9	84.2
16	65.8	89.4
15	70.2	95.4
14	75.2	102.2
13	81.0	110.1
12	87.8	119.3

(# OF CASSETTE COG TEETH — left axis label)

You'll notice that the 39x17 and 53x23 combination as well as the 39x14 and 53x19 combination are similar in size. This is referred to as overlap or gear repetition. Gear redundancy reduces the number of practical gears you have. And while it was once true that riders would shift back and forth between the big and small chainrings and up and down the freewheel as they pursued ideal gear development, they did so only because the jumps between cogs could be as large as three or four teeth per cog on a six-speed freewheel; the shifting was necessary to avoid large jumps in gearing and therefore unpleasant changes in cadence. Today, most riders concentrate their shifting to the rear derailleur except when a major change in terrain calls for a shift between chainrings.

Chainring and Crank Options

The speeds that pros are able to attain are, well, why they are pros. Trying to use the gearing a pro uses is a little like trying to race a top fuel dragster with a moped. You need a pro's engine to make full use of that gearing.

The limitations of the 42/52-t chainring setup led the way to the triple crankset for tourists who needed lower gears. They made loaded touring with panniers over hilly and mountainous terrain possible. Unfortunately, the triple drivetrain has a few liabilities. For starters, each of the components used in a triple drivetrain—crank, front derailleur, and rear derailleur—are all heavier than their racing counterparts. Moreover, the average triple repeats anywhere from six to nine gears. Triples also have a less-than-stellar reputation for shifting performance; the chain can sometimes miss the small chainring when shifting off of the middle chainring.

The compact crank solved these problems by giving riders more gears where they needed them most—at the low end. The upshot is that when a 34/50-t compact crankset replaces a 39/53-t crankset, riders are rewarded with

Compact cranks make great sense for most riders because of their lower and wider gear range.

a 13 percent increase in low-end for climbing while losing less than 6 percent of the high-end gearing. For most roadies—almost everyone except for the top three categories of racers—the compact represents a real advancement in gearing.

While it may seem like it is more appropriate for riders in hilly and mountainous areas, one of the compact's greatest attributes is to give riders more usable gears when in the big ring. Because the vast majority of group rides will unfold at speeds somewhere between 20 and 30 mph, the fact is a 50-t chainring combined with an 11- to 21-t cassette gives riders eight usable gears in that range of speed, while a 53-t chainring combined with the same cassette only gets six usable gears.

Cassette Options

Because cassettes are relatively easy to change, many riders will keep a couple of different cassettes for riding in different circumstances. If you have multiple sets of wheels, equipping each set with a cassette can speed wheel changes before a ride. This can make particular sense if you reserve a special set of wheels just for your hilliest rides, your flattest, fastest rides, or for racing.

With the vast majority of all road bikes being sold with 10-speed drivetrains (that is, 10 cogs on the rear wheel), choosing an appropriate

Most recreational riders aren't as strong as pros and can't make the fullest use of a standard 53/39 crankset.

The triple crank added a third chainring to increase low gearing for climbing big mountains.

cassette really comes down to two questions:

1. What large cog do I need for hills in my area?
2. What small cog do I need for sprints and descents?

Many riders keep a few cassettes around for riding in different terrain.

In response to Question 1, riders in flat areas may need only a 21-t large cog. Riders living in hillier areas have many more choices today than were available a few years ago thanks to advances in rear derailleur design.

In response to Question 2, riders who don't sprint often or descend at high speed may only need a 12- or 13-t small cog. Consider that with a cadence of 120 rpm, a 53x11 gear will propel you at 45.4 mph. If that's faster than your idea of fun, consider running a lower high gear. By choosing a large small cog (such as a 13-t), you will have more usable gears in the middle range of your cassette. The more single-tooth cog jumps your cassette has in its midrange, the more comfortable you will be out on the road.

Refer to the appendix on pages 250–252 for gear charts on some popular combinations, plus a comprehensive gear chart for most possible combinations.

Image: Patrick Brady

Section III
The Lifestyle

Chapter 23
Training: Why, How

The Benefits of Training

As with most things in life, the hardwiring in our brains causes a good thing (cycling) to tickle the pleasure centers. And that same hardwiring has led us to believe more of a good thing (speed, perhaps?) to be a better thing, beer-bust nights in college notwithstanding. Most cyclists need prodding in the none-to-little category to get the idea that going faster on a bike would result in more fun.

So how do you get faster? Training. The benefits of more and better training are weight loss, a stronger heart, and improved eye–hand coordination. The active lifestyle hardly needs a sales pitch; if you're reading this, the signs are pretty clear that you do not want to be a couch potato. The amazing thing about cycling is that because its primary demands are aerobic—that is, dependent on the heart and lungs—even the most out-of-shape couch jockey can realize fantastic gains in fitness. Those gains depend almost entirely on the amount of time you are willing to put in the saddle. While there does come a point of diminishing returns to training, the low-impact nature of the sport makes it easy to do daily.

For you, this means logging miles in the saddle consistently. Naturally, that raises another question: What's consistent? We each have our own constraints in life. A full workweek for some may be 40 hours, but your average lawyer could fit a vacation in working only those hours. Similarly, each cyclist will define his or her ability (availability) to train differently.

If riding with a group or doing organized rides such as centuries is your goal, then riding needs to be a regular part of your week. But you don't have to do what the group does to stay with it. Chris Carmichael, president of Carmichael Training Systems and Lance Armstrong's coach for his seven Tour de France victories, put it this way: "You need not be able to complete a 100-mile ride on your own to be able to complete a century with a group."

To give you some perspective on commitment, an entry-level racer will need to train 10–12 hours per week (yes, that's like a part-time job) to have any success in racing. Racers in the top categories will train upwards of 20 hours per week. A pro racing the Tour de France will train a minimum of 30 hours per week during the season. If you want to do group rides and stay with the group, you will need to train at least 6 hours per week.

As you pursue greater levels of fitness, it becomes important to vary your training. You will want to do long rides and short rides, hard rides and easy rides. How you vary these will make a profound difference in your fitness. By cycling these different efforts properly, you can advance more quickly than a rider with a less-deliberate training regimen.

Defining the Physique of the Racing Cyclist

As a rule, the elite cyclist is a pretty skinny specimen. There is no chance one will ever be confused with a professional wrestler. This is because large amounts of upper-body muscle are unnecessary to make the bicycle go. In fact, except for sprinters, muscle bulk anywhere on the body is generally counterproductive to efficiency. Many racers weigh no more than they did in high school. Women need not worry about losing their figures by riding a bike.

To the noncyclist, every rider looks pretty skinny, but most riders will find they excel at the flats (left), climbing (center) or sprinting (right).

Many cyclists are classified according to their talents. Even though most folks think all cyclists look like famished runway models, they show significant differences in ability. In broad strokes, cyclists can be grouped according to three different builds:

- Climbers look like long-distance runners and are the skinniest of the lot; they have a high strength-to-weight ratio, which helps them go uphill quickly.

- Sprinters look like football players and have the most muscular build among cyclists; they have the strength to make impressive accelerations.

- Time trialists look like track-and-field athletes; also called *rouleurs*, they are riders with the power to be fast on flat to rolling terrain.

Types of Muscle

There are two kinds of muscle fiber, slow-twitch and fast-twitch. If you've ever looked at an anatomic drawing of a muscle, you've probably noticed that some muscle fibers are colored red while others are white. The red muscle fibers are the slow-twitch fibers, which tend to be more plentiful. The white muscle fibers are the fast-twitch muscle fibers.

Slow-twitch muscle fibers do most of the work in cycling. Each ride is made up of thousands of repetitive movements. Cycling is an aerobic sport because it recruits slow-twitch muscle fiber to do most of the work, and the primary energy source for slow-twitch muscle fiber is oxygen. Because you get a fresh supply of fuel with each breath, you can ride at a moderate pace for hours at a time.

Fast-twitch muscle fibers do the hard work. Whenever you make a big effort, such as standing to charge up a hill, you use the less-plentiful fast-twitch muscle fibers. Fast-twitch muscle fibers are said to work anaerobically—without oxygen. Literally speaking, this isn't true, but the real point is that fast-twitch muscle fiber burns glycogen—sugar. Unless you eat during the ride, each "anaerobic" effort gradually empties your bank account. And because there are fewer fast-twitch muscle fibers than there are slow-twitch muscle fibers, these fibers fatigue quickly. Riders will talk about how many "efforts" they have in their legs in acknowledgement of this fact.

Primary Muscle Groups

The quadriceps group of muscles does most of the work of cycling. The "quads" consist of four muscles: the vastus medialis, vastus lateralis, vastus interomedialis, and rectus femoris. These fire on the downstroke of the pedaling motion. Additionally, the gluteus maximus, which is the strongest muscle in the body, helps to extend the hip in the early phase of the pedal stroke and aids hip flexing at the end of the pedal stroke.

The gastrocnemius is responsible for the ankling motion of your foot, specifically, pointing your foot down, while also helping to flex the knee. The gracilis and iliotibial band help to stabilize the knee during extension.

Types of Fitness

The complete cyclist must achieve three different kinds of fitness. Riding in a peloton requires a rider to possess endurance, strength, and speed. These different kinds of fitness each have specific development requirements:

- **Endurance** is the ability to ride for long periods of time without the onset of fatigue. Endurance is gained through long rides. Without endurance, it is difficult to develop other forms of fitness.

- **Strength** is the ability to overcome resistance. Strength is gained through weight training in the gym and large-gear interval training. Without strength, it is difficult to ride fast.

- **Speed** is the ability to move quickly. Think of speed in terms of body movement, not velocity. Speed is gained through strenuous cadence drills and sprints. Without speed, it is difficult to make sudden accelerations.

Data

The Greek philosopher Socrates had it right when he said, "Know thyself." If you wish to achieve serious fitness, you will find attaining that goal difficult unless you make an effort to track your training. What equipment you have will influence just what you can record and how you might record it. Here are your options in rising level of complexity:

- At minimum, you should purchase a cyclocomputer and a simple calendar notebook in which you can write how long each ride was, how hard you went, what the terrain was, and how you felt.

- The addition of a heart rate monitor (HRM) to cyclocomputer and calendar will allow you to add figures about your heart rate (HR). Resting HR, average HR on the ride, and maximum HR during hard efforts are numbers worth recording.

- A GPS device can track all of the above information, map your ride, and download it to any of a variety of software programs that can help you track your efforts.

- A wattage device will give you the highest degree of feedback. The combination of wattage, HR, kilojoules, and time will give you essentially the same information set that pros use. Wattage devices come with software to analyze the data, but a variety of online and software-based coaching programs can help you make sense of the numbers. Some work with GPS devices, giving you the best of both worlds.

Just What Is Hard?

Amazingly, people agree on the difference between hard and easy. Exercise physiologists use a scale called the Borg Rating of Perceived Exertion (RPE). Studies have shown that people correlate effort with surprising consistency on this 20-point scale.

RATING	PURPOSE	EXERTION
6	Recovery	No exertion at all
7	Recovery	Extremely light
8	Recovery	
9	Recovery	Very light
10	Aerobic training	
11	Aerobic training	Light
12	Aerobic training	
13	Tempo training	Somewhat hard
14	Tempo training	
15	Subthreshold training	Hard (heavy)
16	Subthreshold training	
17	Subthreshold training	Very hard
18	Aerobic capacity training	
19	Aerobic capacity training	Extremely hard
20	Aerobic capacity training	Maximal exertion

If you don't have the aid of a heart rate monitor or wattage device, the combination of the RPE scale and cyclocomputer can give a fair assessment of your training.

Heart Rate and Work

Heart rate is a simple indicator of workload. A heart rate monitor is a standard tool for training because it can objectively show just how hard you are working. When training with a heart rate monitor, cyclists divide their training into five discrete zones; these zones correspond with specific points on the RPE scale.

TRAINING ZONE	TARGET HEART RATE (% OF MAX HR)	RPE	TRAINING PURPOSE
One	<65	6–11	Recovery-aerobic
Two	65–80	12–15	Tempo
Three	81–90	16–17	Lactate threshold
Four	91–95	18–19	Aerobic capacity
Five	96–100	20	Sprint

Training zones are not fixed numbers; they are defined relative to your maximum heart rate (max HR). As a result, you need to find out your max HR to give the heart rate monitor's readings context. The traditional rule of thumb regarding max HR is to subtract your current age from 220. For highly trained athletes, this number can be off significantly, but for new cyclists it's a great starting point.

Lactic Acid and Lactate Threshold

Each time a muscle fires, a waste product is produced—lactic acid. Think of it as exhaust, only the tailpipe empties into your bloodstream. When your effort level is low to moderate and your legs are recruiting slow-twitch muscle fiber, your bloodstream can flush away the lactic acid and supply fresh oxygen fast enough to keep up with demand.

If you produce lactic acid too quickly, you will become fatigued. When you pedal at an RPE of 10, your heart rate and lactic acid production will hold steady, but as your RPE increases, so do your heart rate and lactic acid production. When your effort rises to an RPE of 18 or more, you produce lactic acid faster than your bloodstream can flush it from the muscles. The point at which your muscles' production exceeds the bloodstream's ability to flush it away is called your lactate threshold (LT).

Once you exceed your lactate threshold, you are riding on borrowed time. The terminology that cyclists use to describe the experience of exceeding their LT is plentiful and colorful. It is often referred to as "blowing up." The accumulation of the lactic acid in the muscles causes a burning sensation, which is the muscle's way of announcing it needs a break. Once your heart rate drops back below your LT, you will recover. The lower your heart rate drops and the longer you take to recover, the better you will feel. Your LT is the most important determiner of your performance; careful training can raise that number.

To find out your lactate threshold, you can perform a Conconi Test. A Conconi Test will reveal the current state of your fitness as well as tell you the range of heart rate on which you must focus to raise your LT. The protocol for the Conconi Test is included in the Appendix.

The King of Numbers

Not all numbers are created equal. To paraphrase George Orwell from his seminal novel *Animal Farm*, some numbers are more equal than others. More specifically, some numbers are more relevant to judging your fitness than others. For instance, most racers don't track the number of miles they ride each year; rather, they track the number of hours they spend on the bike. Why? Your body doesn't know how many miles it pedaled yesterday, but it can tell the difference between a 1-hour ride and a 5-hour ride. Carmichael confirms, "Your body can't tell how far you rode, but it does understand time. All the pros I coach track their time, not their mileage."

Wattage is the king of all numbers. Simply put, wattage is the purest measure of how much power you can generate on the bike. Heart rate for a given workload can vary depending on not just your current level of fitness, but also your current level of fatigue and even your degree of excitement—adrenalin does wonders. Professional coach and racer Dotsie Bausch of Empower Coaching Systems confirms that wattage is king. "Power-file analysis is the best way to quantify your training. This is an invaluable tool for you to set intermediate benchmarks as you work toward your goals."

Athletes who train by wattage don't have to judge what the numbers mean: Either you hit your target wattage figures during the workout or you don't. Pros are now compared on the basis of how many watts they can generate per kilogram of weight. A top-level pro will generate more than 6 watts per kilogram (watts/kg) for as long as 20 minutes at a time. By comparison, an entry-level racer may only generate 2.5 watts/kg over a 20-minute effort.

Knowing your wattage values for efforts over given terrain (flat or hilly) and duration (5 seconds, 1 minute, 5 minutes, and 20 minutes) will give you a clear picture of your fitness. Bausch says, "Training with wattage eliminates almost all of the guesswork about how you are responding to the training stimulus."

Basics of Training

Track the time you spend riding, not the number of miles you ride. Every hour you spend on the bike matters, and there is a big difference between 40 miles you ride by yourself and 40 miles you do tucked in a group.

Fitness is increased through a cycle of stress, rest, and adaptation. This cycle is used on many levels: during individual workouts, planning your week, your month, and even the year. The body responds to repeated cycles of stress followed by rest by making a physiological adaptation.

The biggest mistake most new cyclists make is to ride too hard most of the time. This happens for two reasons: a lack of understanding about the role rest plays in getting stronger and a lack of planning. Riding hard frequently robs the body of the opportunity to recover from the previous workout.

Pay attention to how you feel. If you're tired, give your body a chance to rest. Go for an easy ride, or skip the ride altogether. You'll feel more energetic once you have recovered.

Plan ahead in order to leave opportunities for rest. Making sure you get adequate rest will ensure you get the most out of each hard ride. This is where having a training diary becomes important.

Macrocycles and Microcycles

Macrocycles and microcycles of stress/rest/adaptation define every aspect of training:

- Training rides are broken up into periods of hard riding followed by recovery.
- Each week of training mixes hard days and easy days.
- Each month of training will feature a series of three hard weeks followed by a recovery week.
- Each year of training will feature periods of intense training followed by periods of recovery.

"Only during ongoing and increasing stimulus and stress can an athlete adapt to the new intensities and then recover, repair, and grow," says Bausch. "Repeating this cycle over and over by injecting new stimulus to challenge the athlete to change and adapt will yield forward progress and results."

The value of the easy recovery ride cannot be overstated, both socially and in allowing overworked muscles to recover.

Basic Workouts

To gain specific forms of fitness, you must do specific workouts. Just as there are different kinds of fitness, there are different kinds of workouts designed to strengthen each of the systems you need to perform at your best. Efforts are categorized relative to stress level and are called training zones, or just zones. The best workouts group specific stresses to fatigue that system or muscle group sufficiently in order to promote adaptation:

- **Base miles** are made up of easy rides that increase the efficiency of the aerobic system. They are the foundation upon which your fitness is built. Zone 2.
- **Intervals** are hard efforts followed by short periods of recovery. These rides are generally flat, and while the length of the effort can vary, the effort and recovery are proportional in length. Zone 4.
- **Hill repeats** are essentially intervals performed on a hill. The number of repeats will be based on the length of the hill. The longer the hill, the fewer the repeats. Zone 4.
- **Sprints** are absolute maximal efforts. While the pace of the sprint might not be that fast compared with a group ride or race situation, a sprint will be as hard as you can possibly go on flat ground for 10–15 seconds. Zone 5.
- **Recovery rides** are easy rides that help flush the lactic acid out of the muscles following a hard ride. These are the easiest rides you will do and the easiest to get wrong by going too hard. Zone 1.

Fatigue and Overtraining

For most of us, the fun of riding inspires us to ride even more. We get stronger and have more fun. And while it's no secret that a hard ride will make you tired, however, what does shock nearly every rider at some point is that after four days of hard rides, the body runs out of gas. Fatigue accumulates like leftovers in the fridge. Unless you are willing to finish off that mu-shu pork, you'll have no room for the new groceries.

Sooner or later, most riders overestimate their body's ability to recover. After a couple of weeks of group rides Tuesday, Wednesday, Thursday, Saturday, and Sunday, there comes a day when the body simply won't go. This lack of planning and simply following whatever the group is doing is sometimes referred to as *ad hoc* training. Group rides are the gateway drug to overtraining.

Carmichael says, "I see overtraining as a problem of too little recovery rather than training too hard. Don't do a hard workout if you are still tired from your last hard workout. You'll get stronger faster if you give your body the opportunity to fully recover."

Nothing, not the cancellation of a favorite show or the breakup of a favorite rock group, can induce an existential crisis in a cyclist as deep as overtraining. You can find yourself wondering why you took up cycling or even hating the sight of the bike itself.

Common signs of overtraining include:

- An excessive desire to nap
- Snacking on foods you can usually resist
- Feeling unexpectedly irritable
- Experiencing restless sleep
- Unexpected weight loss

If you display a combination of these, chances are you are overtrained. Take a week off the bike and then start back slowly with short, easy rides. Skip any hard group rides for at least two weeks.

Flexibility

A flexible muscle is a happy muscle. Cyclists need to stretch in order to promote strength through the full range of the pedal stroke and to reduce the chance of injury. A muscle that is supple due to periodic stretching will display strength through broader range of motion than one that does not experience flexibility training.

Cyclists typically benefit from the following stretches:

- Hamstrings
- Iliotibial band
- Calves
- Quadriceps

Cycling performance benefits from a high degree of flexibility.

"I give all of my athletes a regimen of stretching," says Carmichael. "By maintaining flexibility, they enjoy strength over a wider range of motion and reduce the possibility of injury."

Training Plans

A good training plan will take an assortment of workouts and assemble them in increasing cycles of length, intensity, and rest. There are books out by Carmichael and others that can guide you through the process of creating your own periodized training plan. Alternatively, you can hire a coach who will create a plan for you based on your current level of fitness. For an example 12-week training plan, see the appendix on page 253.

Coaching

Having a coach is like having a tour guide for your fitness. A coach has the ability to look at your experience on the bike and make sense of it through the cycle of stress, rest, and adaptation. While it may seem simple enough to analyze, many cyclists lack the experience and objectivity to properly analyze their current physical state so that they may pursue the best workouts relative to their needs. A good coach can help you turn your dreams into achievable goals.

"A good coach," says Carmichael, "can help you understand your body's response to cycles of training and rest."

Coaching comes in many forms today. Software programs can provide sound feedback based on downloaded GPS or wattage-device data. Coaching services give you the services of a real live coach through a computer interface, e-mail, and phone. And for those who want a traditional hands-on coach, there are usually a few to be found in any metropolitan area.

Commitment and Lifestyle

Before committing to a particular training regimen, give some thought to where you want cycling to fit in your life. Will it be a major priority or just a way to enjoy yourself with a friend or two on the weekend? Naturally, there are no right or wrong answers. If you want cycling to occupy a central role in your life, you'll need to strike some bargains. It's difficult, if not impossible, to ride well on Saturday morning following a late night at the bar on Friday. Similarly, few cyclists can bounce back after a 5-hour ride and have the strength necessary to mow the lawn.

If you are inclined toward a healthy lifestyle and already eat well and get plenty of sleep, the transition into cycling will be easy. But if you have a demanding career and a family, cycling might only fit in at the edges of your day.

Those cyclists who have a career and family enjoy the most success if they've planned their training well in advance and negotiated with their family when they will be on the bike. Riders will frequently refer to the "hall pass" that gives them a finite amount of time to be out. By planning your training around your greatest priorities, you can make the most of the time you have to train.

Image: Patrick Brady

Chapter 24
Diet

Some of the best news you'll get as a cyclist is that while riding you can burn upwards of 500 calories per hour. Exceptionally hard rides can cause you to burn as much as 1,000 calories per hour. *Low-cal* is a word you are allowed to strike from your vocabulary.

Endurance athletes in general and cyclists specifically do not have significantly different dietary needs from the rest of the population. Done right, you'll eat all the same foods you've been eating; you will just increase the serving sizes for some foods.

Don't be Afraid of Carbs

In short, carbs are your friend. Carbohydrates are the basic fuel your body uses to create glycogen, which is the fuel your muscles burn as you exercise. Glycogen (sugar) is to your body what gas is to your car. It is stored in your muscles and your liver, and your body generally holds about 2,000 kilocalories—enough energy to sustain about 2 hours of continuous activity. What happens when you ride for more than 2 hours without replenishing is called "the bonk" and is covered in Chapter 26.

Glycogen is essentially a starch. To produce it, you must eat bread, pasta, rice, and other foods classified as starches. Each gram of carbohydrate contains 4 calories.

Dietary recommendations for cyclists generally advise them to consume somewhere between 45 and 65 percent of their daily calories in carbohydrate. An easy rule of thumb for carbohydrate consumption is to multiply your weight by between 2.72 and 4.54.

Example: a 168-pound rider
168 x 2.72–4.54 = 457–763 grams of carbohydrate per day

Not all carbs are created equal. Complex carbohydrates, such as whole-wheat breads, rice, and potatoes, help prevent spikes and crashes in your blood sugar that can cause you to grind to a halt as suddenly as a car that has run out of gas. For quick energy, foods containing the simple sugars glucose and fructose will bring you around like fresh batteries.

Carbohydrates are the primary fuel a cyclist runs on. You need plenty of them in your diet.

To top off the tank while riding, sugary sports drinks meant to replace depleted carbohydrate stores have been shown to be effective at solution rates around 6 percent; think of how Gatorade tastes—that's a 6 percent solution. Some people can tolerate higher concentrations, but many people will begin to experience gastric distress (burping and stomach upset) at solutions above 8 percent. If your drink tastes sweet, it is too strong.

Be aware that not all carbs are consumed equally, either. Postride refueling is unusually efficient and converts carbs into glycogen at three times the normal rate. For up to 4 hours after the ride, your body works to replace lost glycogen with the ferocity of a Wall Street trader taking advantage of a down market. Those first two hours following a ride are something of a dietary get-out-of-jail card. Almost anything you consume will be used to replace depleted glycogen stores. Get out the chocolate-chip cookies!

consume somewhere between 20 and 25 percent of their daily calories in carbohydrate. An easy rule of thumb for protein consumption is to multiply your weight by .54 to .64.

> *Example:* a 168-pound rider
> 168 x .54–.64 = 91–108 grams of protein per day.

Consuming protein with carbohydrate can aid digestion of the carbohydrate, but research also shows that the protein is used as a fuel source, as well. Most research points to a 4:1 mix of carbs to protein. Carbohydrate/protein drinks have been shown to increase performance, decrease fatigue, and reduce post-exercise muscle soreness. There are a variety of drinks, bars, and gels that provide a mix of carbs and protein at or near this ratio.

Get Plenty of Protein

Protein's primary role in the diet of a cyclist is to help build new muscle and repair muscle tissue damaged in training. It also has two additional roles in the diet of a cyclist; protein helps the body metabolize carbohydrates and serves as a secondary fuel source during prolonged endurance events, meaning events long enough to cause your family to question your sanity, better known as centuries.

Endurance athletes need more protein than couch jockeys, but not so much more that they must resort to protein-packed shakes. The vast majority of riders will do fine with a well-balanced diet.

Dietary recommendations for cyclists generally advise them to

Protein not only builds muscle but it also acts as a supplementary energy source. Some sport drinks blend the two.

Don't Fear the Fat

Forget about eliminating fat from your life. While it's often cast as the villain in any diet, the cause for every weight-loss scheme since the Great Depression, fat serves an important role in a healthy diet.

Fat is an important energy source, giving you staying power between meals. It helps prevent your blood sugar from crashing and causing you to suddenly feel hungry. It is also necessary because some vitamins are fat-soluble and fatty acids are essential for a balanced diet.

Dietary guidelines generally suggest that anywhere from 20 to 35 percent of your daily calories come from fat.

A good diet for a cyclist will include a certain amount of fat, making your meals more enjoyable.

Example: **a 168-pound rider**
168 x .54–1.0 = 91–159 grams of fat per day

Some fats are definitely preferable. Choose olive and canola oils, as well as nuts, seeds, beans, and avocados, to be good to your heart. Other fats, such as those that come from bacon and French fries, should be kept in check.

Stay Hydrated

Proper hydration is essential for optimal performance as a cyclist. An adult human being is composed of 55–65 percent water, with men at the higher end and women at the lower end of that range.

Dehydration begins when you have lost 1 percent of your body weight in fluid. Unfortunately, you can't wait for your body's sense of thirst to guide hydration, as it isn't activated until you have lost 1–2 percent of your body's weight in fluid. Worse yet, with a 3-percent loss

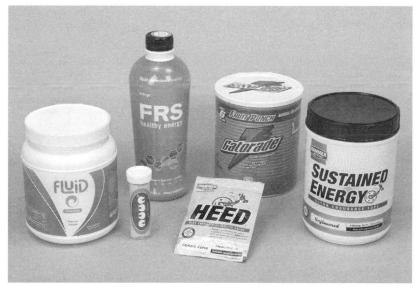

Drink mixes can help you replenish carbohydrates and electrolytes to keep you riding your best.

of fluid, your muscles begin contracting more slowly, limiting performance. A 4-percent loss of fluid causes a decline in performance of 5 to 10 percent.

So you must drink the way dictatorships vote: early and often. Even conservative estimates for cycling indicate that a cyclist should consume 5 ounces of water every 15 minutes while riding. That's one 20-oz. bottle per hour. On hot and humid days and during particularly hard riding, that number rises rapidly. A fast ride on a day with a heat index in triple digits requires 40 oz.—two bottles—per hour.

Be Wary of Alcohol

While a great glass of wine or beer can make a good meal more memorable, alcohol is as good for cycling performance as arsenic. Its presence suppresses the secretion of the hormone ADH, which acts as an antidiuretic. To offset the loss in fluid, you will need to drink an additional glass of water for every two drinks you consume. The calories contained in alcohol constitute a second problem. Unlike the calories found in carbs, proteins, or fat, the calories contained in alcohol are essentially "empty"— they have no nutritive value.

A nice bottle of wine can make any dinner more pleasant, but it won't help you ride your best.

On-the-Bike Foods

If you ride for more than 2 hours, your body will need more calories than can be supplied by a sports drink. Bars and gels are the two most popular forms of sports nutrition after sports drinks. Bars, such as those by PowerBar and Clif Bar, offer a healthy dose of carbohydrate along with some protein. They are excellent for longer rides at low to moderate intensity.

Rides lasting longer than 2 hours will require a bit of refueling, and energy bars are easy to digest.

Gels don't have the caloric wallop of a bar—generally, they have about half the calories, so you must consume more of them. Because they come in liquid form and most contain no protein, they are quick to digest and are easier on the stomach. This makes them ideal for high-intensity rides that last for several hours.

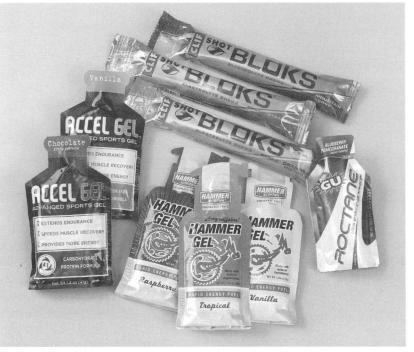

Rides that combine intensity with long distance can make eating difficult. Gels are an easy way to get carbs in while riding hard.

Weight Loss and Cycling

Cycling's low-impact nature makes it an excellent vehicle for any weight-loss goals you have. Even though you may be able to expend 3,500 or more calories in a day, you can't actually lose a full pound each day, not unless you burn actual muscle mass.

The proverbial pound of flesh is equal to 3,500 calories. This is a reasonable amount to try to lose each week. It requires a 500-calorie deficit each day of the week, which is very achievable with a little eating discipline and a 1-hour ride per day. Those who try to push beyond this can push the body into catabolism, a state in which the body consumes muscle protein to meet its caloric needs. This is the same thing that happens when you bonk, and as a weight-loss strategy it is counterproductive in the extreme. Catabolism is like burning your house down instead of having a barbecue. What you want to achieve is a caloric deficit, not starvation.

Nutrition labels contain a wealth of information and can help you track your diet with precision, if you choose.

Chapter 25
The Fred

In cycling, "Fred" is code for newbie—someone whose knowledge is incomplete. Naturally, it's the last thing anyone wants to be called. This book, if it does nothing else, should help you avoid being labeled a Fred.

Riders rarely call someone "Fred" to their face. Even using the term can seem rather third-grade, but riders' regard for the health of the herd trumps their care for any one rider. The issue isn't whether someone is fast enough or has a cool bike, but really one of skill based on the need to stay safe at high speed.

In the view of the group, a Fred is a rider who lacks skill and knowledge, and those deficiencies are seen as potentially dangerous. The logic goes: If you don't know how to dress like the riders in the pack, then you might not know how to ride like them, and you might not be safe to ride near.

There are two ways to be a Fred. The primary way is through your appearance, but a secondary way is through your behavior when riding with others. Your ability to act with consideration for other riders will determine whether they treat you like the Pied Piper or an infectious disease.

Telltale Signs

The biggest problem new riders face when joining a group is simply looking the part. Here are a few simple rules to keep in mind. They are as good as knowing the secret handshake.

Cotton

In short, don't wear it. Cotton offers none of the technical benefits that come from wearing wool or synthetics. When it gets wet, it stays wet and therein lies the rub—metaphorically and literally. Tube socks, T-shirts, sweatshirts, or shorts—they are all the antithesis of technical garments that make comfortable cycling for hours at a time possible.

While great for jeans and T-shirts, cotton doesn't go well with the sweaty business of cycling.

Chainring Tattoo

Nothing says, "I'm new!" like a chainring tattoo. You never see a pro cyclist with a big, black, greasy chainring mark on his right calf. Unfortunately, it's common among new riders. Avoiding this one is easy. If you have a leg over the top tube, keep one foot clipped in. Never straddle your bike with both feet on the ground; it's a recipe for disaster, or at least a badge of dishonor.

Because rest is a big part of going fast, when you are stopped, keep a foot clipped in and sit on your top tube. It doesn't matter which foot remains clipped in; to remain stable, the foot on the ground will be extended out to give you a stable stance; either way, your calf can't hit the big chainring. If you want to stand up with both feet on the ground, get off your bike completely.

The unsightly chainring tattoo is easy to learn to avoid.

Skirts

Riders who wear jerseys two sizes too big are said to wear skirts. A jersey's pockets should sit on your lumbar, not at your hips. Wear a jersey too big, and you are likely to catch the tail of the jersey on the saddle nose when you try to sit down. While some riders may not mind the baggy look, the effect the wind will have on the jersey causes it to flap around like a

The hem of a jersey should sit at your waist rather than cover your rear.

flag, making it harder for riders behind you to see what's going on up ahead. Form-fitting clothing reduces the number of visual distractions other riders must process and cuts down on noise.

Bell Bottoms

Similarly, riders who wear shorts two sizes too big are said to wear bell bottoms. If the leg grippers flare out instead of fitting snugly around the thigh and if the Lycra bunches up rather than running smoothly over the rider's skin, not only is the look terrible, but chafing is inevitable. It's as comfortable as a sandpaper sock.

Loose shorts also present another liability: plumber's crack. When you ride in the drops in a group, no one should see your skin—from your back . . . or elsewhere. Bibs take care of this prob-

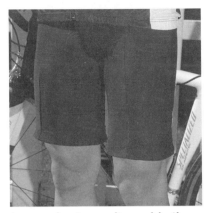

Loose shorts won't provide the support and comfort of a pair that fits properly.

lem and are more comfortable to boot. And again, form-fitting clothing eliminates visual distractions caused by flapping fabric.

Etiquette

Part of not being a Fred is showing consideration for other cyclists. For most of its existence, cycling has been called a gentleman's sport. Much of this is due to rules for racing, both written and unwritten. Contact is forbidden between riders, and it is considered bad form to go hard when another rider needs to heed the call of nature or experiences a flat tire. Even among the nonracing set, there are a number ways you can show your respect for your fellow rider. These gentlemen's rules help to instill a level of civility into the sport and create a strong sense of community. Follow these and your fellow riders will know you "get it."

Announce Turning, Slowing, and Stopping

Riders at the front of a group need to communicate what they are doing. This means they need to announce each change in the ride with both calls and hand signals. Any call to the group should be made with the head turned to help the sound carry to those who need to hear. For the safety of the group, the call and hand signal should be repeated by as many other riders as possible to ensure communication reaches everyone.

When cars approach the group from behind, before they pass the group, it is helpful for one of the riders at the back of the group to call "car back." It lets the riders farther up in the group, who may not hear the car due the sound of the group itself, that a car will be passing. Similarly, on narrower roads and at turns, approaching cars should be called out with a "car up." These calls are pretty universally acknowledged.

Should the group need to slow due to traffic ahead or some other

Take a moment to communicate your intentions to the riders behind you.

reason, the riders at the front need to call "slowing," as well as use a hand signal to reinforce the announcement. As you slow, try to maintain a consistent distance to the rider ahead of you.

The same goes for stopping. The riders at the front should call out "stopping" and give a hand signal. Riders use a variety of hand signals; some will hold their open palm facing back, while others will hold up a closed fist, military-style. It's nice to help relay the call and signals back through the pack, but make sure that you can brake adequately so you don't run into the rider in front of you.

For left turns, the rider closest to the front and left should move out slightly from the group and look back to make sure it is okay for the entire group to move over. Once it is safe to change lanes, the rider will call "clear" and point left. When approaching the turn, the lead rider should again call "clear" only if the entire group can make the turn safely.

For right turns, the rider closest to the front and left will watch the traffic to make sure no cars are entering the intersection in the group's intended lane. Once the rider has verified it is safe to enter the intersection, the rider will point right and call "clear."

Alert Riders to Debris

Debris in the road can disrupt a paceline, cause a flat, or worse, a crash. All riders who see debris, whether it is a piece of broken glass, a patch of sand, or something else, should alert the group. Different groups have different preferences for announcing the presence of debris. Some groups prefer to call everything debris so that people will be more likely to recognize the call even over the din of traffic, however, some groups will call out specifically what is in the road (such as glass, hubcaps, gravel) so that riders can watch for the object(s) more easily.

Take care of the riders behind you by pointing out anything that you choose to avoid.

In addition to calling out the debris, it is helpful to call out its location—"glass left"—and to point to the debris' location with a quick hand gesture. Finally, turn your head in the direction of the debris as you call out its presence; your head motion will reinforce the hand gesture.

Nose Blowing and Spitting

Riding hard can make even the best rider a drippy mess. You'll need to spit or blow your nose from time to time. When you are in a group, consider the riders next to and behind you. If you just spit into the wind, someone will wind up wearing it. Not fun.

When spitting, if possible, move to the side of the group and spit down and away from the other riders. If you are stuck in the middle of the group, lean forward, bring your head as close as possible to the handlebar, and spit just forward of your bar and to the side of your wheel. And while your gloves can be handy for wiping your nose, every now and then the pipes may need clearing with an "air hankie" (aka "snot rocket"). Move to the side of the group, close one nostril with your hand, aim down, and give a hard blow.

Whether you are blowing your nose or spitting, do your best to blow or spit down.

Stop When Others Have a Flat

If someone in your group flats, call it out and stop with the rider. Leaving a rider behind after a flat doesn't serve friendships well. Also, you never know when someone might have a problem with a tube, their pump, or a CO_2 cartridge. Having another rider present with a backup can be a lifesaver.

If you pass a rider who has had a flat or other mechanical, slow down enough to ask if they need anything. Showing some concern for other riders is considered good form; you never know when you might need the favor returned.

No one likes being left for dead. Do your friends a favor and stop while they fix their flats.

Save the MP3 Player for the Gym

The right music can be a powerful motivator. Be aware, though, that on the open road, even low-volume music can drown out many subtle noises that riders use to monitor traffic. From the sudden increase in volume of an approaching car changing lanes into your lane to the low volume of a hybrid car to the sound of another rider approaching from behind, your ears keep you alerted to a lot going on behind you.

Ask Permission to Draft

If you encounter a rider you want to draft, pull alongside and ask permission. Riding in close quarters on the open road—close enough to draft—requires both skill and trust. It's only proper to ask someone if they'd mind you sucking their wheel. A sudden, unannounced turn or stop by the rider in front could send you both to the deck, and if the rider up front didn't know you were there, it would be a rather unpleasant introduction.

Wave to Other Riders

You can never have too many friends. Given that some traffic experiences can be unpleasant, anything you can do to brighten your day or the day of another rider is worth it. Give a little wave as you pass riders. If they are on your side of the road and you catch them from behind, try not to pass too close as that can startle someone, and say hello. Not every mile needs to be filled with the intensity of the competitive drive.

The Call of Nature

Common sense is the rule here. There are times when you will need to go and there may not be a bathroom nearby. Do what you can to be discreet. Obviously taking a leak isn't meant to be sexually provocative, but some members of society will still take offense should someone flout their sense of decency. Cyclists have been arrested for public urination with varying outcomes. Do what you can to make it a private affair, and you probably won't run into a problem.

When you gotta go, you gotta go, but keep it private.

Waving to other riders makes everyone feel like they've got a friend on the road.

STARBUCKS COFFEE

TED DODD
545-6580

Image: Patrick Brady

Chapter 26
Traditional Practices and Occupational Hazards

Traditional Cycling Practices

Cycling has its share of rituals. Some are as obvious as cheese on a pizza. But there are a few practices in cycling that seem to be filled with equal parts mystique and misinformation. They go back for generations and persist in usage for one reason alone: They work. If you are serious about your riding, you should try these; they each have a payoff. Here are the tips and a look under the hood at how they work.

The Ride-Meeting Point

Group rides, by their very definition, must meet someplace. City parks, bike shops, and coffee shops are popular locations.

Sunscreen

Sunscreen should be a part of every cyclist's preride ritual. The only mystery about sunscreen is why more cyclists don't use it with the fervor of a teenage girl who's just discovered lipstick. Your nose, face, forehead, and arms are particularly susceptible to sunburn. Worse yet, if you forget the sunscreen and do get a burn, the helmet tattooed into your forehead will look sillier than a priest in a burlesque outfit. Don't forget your lips, either. Wind-burned lips can crack and peel, making romantic moments less so.

Sunscreen is an absolute necessity to keep your skin healthy.

Leg Shaving

A hairless leg is a cool leg. A common misperception about cycling is that roadies shave their legs to improve their aerodynamics. While there is a slight aerodynamic benefit to be gained by shaving your legs, it isn't the primary reason to do so. The biggest reason to shave your legs is for convective cooling. Hair holds water; think about how much faster your hair dries following a haircut, especially if you haven't had your hair cut in a while. By shaving all the hair off your legs, sweat evaporates directly off your skin, helping to reduce your core temperature on hot days. In the event you crash, it is easier to clean a wound that already has the hair shaved off; the lack of hair means bandages won't rip it out when they are changed, either.

So those are objective reasons to shave your legs, but many cyclists do it simply because hairless legs are part of the look of cycling. To many cyclists, bare legs are a sign of commitment to the sport, and if you shave your legs, the thinking goes, then it's probably safe to follow your wheel.

How high up you shave is a personal choice. Some cyclists only shave beyond where the gripper elastic on their shorts extends, but shorts will wick moisture away from your legs better if you shave to your hip. Should you crash, it's the rare event that doesn't result in some road rash to the hip.

Think of shaving your legs as air-conditioning for your body.

The other benefit to shaving your legs is that it makes massage easier and more comfortable. Without hair on the legs, the hands move more easily with less oil applied.

While most women don't have to be sold on the merits of shaving, guys, you should note that many women who have dated a cyclist report that they quickly develop a preference for hairless gams.

Massage

Leg massage helps promote recovery. By forcing blood through the muscle while at rest, massage can help the body flush lactic acid from tired muscles. Deep-tissue massage breaks up knots in muscles that contribute to tightness following a hard ride.

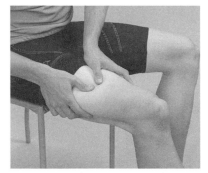
Massage promotes recovery by helping to flush lactic acid from your muscles.

While the best massage is performed by a trained therapist, it is possible to perform self-massage to aid your recovery. There are a variety of foam rollers and balls you can use to help work out the assorted knots, kinks, and sore bits.

Chamois Cream

Chamois cream is a personal lubricant of a nonromantic nature. It helps prevent chafing caused by the saddle rubbing the chamois against sensitive tissues. Back when shorts used a real leather chamois, chamois cream was necessary just to make the chamois soft enough that you could sit on it. Riders noticed that if you used a little extra, the way some folks have coffee with their cream, it reduced chafing as well.

The chamois used in shorts today is plenty soft, but chafing can persist. Some riders apply the cream directly to their skin while others continue to apply it to the chamois itself; it's a matter of preference, really. Most include a little menthol as a natural antibacterial agent.

A good chamois cream can help your shorts keep you comfortable.

Embrocations

An embrocation is a cream or oil applied to the legs to warm them. Much like Bengay, these creams use active ingredients such as capsicum, methyl salicylate, and menthol to generate heat. After being massaged into the skin, they help keep the legs warm while riding without adding the bulk of knee or leg warmers. This can be particularly helpful in wet conditions when the Roubaix Lycra of knee or leg warmers would simply absorb several ounces of water.

Embrocations are just like Indian food: They come in varying grades of heat. Some use a petroleum base; to wash them off, you need a skin-safe soap that can break up grease. Dawn dishwashing liquid works well. Some don't use petroleum and can be washed off with regular soap.

Also known as liniments or Belgian knee warmers, embrocations should be applied after you put on your shorts to avoid getting the embrocation on the chamois. Perhaps you recall the Bengay-in-the-jockstrap practical joke from high school? Slide the shorts' legs up to apply the embrocation. Massage it into the skin gently, then wash your hands with soap. Don't let your legs touch anything in your home

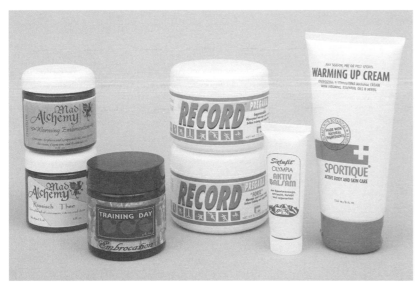

An embrocation is an excellent way to keep your legs warm in cold and especially wet conditions.

before departure, and be prepared to shower the moment you return home; embrocations pick up road grime and can leave your legs looking like you've been rolling in the world's largest pepper mill. It's a gnarly look to be sure, which, of course, makes it something of a badge of honor.

Occupational Hazards

If you ride regularly, you are likely to encounter one or more of the various irritations that go with cycling. These are to cycling what reading glasses are to the over-40 set—a minor, though inevitable, irritation. Suffering these doesn't mean you are clueless; it means you are human.

Sunburn

If you are out in the sun enough, you are likely to get a sunburn once in a while. A minor sunburn really doesn't rise above the level of inconvenience into the status of an injury, but chronic sunburns have the potential to lead to melanoma, a particularly dangerous form of skin cancer.

There are two ways to address the sunscreen issue: Use a sunscreen with a high SPF, seemingly higher than necessary. If you're going to ride more than 3 hours, carrying a small tube of sunscreen in order to reapply it during the ride is helpful. Also, having the sunscreen with you is great if you ever experience early-morning forgetfulness.

Saddle Sores

Cyclists can experience a variety of irritations in their undercarriage. Most get filed under the heading of saddle sores. The issues can include pimples, boils, chafing, and ingrown hairs. While good shorts and chamois cream can take care of most of the issues you might experience, if you do have an irritation, its cause is usually easily tracked.

If you are experiencing pimples or boils, make sure you shower and wash your shorts after every ride. If you are experiencing chafing, check if it happens with all your shorts or just one particular pair. Sometimes an ill-fitting pair of shorts or a rough seam can cause chafing.

The Bonk

Every cyclist bonks; there's a rule somewhere. In return, every cyclist collects a first bonk story. Once you gain enough fitness to ride more than 2o hours at a fairly strenuous pace, you become eligible. It's a rite of passage into serious roadiedom and the stories are invariably hilarious . . . after the fact. From buying a whole watermelon to licking a mashed-up sandwich off the tinfoil, the response to bonking is one of desperation.

Technically speaking, bonking is running out of glycogen—the fuel your muscles run on. This is bad. Your body says, "No firewood? Fine, I'll use your library." The library is muscle protein. Your body can require weeks to rebuild the lost muscle.

Most riders are caught off-guard by their first bonk. Its arrival is as sudden as fireworks and no less spectacular. There are, however, signs that alert you to the situation becoming dire. Early indicators include feeling irritable and indecisive, and sometimes even light-headed. Your pace might slow dramatically. And because bonking is often accompanied by dehydration in new riders, you may notice a normally palatable sports drink suddenly becoming sickly sweet: That's a sure sign you haven't been drinking enough. If you notice this, stop by a convenience store to get a snack and a drink; take a short break.

How do you prevent the bonk? By eating and drinking during the course of any ride lasting more than 2 hours. Drink frequently, and take the opportunity to fuel up at regroup points. Eating on the bike is covered in Chapter 4.

Riding in the Rain

Someday, you are going to get caught in a shower; it may even be this week. Depending on where you live, rain may or may not be a regular part of your riding experience. For those who live in the Pacific Northwest or the Gulf Coast, where rain can be more common than the sun, a few pieces of rain gear can make all the difference in the world: booties, rain pants, a jacket, and fenders.

If you live in a place where rain is less frequent, a simple clip-on fender can be installed in just a few minutes for those days that look iffy. You may still get wet, but you won't get your caboose soaked by spray rooster-tailing off your bike's rear wheel.

The biggest issue with rain has to do with traction. Corners must be taken more slowly as the tires' adhesion decreases. Lean too far and the bike will slip out from under you. "Slipping out," as it's called, isn't good at any time, and is doubly dangerous if traffic is around. Slow down in turns and avoid any manhole or utility covers, as well as painted markings—crosswalk stripes are particularly treacherous.

Residents of the Southwest and West Coast have an entirely different set of considerations. In Los Angeles and other cities where traffic is high and rain infrequent, riding in any amount of rain can be almost as difficult as riding on ice. The buildup of oil on the roads due to the sporadic and seasonal rains means the first time rain does fall, traction drops to ice-rink. In such places, often the best plan is just to wait for the roads to dry. Or buy some skates.

Grates, Manhole Covers, Train Tracks, and Driveway Lips

Not all road surfaces are good for riding. As if the road surface didn't provide enough interest, grates, manhole covers, and driveway lips make opportunities to fall the way James Brown made opportunities to dance. The metal surfaces of manhole covers can be surprisingly slick, even when dry. Storm-drain grates are even worse, as they

Generally speaking, you want to avoid metal surfaces in the road.

feature openings large enough to catch a wheel. Railroad tracks can be problematic whether dry or wet; do what you can to cross perpendicular to the tracks themselves. Similarly, when preparing to ride up a driveway transition, make sure to approach from the sharpest angle possible, preferably 90 degrees; that tiny lip can turn your wheel if you approach from a shallow angle.

Image: Patrick Brady

Chapter 27
Travel

The world is more impressive from the saddle. For those who like to combine their favorite free-time activity with their vacation time, a cycling vacation can be an excellent way to recharge. Bicycle touring used to mean mounting racks and panniers on your bike and sleeping in a tent. These days, tours and touring encompass everything from traditional self-supported tours to guided tours complete with vehicles to top off your drink, hand you a bar, or drive you to the hotel should the need arise.

Getting There

Don't forget your bike. If you are headed to an event or vacation by car, you may be able to pack your bike in your trunk or in the back of the car. If so, always pack some degreaser just in case, as a dirty chain can wreck an interior in a hurry. If you plan to drive with your bike on a regular basis (to training rides, weekend events, and such) you may want to invest in either a rear rack or roof rack

When choosing the type of rack to purchase, give some thought to where you live and drive. If you have a garage or drive under low overhangs, you may want to purchase a rear-mounted rack rather than

a roof rack. Banging your bike into your garage isn't nearly as much fun as getting a tooth pulled . . . and it's a lot more expensive. Conversely, bikes transported on rear racks will suffer more dirt and rocks kicked up from the road.

Racks such as those for the roof or the trailer hitch are a great way to transport your bike to rides and events.

If you plan to fly to a vacation spot, you can use a cardboard shipping box in which new bikes are shipped to cycle shops. They are free, but they don't provide much protection for your bike. A better solution is the bike carrier. They come in a variety of shapes and sizes, but all of them have a few central features. There is a metal frame to which the bike is secured. The bike is disassembled slightly, though not completely; generally the handlebar, wheels, seatpost, seat, and pedals are removed, nothing else. The wheels are inserted in wheel bags to protect them from the frame and vice versa. The bottom of the case features wheels so the case can be pulled rather than carried. The biggest variation between carriers is whether the outside of the case features a hard or soft shell. Some riders have reported that soft-side cases seem to get abused less

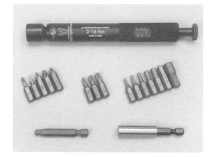

Carbon fiber stems, handlebars, and seatposts should be tightened to proper torque specs.

because other luggage can't be stacked on them the way they can on hard shell cases.

Velo Classic Tours is a New York–based bicycle touring company specializing in European destinations. Its owner, Peter Easton, has advised many clients on whether to bring a bike or rent. "There are merits to both," he says. "The more experienced cyclist is going to be more particular, so I typically don't recommend a rental bike unless it's done at a professional level, that is, a complete size run of frames available, with optional stem lengths available. With that said, the cost of traveling with a bike is becoming increasingly expensive, so high-end alternatives for hire is a growing market. If you're a casual cyclist or just getting started, there are more options, as your comfort-level range is greater."

On Your Own or With Friends

If you are traveling on your own or with another person but only taking one bike, you may not need a bike rack. Aside from potentially offering your bike increased safety from theft and impact (almost everyone who has a roof rack has a bike–overhang story), your car will get better gas mileage on the way, and you'll be relieved of the chore of cleaning bug carcasses off your bike after you arrive.

You may want to inquire with a local shop about group rides that meet nearby or pick up a guidebook to good rides in the area. Such information can lead you to roads with less traffic and more scenic vistas. You can rest assured the locals will be riding the best cycling roads there are and won't be shy to share their knowledge.

Traveling with friends can be a great way to take a great activity—group riding—and use it to explore a new locale. The challenge is to make sure everyone has the same sort of rides in mind. If you're not headed off for an organized event with a group committed to a particular length, be sure to communicate ahead of time about ride length and terrain so everyone is on the same page before rolling out. One rider's short spin can quickly become another rider's forced march.

Special travel cases can allow you to pack your bike for safe travel.
Image: Patrick Brady

Guided Tours

Why not let an expert show you the area's best roads? Bicycle-travel companies proliferated at the turn of the 21st century after Lance Armstrong won his first Tour de France. Americans developed a taste for riding the great climbs of the Alps and through the vineyards of Provence and Tuscany.

As a result, a bicycle tour has come to mean a tour in which you ride out-and-back loops or point-to-point from hotel to hotel. All your gear is transported for you, allowing you to focus on the riding.

While guided-tour companies have existed since the 1970s, the big changes have been to follow bike races, giving avid roadies a chance to see the pros in action, and to accommodate their greater ambitions and endurance. And while it might seem that it would have been easy for tour companies to accommodate riders who think 70 miles on a bike is more fun than a day at Disneyland, neither the hybrid bikes the companies often used nor the guides were suited to it. Because the average

Bike touring gives you a different perspective on foreign countries.
Image: Patrick Brady

A bike tour is a guaranteed way to see a beautiful slice of the world.
Image: Patrick Brady

SECTION II The Lifestyle

noncycling guide confused a paceline with a chain gang, a whole new breed of tour company had to emerge to cater to these clients.

Today, there are companies covering almost every angle of bicycle touring. From riding portions of the Tour de France route and watching the racers go by to meandering through vineyards and experiencing the local wines, you can have a big day on the bike. If your spouse thinks that's a bit much, he or she can take in a shorter ride, local museums, or even a cooking class.

Easton advises people to experience other cultures. "I typically recommend a foreign destination. Noncycling attractions are important to get an insight into local culture, to experience the authenticity of a region—whether it's a museum, an historic landmark, or visiting a World Heritage site."

Destinations

Pretty destinations are to tour companies what Birkenstocks are to hippies. If you can think of a pretty place, there is almost certainly a tour company guiding cyclists through it. In choosing a destination, there are a few facts to keep in mind:

- If you are traveling with another person, the more you have in common on and off the bike, the easier it will be to find a tour company that fits your needs.

- Though it can be as expensive and difficult to transport as a baby, you will have a more pleasant riding experience if you take your own bike.

- The more popular the destination is among tourists in general, the more options you will find among tour companies—that is, if you want a bike tour that includes cooking classes, you'll be more likely to find it in Tuscany than in North Africa.

Easton says he tells clients, "Ask yourself what interests you. Food, wine, art, architecture, shopping, music, all of this can be accessed to highlight any trip that includes a bike."

Because topography can dictate the difficulty of a ride and ultimately affect how much riding you do each day, take some time to look at a map before picking your destination. The mountains are beautiful, but the riding can be daunting.

Easton says, "For terrain, it's different for everyone, but again, a little bit of research goes a long way—get a good topography map and take a look—if the road looks like a snake, you can bet it goes up before it goes down!

Overdoing It

Vacations are great because they give you time to binge on your favorite thing. Kids get excited at the prospect of a whole day at Disney World, beach bunnies salivate for a full day of sea and sand, and cyclists dream of more calories burned than the average person can eat in a day.

If you plan to ride more than four days, remember that your body can't combine both long miles and intensity ad infinitum. Plan some

Make sure to take some days easy while on your trip.

short, easy days during your vacation so that your final day of riding isn't a death march. And if you are traveling with someone who isn't as avid a cyclist as you are, those shorter days can help prevent your companion from perceiving the trip as one big bike ride.

"I tell people the ideal is seven to eight days, with a day in the middle either off the bike or real easy," recommends Easton. "A large percentage of cyclists, unless you're a professional, don't ride more than two days in a row, so after three and four days, fatigue becomes a big factor. A chance to regenerate with a day off provides the opportunity to enjoy the remaining days and go home feeling invigorated instead of exhausted."

Flexibility

A bicycle tour isn't the sort of excursion that can be run with the precision of a Swiss train. Flats interrupt the miles, hunger takes over from time to time, and if you're open to it, amazing experiences can unfold when you least expect it. Leave yourself time and room to color outside the lines.

Velo Classic's Easton says, "I encourage people to research and figure out what they really want to get out of a bike trip, not just what they want to brag to their riding buddies about doing. There is nothing wrong with rolling along at 15 mph on a brilliantly sunny day in some foreign land, seeing things you've never seen before, and coming across the surprises that define unique encounters with new cultures—the people, the foods, the smells, the sights, the opportunities. You never know who'll you meet and where you'll end up, if you're open to it. I've had some of the most rewarding experiences in my life when I've least expected it, and I cherish the thought that I was so willing to allow myself to venture out of my comfort zone."

Make sure to stop and smell the bakery . . . and enjoy a croissant or two. Image: Patrick Brady

Chapter 28
Cycling Clubs and Organizations

What They Offer

A cycling club is an instant group of friends. That's probably reason enough to join a club in your neighborhood, but the practical benefits play out in a number of ways.

Training Partners
The fastest route to getting stronger is by training with riders stronger than you. Joining a club will give you instant access to a number of riders who can drop you faster than an ex-friend on Facebook. Most riders will tell you that committing to meet club members at a group ride will also help get you out of bed on early mornings when the will flags.

Riding with friends can help you get stronger, faster. Image: Patrick Brady

New Routes

Riding with more experienced riders will introduce you to roads you never knew existed. From steep hills to flat roads with no traffic, riding with experienced club members can increase your vocabulary of cycling-safe roads.

No one knows the locals roads suitable for cycling like an experienced rider. Image: Patrick Brady

News of the Local Cycling Community

Most clubs offer a newsletter, a website, and an e-mail distribution list. Increasingly, e-mail distribution lists are becoming one of the most valuable ways to interact with the club. From meeting up for impromptu group rides to equipment for sale and special deals from club sponsors, the e-mail list can be one of the most valuable club benefits. Large clubs will often include reference material about area rides, local bike shops, and links to sponsors on their websites for new or visiting riders.

Socializing

Through the course of each season, most clubs will sponsor a few social events where members can get together as normal adults, that is, in cotton and in shoes with laces. Many clubs will have an annual awards ceremony where they recognize riders who have made significant contributions to the club or advancement in ability.

A get-together with your riding friends off the bike from time to time will strengthen your friendships.

Learning Opportunities

Many clubs relish their role in the cycling community as an opportunity to increase the skills, fitness, and enjoyment of their members. Some clubs will offer weekly group rides for riders just becoming accustomed to riding in a peloton. Other clubs will offer clinics for beginners that teach them everything from fixing a flat to riding in a paceline.

Some clubs invite current and former pros to speak at their meetings.

Traveling Companions

Whether you are heading off to a charity ride, century, or race, traveling with friends makes the drive more enjoyable and affordable. And riding the event with friends makes the event itself more memorable.

Some clubs organize annual trips to destinations farther afield. Traveling with friends to a tour in Europe can cut many of the logistical issues and, again, make getting there all the more enjoyable.

Club Clothing

After tubes and tires, cycling clothing is most riders' largest annual cycling-related expense. Club-cycling clothing is generally high in quality and usually less expensive than the top-shelf clothing available through most shops. Wearing your club's kit can help your friends find you in a group where many clubs are present and give you a feeling of inclusion as well.

A club-cycling kit is a great way to get high-quality cycling clothing without spending a fortune.

A unified cycling kit has a much sharper look that most off-the-rack clothing because of the coordinated design. Many clubs will not only offer shorts and jerseys but vests; windbreakers; arm, knee, and leg warmers; and sometimes even gloves, cycling caps, and winter jackets. You may not be as fast as a pro, but at least a club kit will make you look like one.

Discounts on Cycling Gear

Most clubs enjoy sponsorship with some of the industry's manufacturers. Members usually receive opportunities to purchase bikes, equipment, sports drinks, and energy bars at a noticeable discount. Typically, a club will also feature sponsorship from a local shop, and members will often receive a discount on bikes, parts, food, and sometimes even repair labor. The exact nature of the discounts can vary substantially from manufacturer to manufacturer, shop to shop, and even club to club. Usually, the bigger the club, the better the deals.

Social Networking

Club friendships can offer another valuable resource: referrals. From looking for cycling-specific needs such as a coach, chiropractor, or physician to such noncycling things as a new vet or auto mechanic, your cycling friends often understand your needs in a way few others do.

Other Benefits

Each club defines itself differently and will offer a broad array of benefits. Some clubs are so large (400 or more members) that they have taken the step to purchase equipment that can be loaned out to members for special purposes, such as disc wheels or bike carriers for travel.

How to Find a Club

So long as you don't live under a rock, at the bottom of the ocean, or on the moon, it won't be hard to find a bike club. Heck, Wyoming, the most sparsely populated state in the union, has more than a half-dozen bike clubs. A Google search for "bicycle club" and your city should net great results, but just in case, you'll find a few links in Chapter 30: Further Reading, beginning on page 231.

The Internet has proved to be a powerful tool for finding bicycle clubs.

Organizations

There are a number of advocacy groups that work to promote cycling as a safe and green alternative form of transportation. If you want to help ensure cyclists are represented well in Washington or want to become more involved in touring or racing, consider joining one of these organizations.

Adventure Cycling Association (AdventureCycling.org): This group's nonprofit mission is to inspire people of all ages to travel by bicycle for fitness, fun, and self-discovery. Founded in 1973 as Bikecentennial, Adventure Cycling is the premier bicycle-travel organization in North America with 44,500 members nationwide.

The association researches and produces cycling maps for its Adventure Cycling Route Network, one of the largest route networks in the world at 38,158 miles (and growing). It publishes *Adventure Cyclist* magazine for its member-

Adventure Cycling Association

ship, leads bike tours, works on bicycle-advocacy projects such as the U.S. Bicycle Route System, sells bike-travel gear, and provides trip-planning resources for bicycle travelers. As a nonprofit organization, the ACA's proceeds from tours, sales, and membership go directly back into supporting its mission and programs.

Bikes Belong Coalition (BikesBelong.org): Works to put more people on bicycles more often. From helping create safe places to ride to promoting bicycling, they carefully select projects and partnerships that have the capacity to make a difference.

Bikes Belong concentrates its efforts in four areas:

- Federal policy and funding
- National partnerships
- Community grants
- Promoting bicycling

In addition, they operate the Bikes Belong Foundation to focus on kids and bicycle safety.

League of American Bicyclists (BikeLeague.org): Exists to promote bicycling for fun, fitness, and transportation and work through advocacy and education for a bicycle-friendly America.

People Powered Movement (PeoplePoweredMovement.org): Formerly known as Thunderhead Alliance, this group is the North American coalition of grassroots bicycle- and pedestrian-advocacy organizations. They *unite* advocacy leaders to help them become more effective by sharing best practices and innovations. They *strengthen* organizations through resource sharing and training opportunities. They help advocates *create* organizations in underserved communities. Alliance organizations are working together to transform communities into great places to bike and walk.

USA Cycling (USACycling.org): Governs road, mountain, track, cyclocross, and BMX bicycle racing in the United States. In addition to sanctioning the races through permits, it licenses racers, officials, mechanics, and coaches. USA Cycling develops athletes through the National Team system and selects the athletes who represent the United States at the Olympic Games.

Image: John Pierce, Photosport International

Chapter 29
Pro Racing

If you plan to watch races on TV or you've read about racing in the past, it is helpful to have some idea of the constellation of great racers and the events that have made their reputations.

The Grand Tours

There are many bike races, but the top of the heap are the Grand Tours, races that unfold over three weeks. There are only three in the world, taking place annually in France, Italy, and Spain. The Grand Tours include 21 stages with two rest days.

Tour de France: The Tour, as it is known, is the world's largest annual sporting event in terms of TV and live viewership and the most prestigious of all bike races. Each day a new race—called a stage—is run, often between two cities.

The race begins with a short time trial, called the prologue. The riders' varying times give each competitor an overall placing and also indicate who some of the strongest contenders may be. In some years there is a team time trial, in which each team's nine riders ride a time trial working together in a paceline.

Stages take several forms. Most are mass-start events and often cover more than a hundred miles in distance. Some stages climb the high mountains of the Alps and Pyrenees. Climbs are classified from 4 (the lowest) to 1 (very high) and even those called *hors categorie* (H.C.—beyond category), reserved for the very highest mountains. Each year several stages will finish atop mountains.

The race is judged on overall accumulated time. The rider with the lowest accumulated time is the race's General Classification (GC) leader and wears a yellow jersey. The race awards jerseys for three other classifications. The points competition gives a green jersey to the best sprinter. The mountains competition (often called the King

The Tour de France
Image: Patrick Brady

of the Mountains) gives a red-and-white polka-dot jersey to the best climber. The young-rider competition awards a white jersey to the best overall rider under the age of 25.

Because of the incredible prestige a win in the Tour de France carries, riders from all over the world make it the focus of their season. Not a single French rider has won the Tour de France since 1985.

The Tour de France was first run in 1903 and has only been suspended 11 times, during World Wars I and II. Initially the race had few stages (the 1903 edition had just six), but the stages ranged between 167 and 263 miles in length—long by today's standards (the race totaled 1,509 miles). In 2008, the Tour had 21 stages; the mass-start stages ranged between 89 and 144 miles for a total of 2,212 miles.

Tour of Italy: The Giro d'Italia is the second oldest and second most-popular of the Grand Tours. The Giro is held in late May and June.

The Tour of Italy has never carried the worldwide adulation that the Tour de France enjoys. As a result, it remains a bigger priority to Italian riders than non-Italian riders, which explains why the majority of Giri have been won by Italians, including an 11-year streak from 1997 to 2007.

The race is judged on overall accumulated time. The rider with the lowest accumulated time is the

The Tour of Italy Image: John Pierce, Photosport International

race's General Classification (GC) leader and wears a pink jersey. The race awards jerseys for three other classifications. The points competition gives a mauve jersey to the best sprinter. The mountains competition (often called the King of the Mountains) gives a green jersey to the best climber. The young-rider competition awards a white jersey to the best overall rider under the age of 25.

The Giro was first run in 1909 and has been suspended only nine times, during World Wars I and II.

Tour of Spain: The Vuelta a España is the third oldest and third most popular of the Grand Tours. Originally held in April, the Vuelta was moved to September in 1995.

The Vuelta a España has also never commanded the worldwide attention that the Tour de France enjoys. As a result, it remains a bigger priority to Spanish riders than non-Spanish riders, which explains why 9 of the last 20 Vuelta have been won by Spaniards.

The Tour of Spain
Image: John Pierce, Photosport International

The race is judged on overall accumulated time. The rider with the lowest accumulated time is the race's General Classification (GC) leader and wears a red jersey. The race awards jerseys for two other classifications. The points competition gives a mauve jersey to the best sprinter.

The tour was first held in 1935, though intermittently; it has been held annually since 1955.

The Monuments

Five races—Milan–San Remo, the Tour of Flanders, Paris–Roubaix, Liège–Bastogne–Liège, and the Tour of Lombardy—carry the distinction of being called the Monuments. They are so named because they began prior to World War I; the youngest of the events, the Tour of Flanders, was first run in 1913. The roads they travel were used during the World Wars, and now the courses are lined with memorials to the war dead.

Milan–San Remo: At 298km (185 miles), Milan–San Remo is the longest of the five Monuments. Traditionally run the third week of March, Milan–San Remo signals the shift into high gear for the Spring Classics. The race is held in Italy, and its course runs from the city of Milan to the small town of San Remo on the Ligurian coast near the French border. Conditions are generally cold at the start but with the run to the coast, the finish is much warmer. The course features several significant climbs, and the final two, the Cipressa and Poggio, are effective at thinning the pack so that only the strongest sprint for the finish. Italians have won the race in 50 of the 99 editions. Belgian Eddy Merckx holds the record for the most wins with seven.

Tour of Flanders: The Ronde van Vlaanderen is the first of the Northern Classics. It is generally run the first Sunday in April, one week before Paris–Roubaix. It cov-

Milan–San Remo Image: John Pierce, Photosport International

ers a 262km (163-mile) course from Bruges in the north to Ninove outside of Brussels. It is famous for its 17 hills, which range in length from 375 meters (410 yards) to 2.2km (1.4 miles). The climbs are called *muur* (wall) because many are steep at some point; 11 of the hills have sections with gradients of 11 percent or more, and 8 have sections made up of cobblestone. If the roads are damp, riders are frequently forced to dismount their bikes on the steepest sections of hills and walk up.

The Tour of Flanders Image: John Pierce, Photosport International

It's a bit like trying to climb a mountain in your dancing shoes. Many Belgian riders have said that winning Flanders is more important to a Belgian than wearing the yellow jersey of the Tour de France. Belgians have won the race 65 of the 92 times it has been run. Achiel Buysse, Fiorenzo Magni, Eric Leman, and Johan Museeuw are tied for the record of most wins, with three apiece; all are Belgians except for Magni, an Italian.

Paris–Roubaix: Considered the "Queen of the Classics," Paris–Roubaix is the only Monument run in France. Best known as the "Hell of the North" for the sections of cobblestone roads it traverses in Northern France, it is held the second Sunday in April.

Over its 260km (162-mile) course, Paris–Roubaix submits riders to 28 sections of *pavé* (French for cobblestone). The sections of pavé range in length; some are as short as 200 meters (218 yards), while the longest are 3.7km (2.3 miles). The sections are rated in difficulty from one star (easy) to five stars (reserved for the most difficult sections). These are the same cobblestone roads used in World War I. The most famous (and difficult) sections—the Arenberg Forest, Mons-en-Pévèle, and

Paris–Roubaix Image: John Pierce, Photosport International

Carrefour de l'Arbre—are traditionally the site of attacks that can tear the race apart. The cobblestones jar the body terribly, can be slippery, and are the source of untold numbers of punctures. Riders will run exceptionally low tire pressure (sometimes as low as 50 psi) in an effort to cushion them from the rough surface and reduce the likelihood of a puncture. Most don't finish the race due to one or another of the many setbacks a rider can encounter. As a result, riders speak of the luck required to win at the velodrome in Roubaix. Crashes are frequent and often spectacular; it's kind of a full-contact roulette.

The day's weather can make a big difference in the race; if there's rain, racers can be forced to ride through mud, while on dry days dust can affect racers' breathing and vision. (Imagine trying to skateboard through a quarry and you'll have the idea.) Though the race is French, it is a particular favorite of the Belgians, who have won it 52 times in 106 runs. Roger De Vlaeminck holds the record for the most wins: four.

Liège–Bastogne–Liège: As the oldest of all the Classics—first held in 1892—Liège–Bastogne–Liège is also known as "La Doyenne" (a sign of respect, something like "grand dame"). It is one of two Classics held in the Ardennes region of Belgium (the other is La Flèche Wallonne) and is known for an exceptionally hilly course with 12 notable climbs. Liège–Bastogne–Liège is held the last Sunday in April over a 261km (162-mile) course. The course only takes in two of the 12 climbs in the 105km run from Liège to Bastogne on the trip south, but after leaving Bastogne, the riders are taken on a circuitous route over 10 of the 12 climbs. And while the race is called Liège–Bastogne–Liège, the race's finish is in the town of Ans, which is

Liège–Bastogne–Liège
Image: John Pierce, Photosport International

a bit like having a race called Denver–Colorado Springs–Denver finish in Boulder. Belgians haven't fared so well in their race since Eddy Merckx's last of five wins (the record) in 1975. Since then, only four Belgians have given a salute in Ans.

Tour of Lombardy: The "Race of the Falling Leaves" is the only one of the Monuments held in the fall. The running of the Giro di Lombardia signals the end of the season for most top riders. Generally held the second or third week of October, the Tour of Lombardy was originally

The Tour of Lombardy   Image: John Pierce, Photosport International

called Milan–Milan, the course has changed many times; today the start takes place in Varese, and the 242km (150-mile) race finishes in Como on Lake Bellagio. The race contains a number of significant climbs, with six of them notable for their length. The race's most difficult challenge is the climb up to the historic chapel of the Madonna del Ghisallo, which holds bikes and memorabilia of many great former riders. The 8.6km (5.3-mile) climb contains a maximum grade of 14 percent. The race is an overwhelming favorite of Italian racers, who have won 67 of 102 races. Fausto Coppi holds the record for the most wins: five.

World Championships

Unlike some sports where the World Championship is awarded based on points accumulated over the course of the season in important races, in cycling the World Championship is awarded based on a single race which moves location each year. First held in 1927, the race was held in August after the Tour de France, but was pushed back to September following the 1995 move of the Vuelta a Espana to August. Most of the prominent cycling countries have hosted the World Championships at one point. The United States hosted the World Championships in Colorado Springs in 1986. Because the course changes each year, its challenges and length do as well; in some years the race is flat and ends in a sprint, while other years feature hills that can result in a solo breakaway. The World Championship road race is the one time each year riders set aside their team affiliations and race under the flag of their country; this temporary change of affiliation isn't without its problems,

The World Championships
Image: John Pierce, Photosport International

but riders often come together to form a remarkable alliance. A World Championship is held in both the road race and time trial, and the winner wears a rainbow jersey for the next year. Four riders have each won the World Championship road race three times: Alfredo Binda, Rik Van Steenbergen, Eddy Merckx, and Oscar Freire.

Top-Tier American Races

The United States has had a number of high-quality races that have attracted top international fields. The first great U.S. stage race was the **Coors Classic** (which started as the Red Zinger in the mid-1980s). It was followed by the **Tour DuPont**, the **Tour de Georgia**, and now the **Amgen Tour of California**.

With eight days of racing, the Tour of California is one of the longest stage races run on American soil, and other than the 1986 World Championships in Colorado Springs and 1996 Olympic Games in Atlanta, it draws the strongest international field of racers assembled in the States. The race has been hailed for spectator-friendly and challenging courses, great organization, and fantastic racing, as well as occasionally stellar weather.

After many years in Philadelphia, the **National Championship Road Race** is now held in Greenville, South Carolina, over a demanding course in hot and humid conditions.

Races in America tend to have unfortunately short life spans because they rely on corporate sponsors for their existence. As soon as their marketing priorities change, the races often fold due to an inability to replace the title sponsor willing to put up the bulk of the necessary funding. The pullout of a sponsoring corporation has made races disappear faster than a Star Trek crew member from the transporter room.

Image: John Pierce, Photosport International

Who's Who

So who's best? It is difficult and unfair to judge one man by another's era, but a win is a win, and those can be counted. Here are the international riders who have had a lasting influence and the Americans who paved the way for Lance.

Eddy Merckx (1945): Easily the greatest racer ever, Merckx amassed 525 wins as a professional cyclist. His professional career spanned the years from 1965 to 1978, with his greatest success coming from 1969 to 1975. He won the Tour de France five times, with 34 stage wins (a record) and 96 days in the yellow jersey (also a record), not to mention the most stage wins in a single edition of the Tour de France: eight. He won the Tour of Italy five times with 24 stage wins, the Tour of Spain once with 6 stage wins, Milan–San Remo seven times, the Tour of Flanders twice, Paris–Roubaix three times, Liège–Bastogne–Liège five times, and the Tour of Lombardy twice.

Eddy Merckx
Image: John Pierce, Photosport International

He was World Champion three times. He also set the World Hour Record. Other records include the most victories in a single season—54—and the most victories in the Classics—28. A Belgian magazine named him the greatest Belgian ever. Merckx tested positive for drugs at the Giro d'Italia in 1969 and was kicked out of the race, but he always proclaimed his innocence, and argued the sample had been tainted. Few riders had the courage to take on Merckx directly; he was royalty to the peloton. His nickname: The Cannibal.

Fausto Coppi (1919–1960): Coppi was the first cyclist ever to win seven Grand Tours. His career spanned from 1940 to 1959, although interrupted for four years by World War II. He won the Giro d'Italia five times, taking 22 stages, as well as earning the King of the Mountains' green jersey three times. He also won the Tour de France twice, took nine stages, and received the King of the Mountains' polka-dot jersey on each of the two occasions that he won the race overall. He won three of the five Monuments: Milan–San Remo (three times), Paris–Roubaix (once), and the Tour of Lombardy (five times—a record). Coppi won the World Championship Road Race once and was the Italian National Champion in the road race four times. He even set the Hour Record with a mark that stood for 13 years. Despite his admission that he used amphetamines, Coppi was revered by riders and

Fausto Coppi
Image: John Pierce, Photosport International

fans alike until he had an affair with a married woman, called the "lady in white." Unfortunately, he contracted malaria while on a combination bike race and safari trip to Burkina Faso in 1959 and died at age 40. His nickname: Il Campionissimo—the champion of champions.

Lance Armstrong (1971): Because he won the Tour de France seven times, Armstrong is often referred to as the greatest cyclist ever. He turned pro in 1992 following the Olympics and retired following the 2005 Tour de France; he came out of retirement in 2009, some 17 years after he first turned pro. Beginning with his first win in the Tour de France, in 1999, Armstrong amassed a string of seven consecutive victories in the Tour. He won 22 stages in all and spent 75 days wearing the leader's yellow jersey (third highest). In addition to winning the Tour, Armstrong won the World Championship in 1993; at 21 years old, he was the youngest World Champion ever. He won the U.S. National Cycling Championship, the Clásica San Sebastián, La Flèche Wallonne, the Tour de Suisse, and twice won the Critérium du Dauphiné Libéré. He represented the United States three times at the Olympic Games:

in 1992, 1996, and 2000. He earned a bronze medal in the individual time trial in 2000. He is the only rider since Gino Barali (in 1948) to win three consecutive mountain stages of the Tour de France, a feat he managed in 2004. He has been accused by some of drug use, but no allegations have been proven. Armstrong wasn't always liked by his competitors, but he was respected for his work ethic and determination. Following his second victory in the Tour, most riders figured they were racing for second place. While he was often compared to Greg LeMond as a rider, Lance Armstrong bears more in common with our next great, Bernard Hinault, than with LeMond. His nickname: Mellow Johnny, a play on *maillot jaune*—the Tour leader's yellow jersey.

Lance Armstrong
Image: John Pierce, Photosport International

Bernard Hinault (1954): The third man to win the Tour de France five times was Bernard Hinault. Over the course of his career, which spanned 11 years, from 1975 to 1986, the Frenchman celebrated 250 victories, among them 10 victories in Grand Tours. He claimed 28 stages of the Tour de France—13 in individual time trials, and wore the yellow jersey for 78 days. In addition to five Tours, he won the Giro d'Italia three times and the Vuelta a Espana

Bernard Hinault
Image: John Pierce, Photosport International

twice, making him the only cyclist to have won each Grand Tour more than once. Hinault enjoyed success in one-day races as well, with two victories in Liège–Bastogne–Liège and one World Championship, as well as a victory at Paris–Roubaix. Hinault was the prototypical patron of the peloton; he could dictate the pace through sheer intimidation. His nickname: The Badger, because he became more ferocious when he felt cornered.

Jacques Anquetil (1934–1987): As the first cyclist to win the Tour de France five times, this Frenchman achieved what was thought to be impossible. He raced as a pro from 1953 to 1969, a long career by modern standards. In that time, he won 200 races, including 16 stages of the Tour de France. He wore the yellow jersey for 50 days over his career. Anquetil specialized in the Grand Tours and was the first rider to win all three: the Tour de France (five victories), the Giro d'Italia (two victories), and the Vuelta a Espana (one victory). In 1961, Anquetil wore the Tour de France leader's yellow jersey for the entire length of the race, from

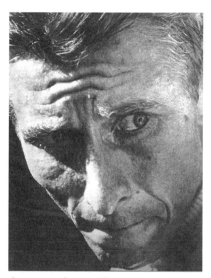

Jacques Anquetil
Image: John Pierce, Photosport International

start to finish, a feat only one other rider has duplicated. Anquetil's only win in a Spring Classic came at Liège–Bastogne–Liège, one of the hilliest Classics. He is remembered as a gifted time trialist and won the Grand Prix des Nations time trial an incredible nine times. He also set the Hour Record in 1956. Of drug use, Anquetil said racers could not manage the Tour without help, but refused to be tested, claiming it an invasion of privacy. Anquetil was considered distant by the French and didn't enjoy as much popularity as other riders; yet he was also known to party into the night. His nickname: Monsieur Chrono, due to his time trial ability.

Miguel Indurain (1964): The only Spanish cyclist to win the Tour de France five times, Indurain was the first rider to win his five Tours in successive years, from 1991 to 1995. He turned pro in 1985 and retired 11 years later, in 1996. Indurain also won the Giro d'Italia twice. Along the way he collected 12 stage wins at the Tour and another four stage wins in the Giro. He never won any of the Monuments, but did win Olympic gold and the World Championship in the individual time trial. He was

Miguel Indurain
Image: John Pierce, Photosport International

large and powerful, standing 6 feet 2 inches tall. Time trialing was his great talent and the key to most of his victories. His one significant victory in a one-day Classic came at the Clásica San Sebastián. Indurain was legendary for his silence; he was considered something of an enigma. His nickname: Big Mig.

Louison Bobet (1925–1983): In the modern era of bike racing (post World War II), Bobet was the first rider to win the Tour de France three times. He also won four of the five Monuments—Milan–San Remo, the Tour of Flanders, Paris–Roubaix, and the Tour of Lombardy—as well as the World Championship. His career spanned from 1947 to 1962. He won 11 stages of the Tour de France as well as the King of the Mountains' polka-dot jersey once. Other significant wins include the World Championship Road Race and the French National Championship on two occasions. He was respected as a rider, especially given that his career was book-ended by Fausto Coppi's and Jacques Anquetil's careers. He was known as a stylish dresser, something other riders sometimes ridiculed. His nickname: Zonzon.

Greg LeMond (1961): LeMond made history by becoming both the first American and the first non-European to win the Tour de France. He won the Tour three times in his career and was thought to have had the ability to win more had he not been shot in a hunting accident. His career ran from 1981 to 1994. He spent 22 days wearing the yellow

jersey and won six stages. He also won the World Championship Road Race three times, first as a junior, then twice as a pro. While he is primarily remembered as a stage racer, LeMond had three top-four finishes in the Monuments before his hunting accident. LeMond's 1986 and 1989 Tour de France victories are remembered for being dramatic battles against beloved Frenchmen: Bernard Hinault (his teammate in '86) and Laurent Fignon (in '89), with the '89 race being the closest in history; the margin of victory was just 8 seconds. His nickname: Just Greg (or just Greg).

Greg LeMond
Image: John Pierce, Photosport International

Rik van Looy (1933): Van Looy was the first professional to win the five monuments and the only cyclist ever to win all of the Classics. His career spanned an unusually long time, from 1953 to 1970. During that time, he won an impressive 379 races on the road (van Looy was also successful on the track). He was known as a specialist in the Classics and never won a Grand Tour. He won Milan–San Remo (once), the Tour of Flanders

Rik van Looy
Image: John Pierce, Photosport International

(twice), Paris–Roubaix (three times), Liège–Bastogne–Liège (once), and the Tour of Lombardy (once). He also won the World Championship twice, the Green Jersey of the Points Classification of the Tour de France twice, and the Belgian National Championship twice. He won stages of the Tour de France, the Giro d'Italia, and the Vuelta a Espana. His nickname: The Emperor of Herentals, or just "The Emperor" for short.

Roger De Vlaeminck (1947): De Vlaeminck is remembered for two achievements: He holds the record for the most victories in Paris–Roubaix—four wins—and he is one of three riders (the others being Merckx and Van Looy) to win each of the Monuments. He enjoyed a long career, from 1969 to 1984. Like his mentor Van Looy, De Vlaeminck was a Classics specialist. In addition to his wins in Roubaix, he won Milan San Remo (three times), the Tour of Flanders (once), Liège–Bastogne–Liège (once), and the Tour of Lombardy (twice). He claimed one stage win at the Tour de France and 22 stage wins in the Giro d'Italia as well as the points leader's jersey on three occasions. He was twice Belgian National Champion in the road race. He was admired by his fellow competitors. His nickname: Monsieur Paris–Roubaix.

Sean Kelly (1956): Though he was initially known as a sprinter, Irishman Sean Kelly became one of the most complete riders of his generation, earning the distinction of being the greatest cyclist the British Isles have produced. His career spanned 17 years, from 1977 to 1994. In that time he won a Grand Tour—the Vuelta a Espana—and won four of the five Monuments: Milan–San Remo (twice), Paris–Roubaix (twice), Liège–Bastogne–

Roger De Vlaeminck
Image: John Pierce, Photosport International

Sean Kelly
Image: John Pierce, Photosport International

Liège (twice), and the Tour of Lombardy (three times). He won the green jersey of the leader of the Tour de France's points competition four times, notching five Tour stage wins along the way and spending one day in the leader's yellow jersey. Other riders held him in high regard; he was universally respected. His nickname: King Kelly.

Joop Zoetemelk (1946): This Dutch cyclist achieved several unusual distinctions in his career. In addition to winning two Grand Tours (the Tour de France once and the Vuelta a Espana once) he was second six times and completed the Tour 16 times, both records. Zoetemelk's career lasted 18 years, from 1969 to 1987. He was, at the age of 38, the oldest cyclist ever to win the World Championship Road Race. He won 10 stages of the Tour de France and spent 22 days in the yellow jersey; he also won the National Championship road race of the Netherlands twice. He won the gold medal at the 1968 Olympic Games in the team time trial. His nickname: The Wheel-Sucker—a name Merckx gave to him for his frequent second-place finishes.

Jan Ullrich (1973): Ullrich is arguably the finest cyclist Germany ever produced. Part of the sports-education schools of the German Democratic Republic, Ullrich benefited from the reunification of Germany, which allowed him to compete in races throughout Western Europe. He won two Grand Tours (the Tour de France once and the Vuelta a Espana once) and earned nine stage wins (seven at the Tour and two at the Vuelta). While he is sometimes better remembered for his five second-place finishes at the Tour de France, Ullrich did enjoy some success at the Olympics—where he won the road race in 2000—and the World Championships—where he twice won the individual time trial. Ullrich came

Jan Ullrich
Image: John Pierce, Photosport International

under fire for doping allegations as a result of Operation Puerto and ended his career prematurely in an effort to avoid further investigation. He was respected for his strength but also frequently criticized for overeating and gaining weight during the winter. His nickname: Der Kaiser.

Erik Zabel (1970): This German rider is considered one of the finest sprinters of his generation. He won the green jersey of the Tour de France's points competition a record six times. He took 12 stage victories at the Tour and another 8 at the Vuelta. He also won the points competition of the Vuelta a Espana three times. At Milan–San Remo he scored four wins, as well as three wins at Paris–Tours and a victory at the Amstel Gold Race. His career ran 15 years, from 1993 to 2008. He was twice German National Champion. In 2006, he confessed to using EPO (see definition on page 228) briefly during an earlier portion of his career. Zabel was liked and respected by his fellow competitors.

Erik Zabel
Image: John Pierce, Photosport International

Richard Virenque (1969): This Frenchman was the darling of France, a true King of the Mountains. A gifted climber, Virenque won the Tour de France's polkadot jersey seven times, a record. He focused on the climbing competition during his career, which ran from 1991 to 2004. Though he did wear the leader's yellow jersey twice, and finished second and

Richard Virenque
Image: John Pierce, Photosport International

third overall, he was never able to win the Tour de France. He took seven stage wins at the Tour and one stage of the Giro d'Italia. While Virenque is the best climber on paper, most aficionados of climbing say three men were better: Lucien van Impe, Charly Gaul, and Federico Bahamontes. Virenque was at the center of the Festina Affair (see page 229 for more), and despite initially claiming he was clean, he later admitted to taking the drug EPO. Following the Festina Affair, Virenque gained a reputation as a lovable, though naïve, hypocrite. His nickname: Richard the Lion-Hearted.

Andy Hampsten (1962): Hampsten is the only American and non-European ever to win the Giro d'Italia. After Armstrong and LeMond, he is third on the list of America's greatest cyclists and is remembered as an extremely gifted climber. His career spanned from 1985 to 1994. On his way to winning the Giro, Hampsten won two stages and the green jersey of the mountains competition. His win in the Giro came following a legendary stage over the 9,000-foot Gavia pass in blizzard conditions, to this day considered one of the greatest days of bicycle racing. Hampsten

Andy Hampsten
Image: John Pierce, Photosport International

twice finished fourth at the Tour de France and won one mountain stage. He also enjoyed great success in shorter stage races, with wins at the Tours de Suisse and Romandie. Hampsten was a favorite of the media for his thoughtful answers and introspective nature, and was well liked by other riders. His nickname: Ernie.

Tyler Hamilton (1971): While other Americans have won some significant semiclassics, Hamilton is known for being the first American to win one of the Monuments, Liège–Bastogne–Liège. His career spanned from 1995 to 2009. He won Gold at the 2004 Olympic Games in the individual time trial and also the U.S. National Championship. He won a stage of the Giro d'Italia and finished second overall despite having broken his shoulder in a crash. He finished fourth in the Tour de France, even after breaking his collarbone in the opening stage. He made a dramatic breakaway for a stage win in the Tour that year. Hamilton tested positive for doping and served a two-year suspension; he returned to racing but continued to be dogged by allegations of doping with regard to a case known as Operation Puerto. He tested positive again in 2009 and retired immediately after the announcement. Hamilton was universally liked and respected for his kind manner and legendary ability to continue riding through injury, though the doping issues dulled his luster. His nickname: Ty.

Levi Leipheimer (1973): Leipheimer is arguably the best cyclist America has produced who hasn't won a Grand Tour. After turning pro in 1998, he has finished third at the Tour de France and second and third at the Vuelta a Espana. He also won a stage of the Tour and two stages of the Vuelta. Winner of the Tour of California three times, as well as the U.S. National Championship in the road race and time trial, Levi was the bronze medalist in the individual time trial at the 2008 Beijing Olympics. His nickname: just Levi.

Tyler Hamilton
Image: John Pierce, Photosport International

Levi Leipheimer
Image: John Pierce, Photosport International

Bobby Julich (1971): Proclaimed "the next Greg LeMond" repeatedly, Julich finished third at the Tour de France in 1998, making him only the second American to finish on the podium. Julich turned professional in 1992 and retired at the end of the 2008 season. His biggest wins came at short stage races: the Critérium International, Paris–Nice, and the Eneco Tour of Benelux. He earned the bronze medal in the individual time trial at the 2004 Athens Olympics. His nickname: Bobby J.

Bobby Julich Image: Patrick Brady

George Hincapie (1973): Depending on your view, George Hincapie had either the good or bad fortune to spend most of his career in service to Lance Armstrong. An immensely talented rider who excelled in the Spring Classics, Hincapie rode the Tour de France 15 times, finishing it 14 times, and was the only rider to serve Armstrong during each of his seven wins. While he was tipped as a potential winner of Paris–Roubaix or the Tour of Flanders for many years, Hincapie never enjoyed victory in those races. His biggest victories came in at the Tour de France, where he won four stages (three were in team time trials, while one was a mountain stage in the Pyrenees), as well as the early-season Classics Ghent–Wevelgem and Kuurne–Brussels–Kuurne. He won the National Championship Road Race three times. His nickname: Big George.

George Hincapie
Image: John Pierce, Photosport International

SECTION II **The Lifestyle**

Davis Phinney (1959): Phinney has scored more wins than any other American rider, 328 in all. His career spanned from 1981 to 1993. He was the first American to score a stage win at the Tour de France and he won the U.S. National Championship once. Phinney was diagnosed with early-onset Parkinson's disease in 2000; he now heads the Davis Phinney Foundation, which seeks to help people with the disease. Phinney married 1984 gold medalist Connie Carpenter, and their son, Taylor, is on his way to become the next big thing in American cycling. Davis' nickname: The Cash Register.

Jonathan Boyer (1955): Not only was Boyer the first American to race the Tour de France, he was also the first to finish the race in the top 20, finishing 12th on one occasion. He raced 11 seasons, from 1977 to 1987. His greatest success was winning the Coors Classic, the largest race in the United States at the time. His nickname: Jacques.

Davis Phinney
Image: John Pierce, Photosport International

Jonathan Boyer
Image: John Pierce, Photosport International

George Mount (1955): Mount was the first American cyclist to race the Giro d'Italia. Following his sixth place in the road race at the 1976 Olympic Games, Mount turned professional and joined an Italian team. He raced the Giro d'Italia and twice finished in the top 30. He won what would become the Coors Classic as well as a gold medal at the Pan American Games. He won more than 200 races on three continents. His nickname: Smilin' George.

Mike Neel (1951): Neel was the first of the trailblazing American cyclists to head to Europe to find fortune in bike racing. Following the 1976 Olympics, Neel turned pro and raced in Europe from 1976 to 1978. He signed to an Italian team and became the first American to ride the Vuelta a Espana and finished 10th at the World Championship in 1976.

George Mount
Image: John Pierce, Photosport International

Other Notables

These former riders (four pros and an amateur) are significant personalities as team directors and race commentators. Here's why they are worth paying attention to:

Johann Bruyneel (1964): A fine rider in his day who once finished seventh at the Tour de France, Bruyneel is more famous as the architect of Lance Armstrong's seven Tour de France wins. He has since guided Alberto Contador to three more Grand Tour victories, one each in the Tour de France, the Giro d'Italia, and the Vuelta a Espana, giving him 10 victories total. No other team director in the modern era can claim such a record.

Johan Bruyneel
Image: John Pierce, Photosport International

Jonathan Vaughters (1973): A former teammate of Lance Armstrong's who was known as a gifted climber (he held the record for the fastest climb up the famed Mont Ventoux), Vaughters is better known today as the director for the Garmin/Slipstream Team. Vaughters is at the vanguard of teams actively promoting doping-free racing by pursuing unparalleled testing of his riders.

Jonathan Vaughters
Image: John Pierce, Photosport International

Phil Liggett (1943): The grand statesman of English-language cycling broadcasters, Liggett was an amateur racer in the United Kingdom who was offered a contract to turn pro in 1967. Instead, he chose to begin reporting on bike racing for cycling magazines and newspapers.

Today he is best known for his broadcast work for CBS, Versus, and ITV. He is known for his witty expressions such as "the suitcase of courage."

Paul Sherwen (1956): Sherwen rode as a pro for 10 years, from 1978 to 1987, before becoming a cycling commentator. The former British road-race champion knows the suffering of the riders on which he reports. Though he rode as a *domestique* (see description of team members' functions on the next page), he finished as high as 11th at Milan–San Remo and 15th at Paris–Roubaix. He finished the Tour de France three times. Today he works with Liggett commenting on races for CBS, Versus, and ITV.

Bob Roll (1960): TV's most colorful English-language cycling commentator, Roll was a domestique for some of the best American riders of his generation, including Andy Hampsten and Davis Phinney. He finished the Tour de France twice and the Giro d'Italia three times as well as five finishes at Paris–Roubaix and two finishes at Liège–Bastogne–Liège. He frequently works with Liggett and Sherwen announcing races for CBS and Versus. He is the author of four books, including *Bobke: A Ride on the Wild Side of Cycling* and *Bobke II*. His nickname: Bobke.

Phil Liggett
Image: John Pierce, Photosport International

Paul Sherwen
Image: John Pierce, Photosport International

Bob Roll
Image: John Pierce, Photosport International

SECTION II The Lifestyle

Teams

Cycling can be a confusing sport to watch on TV because teams compete in a race, while an individual wins the race. The role of teams in the success of the winning rider should not be underestimated. Teams work to control the race so their rider will have ideal conditions to win the race. Here are the roles riders may play within a team:

Leader: This alpha-male of the team provides a rallying point for the team as its designated go-to guy. He is the GC rider for the Grand Tours as well as the intended winner of his other target races.

Sprinter: In addition to a GC leader, many teams will have a sprinter on whom they pin their hopes for those fast finishes in flat stages and certain one-day races. Their finishing kick can deliver valuable exposure for the team sponsor when they win.

Domestique: Literally, it means "houseboy". This servant of the peloton will drop back to cars for water bottles, food, or even clothing for his leader. Domestiques will ride at the front of the peloton to control the pace of the race by keeping the pace high to discourage attacks, or higher still to bring back a breakaway. Often, these riders jump into early breakaways to give their teams TV exposure; they may work in a small breakaway for 6 hours before being pulled back. If the team contains a great sprinter, several domestiques will form a leadout in the final kilometers, a kind of supercharged team time trial at the front of the race with the last rider being the sprinter, who explodes off the front with 150–200m to go. The job is all toil, and the glory comes only if your man wins.

Climbers: In the Grand Tours, climbers serve as domestiques of a different feather as they pace their leader up the long climbs and discourage attacks by the other riders. They may also be called upon to attack in order to wear down other riders by making them chase.

Drugs

While performance-enhancing drugs (PEDs) have been used in nearly every sport, cycling garnered the unfortunate distinction for making winning nearly synonymous with drug use. Historic records and interviews show that drug use goes back to the early 20th century at the least. Some of the sports' biggest names—Fausto Coppi and Jacques Anquetil among them—have either openly acknowledged or made veiled references to their own drug use.

Cyclists have tried and used most everything:

- Amphetamines and other stimulants—think instant turbo unit
- Anabolic steroids and testosterone—to build muscle more easily and recover more quickly
- Corticosteroids and opiates—no pain means . . . no pain

EPO

Erythropoietin (EPO) is a hormone that controls red-blood-cell production. Synthetic EPO and its relatives increase the number of red blood cells in the user's bloodstream. It is made for cancer patients experiencing anemia caused by chemotherapy. It also happens to be useful to endurance athletes. By increasing a rider's population of red blood cells, EPO raises the rider's aerobic capacity, giving the cyclist the ability to ride faster and recover more quickly due to less lactic acid production.

EPO changed the nature of drug use in cycling. Unlike amphetamines and steroids, which had known side effects and had to be used sparingly, EPO could be used throughout the season. Unlike other drugs that could be used by athletes largely at will (steroids require some planning), EPO requires carefully spaced injections and monitoring by a doctor to make sure that a rider's hematocrit (percentage of red blood cells) doesn't rise too high. In the early 1990s, several Dutch cyclists died from heart attacks in their sleep, which are believed to have been caused by an EPO-induced excessively high hematocrit.

Because of the expense and planning required, teams began overseeing their riders' EPO administration, contracting with doctors and purchasing the drugs on behalf of the riders, usually from an account funded by the riders.

To protect a rider's health (and because no test existed to find EPO for several years), the UCI mandated that a rider's hematocrit could not rise above 50 percent. Any rider with a hematocrit higher than 50 would be suspended for two weeks—for his health.

Major Drug Scandals

The Festina Affair

In 1998, Festina Team *soigneur* (a team employee who handles everything from massage to making food for the riders) Willy Voet was stopped while on his way to the start of the Tour de France by customs agents at a border crossing. Voet had drugs enough to march a team of elephants to the moon. The ensuing scandal caused the Festina Team to withdraw from the Tour de France and nearly derailed the race itself. More importantly, it exposed the depth to which drugs were used by the peloton. Drug use was an integral part of most professionals' preparation for major races, Grand Tours especially.

Until the Festina Affair, the public was largely ignorant of drug use, and those who had any awareness generally turned a blind eye to it. Race organizers had tacitly condoned drug use, sometimes even assisting riders in their efforts to evade detection. Public outcry over the Festina Affair threatened the reputation of the Tour de France itself. As a result, the Tour took firm steps to eliminate any rider or two that might besmirch its lofty reputation. Drug testing got serious.

Operation Puerto

Once a test for EPO was created, many riders who wanted the same benefit began resorting to blood doping. A doctor would draw blood from the athlete, concentrate the red blood cells, and store the blood in a refrigerator or freezer. The blood cells could be transfused at a later date, such as the day before an important race.

In May of 2006, Spanish police raided the clinic of Dr. Eufemiano Fuentes and found large stores of blood allegedly belonging to a variety of athletes, including cyclists, football (soccer) players, and tennis stars. Fuentes used simple codes—such as the name of the rider's dog—to label the blood of the athletes.

Files indicate some of the biggest names in the sport—including Jan Ullrich—may have been involved, and though the case has been opened and closed more times than a refrigerator door in a houseful of kids, the case now appears to be closed for good.

Floyd Landis

Landis was a lieutenant on Lance Armstrong's U.S. Postal Service team from 2002 to 2004, helping Armstrong win the three Tour de France times. Landis moved to the Swiss Phonak team and won the 2006 Tour de France, only to test positive the day after the race ended, making him the only rider ever to be stripped of a Tour de France victory. He mounted the most expensive doping-defense case in history, even penning an autobiography pleading his innocence. He ultimately lost the case.

Floyd Landis
Image: John Pierce, Photosport International

In May, 2010, following a lackluster return to the sport once his two-year suspension ended, Landis sent e-mails to several cycling officials. He made accusations of doping against Armstrong and other former teammates, as well as his team director, Johan Bruyneel. He even alleged that Armstrong bribed the former head of cycling's governing body, UCI President Hein Verbruggen, to quash a positive dope test.

Federal officials are investigating the allegations. The stakes are high; at risk is Armstrong's legacy within the sport. Landis may be granted federal-whistleblower status when he testifies.

CYCLE SPORT
AMERICA
Tour de France 2008

Best ever Tour stages
30 years of classic action
Up-to-the-minute form guide

The road to Pa...
The race

NEW YORK TIMES BESTSELLER
LANCE ARMSTRONG'S WAR
One Man's Battle Against Fate, Fame, Love, Death, Scandal, and a Few Other Rivals on the Road to the Tour de France
DANIEL COYLE

PARIS-ROUBAIX
A JOURNEY THROUGH HELL
PHILIPPE BOUVET
PIERRE CALLEWAERT
SERGE LAGET

INSIDE EUROPE'S BEST BIKE FACTORIES
ROAD BIKE
ACTION MAGAZINE
LANCE VS. CONTADOR:
ARE THEY REALLY TEAMMATES?

Breaking the Chain
DRUGS AND CYCLING: THE TRUE STORY
Willy Voet

HEROES OF THE POSTWAR ERA, 1946-1967
Cycling's Golden Age
THE HORTON COLLECTION

A DOG IN A HAT
An American Bike Racer's Story of Mud, Drugs, Blood, Betrayal, and Beauty in Belgium
Joe Parkin

LANCE ARMSTRONG
with Sally Jen...
Every Second Counts

bicycle

TIM KRABBÉ
THE RIDER
A CYCLING CLASSIC BY THE AUTHOR OF
THE VANISHING AND THE CAVE

The Story of the Tour de France
How a Newspaper Promotion Became the Greatest Sporting Event in the World
Volume 2: 1965-2007
By Bill and Carol McGann

Mike and the Bike
Written by Michael Ward • Illustrated by Bob Thomson • Foreword by Lance Armstrong
CD Included!

Chapter 30
Further Reading and Involvement

English may not be cycling's first language, but that doesn't mean the sport is without some excellent and significant works devoted to the sport.

Internet

Wikipedia.org: From racers to races to manufacturers, nearly everything in cycling enjoys a rich entry on the site.

CyclingNews.com: Up-the-minute news on cycling, primarily road racing, updated at least twice daily.

VeloNews.com: Road and mountain bike racing, tech, and fitness, updated daily.

VeloNews

USACycling.org: The governing body for all forms of bike racing has an excellent page for finding bicycle clubs.

Bicycle Clubs USA (www.geocities.com/Colosseum/6213): A huge database of bicycle clubs around the country; most are linked.

BikeRadar.com: Interviews, gear, and other cycling content, updated several times daily.

MapMyRide.com: Download GPS routes and see them mapped and illustrated with elevation profiles; share them with friends.

CompetitiveCyclist.com: The best online shopping resource on the Web, with knowledgeable product descriptions.

BikePortland.org: A model for how bicycle advocacy should be done in every city.

Map My Ride

Bikesnobnyc.blogspot.com: The funniest cycling blog on the Internet; style police to the rescue.

RedKitePrayer.com: The author's blog, devoted to race analysis, technology developments, and insight into the cycling life.

Active.com: A national online event-registration site; a great way to find organized rides in your area.

Red Kite Prayer

BikeReg.com: Another national online event-registration site with many event listings; particularly strong in racing and on the East Coast.

Sportsbaseonline.com: This online event-registration site is heavy on racing in the Southwest.

Western States Ride Calendar (**www.bbcnet.com/RideCalendar/ridelistdate.asp**): Centuries and other organized rides (no races) on the West Coast.

BikeRide.com: Listings of cycling events around the country.

ClassicRendezvous.com: Devoted to vintage lightweights and other handbuilt bikes.

SheldonBrown.com: The most comprehensive resource of bicycle technical information on the Internet; don't let the clunky look fool you; it's a remarkable work of passion for the bike.

eBay.com: Cycling is eBay's single most popular sales category; you can find almost anything new or used here.

CyclingForums.com: The Usenet forums have been around for ages and are a resource for everything from racing advice to technical questions.

VelocipedeSalon.com: This forum is particularly popular with fans of handcrafted frames and is moderated by some of the best in the biz.

Magazines

Bicycling: As the largest-circulation magazine devoted to cycling in the United States, *Bicycling* is the *People* of bike magazines. Personalities, equipment, tips, and a little dash of racing.

VeloNews: This is the bible of bike racing. It covers road and mountain bike racing in the United States and around the world. In recent years it has expanded its content on equipment, training, and maintenance. It is photographer Graham Watson's American home, and thanks to its large format makes cycling look as dramatic as it actually is. Virtually indispensable to bike racers.

Cycle Sport: If your concern is European road racing, then this is the magazine of record. Singular in its focus, it is on a first-name basis with the sport's stars.

Road Bike Action: RBA is a primarily product-oriented magazine but also includes training advice, race analysis, and cycling-lifestyle features. A must-have if you are shopping for anything in cycling.

Road: With the American road-racing scene as its primary focus, *Road* does what it can to make stars of the fine domestic riders who have yet to make the jump to the Europe. It also features some product reviews and training information.

Books

Every cyclist needs a library of great cycling books. Taken as a whole, these will give you a great look at the sport's most exciting and necessary elements.

Repair Manuals

Big Blue Book of Bicycle Repair, Calvin Jones (Park Tool, 2008): Park is the industry's largest producer of bicycle tools, and Jones is Park's resident talking head of wrench wisdom. He teaches USA Cycling's licensing course to aspiring race mechanics. The Park volume is well written, features clear photos in color, and informs the reader which tools will be necessary at the beginning of the process.

Zinn and the Art of Road Bike Maintenance, Lennard Zinn (VeloPress, 2005): Zinn is a framebuilder who has been writing technical articles on repairs for *VeloNews* for more than 10 years. He is the Zen master mechanic with an understanding of the real world.

Sutherland's Handbook for Bicycle Mechanics, Howard Sutherland (Sutherland's, 2004): Sutherland's produces resources for bike shops, from repair tickets to this reference manual. Howard Sutherland put this tome together as the ultimate resource of bicycle data for the working mechanic. For the über-geek exclusively.

Training

The Cyclist's Training Bible, Joe Friel (Velo Press, 2009): Friel's work is based on the groundbreaking research of his mentor, Tudor Bompa, the father of periodized training for athletes. Friel's writing is clear and the information is extraordinarily well organized. This is the single most comprehensive book on the subject.

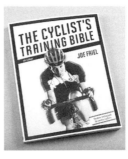

Serious Cycling, Ed Burke (Human Kinetics, 2002): Burke was renowned for his work as a coach and a researcher into training techniques for cyclists. His gift was to weave the details of training into a comprehensive plan.

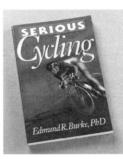

The CTS Collection: Training Tips for Cyclists and Triathletes, Chris Carmichael (Velo Press, 2001): As Lance Armstrong's coach through his seven Tour de France victories, Carmichael knows a thing or two about what it takes to make a cyclist fit. He has a rare talent for making complex fitness concepts simple to understand for the new cyclist. The perfect first book on training.

Bicycle Road Racing: The Complete Program for Training and Competition, Edward Borysewicz (Vitesse Press, 2010): In the 1980s and early '90s, former U.S. Olympic Team coach Eddie Borysewicz (best known Eddie B.) was the last word on training. The former Polish National Team coach defected to the United States and brought with him a number of old-world ideas about training—some great, some odd (such as the advice to eat horse meat). It's still relevant for its old-school approach.

SECTION II The Lifestyle

Andy Pruitt's Complete Medical Guide for Cyclists, Andy Pruitt (VeloPress, 2006): The Boulder Center for Sports Medicine is the place cyclists with hard-to-fix medical problems go, and Pruitt heads the treatment for all cyclists there. He's a brilliant biomechanist and physician, and he understands the aches, pains, and injuries associated with cycling better than anyone else writing on the subject. This is a must-have.

Biographies

It's Not About the Bike: My Journey Back to Life, Lance Armstrong with Sally Jenkins (Berkeley Trade, 2001): From top of the world to death's door, Armstrong has lived it, and his story is as miraculous and inspiring as they get. Surely you've read this already.

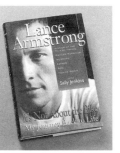

Every Second Counts, Lance Armstrong with Sally Jenkins (Broadway, 2004): For all the rest of us who haven't actually recovered from cancer and wonder how we might refocus our lives were we given a second chance, this is a must-read. Truly, this is the book that makes Armstrong's experience relevant to our lives.

Eddy Merckx, Rik Vanwalleghem, trans. Steve Hawkins (VeloPress, 2000): Merckx is the greatest cyclist ever, and if you've ever wondered how people can say he's better than Armstrong, this book will show you exactly why. More remarkable are Merckx's existential crises that followed each and every win—the anxiety that fueled every win. What else could possibly drive a man to win everything in sight than the question, "Will I win again?"

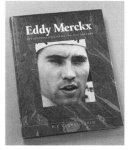

A Dog in a Hat, Joe Parkin (VeloPress, 2008): Parkin went to Belgium with a phone number and a bike. He made friends, got a pro contract, got the shaft repeatedly, all while chasing an unrealized dream: the big win. Along the way he saw it all—doping, greatness, hard work, heartbreak. He passes judgment on no one and lets the reader decide how to feel about the characters. If you've ever wondered what being a pro is like for everyone who isn't Lance, this book shows it in Technicolor. The best autobiography in the biz.

Racing and Doping

Lance Armstrong's War, Daniel Coyle (Harper Paperbacks, 2006): Coyle is a contributing editor to *Outside* magazine, which is to say he's an exceptionally talented writer. For an intimate look at Lance Armstrong and the U.S. Postal Team preparing for and winning a Tour de France, don't miss this volume; it's a fantastic read.

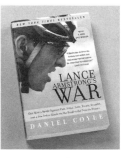

Breaking the Chain, Willy Voet (Random House, 2002): Busted. Betrayal. Heartbreak. Voet was a staff member of the Festina Team in 1998 on his way to the start of the Tour de France when he was stopped at a border crossing with a carload of doping products. He was a decent man doing a dirty job, and his arrest gave the world its first real look at doping in the pro peloton.

History

Bicycle: The History, David Herlihy (Yale University Press, 2006): Herlihy begins with a thesis: The history of the bicycle really begins with the modern chain-driven bicycle. Everything else was just research. He follows its evolution with a scholar's eye, and what emerges is a picture of the bicycle as a social phenomenon rather than just an interesting machine.

Cycling's Golden Age: Heroes of the Post-war Era, 1946–1967, Brett Horton and Owen Mulholland (VeloPress, 2006): Horton realized that someone needed to begin to track and collect the artifacts of cycling so that a Tour de France trophy doesn't wind up in a grandchild's attic gathering dust. His collection encompasses the full breadth of the sport's existence, and this volume tells the story of one period of the sport's immense history. The writer, Mulholland, is the perfect man for the job—a true cycling historian with a flair for the profound and dramatic. There isn't a richer presentation of cycling in print.

Paris–Roubaix: A Journey Through Hell, Philippe Bouvet, Pierre Callewaert, Jean-Luc Gatellier, and Laget Serge (VeloPress, 2007): There's a reason why Paris–Roubaix is the sport's greatest Classic. This amazing volume sells you on that idea in the first page and dazzles you with each successive one.

The Story of the Tour de France, Vol. 1 & 2, Bill and Carol McGann (Dog Ear Publishing, 2006, 2008): The McGanns have created the ultimate survey of the history of the Tour de France. Were the Tour de France taught in college, these would be the textbooks. Using novelistic techniques, a keen eye for characters and their motivations, an intimate understanding of the bicycle and racing strategy, not to mention tragedy with a capital *T*, the McGanns tease out only those details that are essential to the quest. Along the way, they weave in the World Wars, the economy, and the occasional social unrest. What emerges is a mythology that explains how all of Europe catches its breath each July.

Campagnolo, Paolo Facchinetti and Guido Rubino (VeloPress, 2008): No other manufacturer in cycling commands the awe and reverence that Campagnolo attracts. Campy's 75 years of manufacturing are celebrated here in rich color, and the reader sees that the company's history is the history of the bicycle itself.

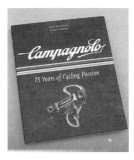

Photography

Landscapes of Cycling, Graham Watson (VeloPress, 2004): To most Americans, Graham Watson is the photographer of record for pro cycling. His long tenure at *VeloNews* has made his images our mind's-eye memory of the race itself. This retrospective runs the whole of his career, back to the time of Sean Kelly and Greg LeMond. The perfect starting point for Watson's work.

Tour de France: The 2005 Tour de France in Photography, James Startt (Cycle Publishing, 2006): Lance Armstrong's historic seventh Tour de France win came in 2005. Startt has been documenting Armstrong's exploits since the early 1990s, and this is a fine and original collection of photographs. Startt's take on photography carries the drama of the motion itself; these images are unforgettable. Any of his books are worth picking up.

Fiction

The Rider, Tim Krabbe, trans. Sam Garrett (Bloomsbury USA, 2003): There are a few works of fiction devoted to cycling. This one stands head and shoulders above the others. Krabbe explodes a single day, a single race, onto the page. His presentation is cinematic and at times surreal. With mere pages left, you'll be at the proverbial edge of your seat hoping he gets the win. Be sure to pick this up.

Science

Bicycling Science, David Gordon Wilson (MIT Press, 2004): Strictly for the geeks. Great fun at times, but surprisingly little light is shed on how a bicycle's geometry really determines its handling.

Law

Bicycling and the Law, Bob Mionske (VeloPress, 2007): Mionske is a former pro and two-time Olympian whose second act was a career as a lawyer. He writes a column for *VeloNews* on the law and authored this volume as a practical education into the rights and responsibilities every cyclist faces with regard to the law. Taken as a whole, Mionske has created a work that illustrates the bicycle's precarious place in American culture. Truly indispensable for any cyclist on the road.

For Kids

Mike and the Bike, Mike Ward, Bob Thomson and Phil Liggett (Cookie Jar Publishing, 2005): If you have your own team started or plan to in the future, this is the perfect book to present bicycling just the way you'd like to see your kids experience it. At once responsible and fun, it's a take on cycling for children that only a devout roadie could conjure. This book should accompany every children's bike sold.

Lexicon

A cyclist's vocabulary is equal parts technical terminology and insider slang. As with most communities, speaking the native tongue is half the key to acceptance.

A

Ad hoc training: This is what happens when you train without any plan; it usually results in too many hard days of riding and can lead to overtraining.

Allen wrench: Most of the bolts on a bicycle are adjusted using Allen wrenches. These hexagonally shaped wrenches come in a variety of sizes. The most common sizes used on bicycles are 2, 4, 5, 6, 8, and 10mm. More generically, these are also called hex keys.

Alloy: Most parts on a bicycle are made from aluminum alloy but may be referred to as just alloy in construction. If someone calls something alloy, what they mean is the part is made from aluminum. See also: aluminum.

Aluminum: Aluminum has been used to make bicycle frames for many years, though it gained its greatest acceptance in the last 20 years. Often it will be referred to by the specific designation of the alloy in use, such as 6061 or 7075. Frames made from aluminum are often more affordable than those made from titanium and carbon fiber and can even be less expensive than some steel bikes.

Ankling: Every rider has a unique pedal stroke. Where this becomes most apparent is in the movement of the foot as it travels through the pedal stroke. Whether a rider drops his heel, raises it, holds it steady, or uses some mixture of these movements, the action is referred to as ankling.

Arm warmers: These sleeves are made from heavy Roubaix Lycra and enable you to wear a short-sleeve jersey in cooler conditions, but because they are easily removable, you can take them off if the temperature rises.

Attack: In races and on competitive group rides, a sudden acceleration by someone at the front, especially one that sees a rider leave the group, is called an attack. See also: pain cave.

Au bloc: This is a French term that means going "all out." It's when you give everything you've got and can go no harder. You're most likely to hear it used by television commentators such as Paul Sherwen. Say it with a long O, *O-bloc*.

Axle: The axle passes through a wheel's hub and clamps into the dropouts. It remains stationary while the bearings turn on it.

B

Bearings: Bearings are used to allow certain components of the bicycle to turn or roll easily. They are used in the wheels, the headset, the freehub, the bottom bracket, and the pedals. Some bearings use loose balls, which must be adjusted, while others use precision-sealed bearings, which come in a cartridge and require no adjustment.

Bell bottoms: Cycling shorts that don't fit properly can cause chafing and are said to be bell bottoms.

Bib shorts: High-end cycling shorts often include suspenders to keep them in place while you ride, ensuring that the pad doesn't move and chafe you. By the way, the bibs go *under* the jersey.

Big ring: Riders will often refer to the large chainring as the big ring. It speaks to a hard effort.

Blowing up: This is a slang term for what happens when a rider exceeds his body's lactate threshold for too long. It goes by many names, including hitting the wall and detonating, but the feeling is the same for everyone.

Bonk: Your body stores energy in your muscles and liver. When you begin a ride there are stores enough for 2–3 hours of hard riding. If you don't refuel with drinks, bars, or other food on a ride, you can run out of the fuel—muscle glycogen—and when you do, you are said to bonk. Bonking can leave a rider irritable, confused, and almost unable to ride. It has one solution—calories. Bonking is also known as hitting the wall.

Bottom bracket (component): The bottom bracket is made up of two bearings and a spindle (or axle) to which the crankset is attached. It is inserted in the bottom bracket shell.

Bottom bracket height: Bottom bracket height is the distance from the center of the bottom bracket shell measured on a line that is perpendicular to the ground. Most road bikes have a bottom bracket height of 27cm; some bikes will be higher than this by a few millimeters for added stability, and some bikes can be 5–10mm lower than this for increased maneuverability.

Bottom bracket shell: The bottom bracket shell is located at the juncture of the seat tube, down tube, and chainstays. Its height above the ground (measured in centimeters) dictates much of a bike's handling characteristics.

Brake caliper: The brake calipers do much of the work of actually stopping a bike. They are mounted on the fork and the seatstays.

Brake pad: To stop a bicycle, two pads make contact with the rims of the wheels. Most are made from a rubbery compound, and riders who live in hilly or mountainous regions will need to replace them regularly.

Brazing: Steel bicycles are often built using a technique similar to how plumbing is assembled. In brazing, two tubes are mitered and then inserted into a fitting called a lug. A builder heats the joint with a torch and then feeds a rod of silver or brass into the hot joint to essentially glue the tubes to the lug. See also: lug.

Breakaway: If an individual or a small group of riders manages to ride away from the peloton during a group ride or race, the group in front is called a breakaway. Riding in a breakaway requires an all-in effort and suffering by the bushel but is cause for bragging rights afterward.

Broom wagon: This is the vehicle that follows at the back of a race and picks up riders who are too tired to continue.

Butted: When the end of a piece of tubing is thicker than its midsection, it is said to be butted. A tube that is butted at both ends is double-butted. The thin midsection of a double-butted tube reduces the amount of vibration that reaches a rider and cuts weight without sacrificing strength.

C

Cadence: The rate at which a rider pedals, as measured in rpm, is called the rider's cadence or pedal cadence. Most riders target a range of 90-105 rpm on the road.

Calf: The calf is made up of a pair of muscles that extend the foot during the pedal stroke, creating the motion that is referred to as ankling. See also: ankling.

Calorie: This is a measure of the amount of energy required to heat one gram of water one degree Celsius, and the primary way most people track food intake. The number of calories in a pound varies; one pound of muscle contains 600 calories, while one pound of fat contains 3,500 calories. There are 239 calories in one kilojoule.

Cantilever brake: This special brake is used most often on touring and cyclocross bikes. It can accommodate larger tires than standard caliper brakes can and offers excellent stopping power.

Car back: Riders at the back of a group have a duty to let the rest of the group know when a car is approaching from behind. The call is simple: "Car back." The appropriate response is to move as far as possible to the right to allow the car to pass.

Car up: When approaching turns, riders at the front will announce oncoming traffic that may delay the group from making its turn by a few seconds. The call is simple: "Car up." The appropriate response is to be ready to brake or even stop.

Carbon fiber: Carbon fiber is used to make an ever-increasing number of bicycle parts. Frames, forks, handlebars, stems, seatposts, wheels, bottle cages, and even derailleurs are made from the material. It can be used to make parts that are at once very stiff, lightweight, and yet fragile. Oh, and as expensive as a European vacation.

Cassette: This is the collection of cogs mounted on the rear wheel. Cassettes come in many configurations, with as few as 8 cogs or as many as 11. They also come in many different gear ratios, to accommodate a rider's use on flat land, hilly country, or the high mountains.

Center of gravity: The center of gravity is the point at which weight is centered. As a rider moves on the bike, shifting his hands from the drops to the bar tops or to the hoods and standing up, his center of gravity shifts and the way the bicycle handles will change.

Century: A century is a 100-mile ride. While it is possible to do a century on your own, it most commonly refers to an organized event with periodic rest stops, or sags. A 100km ride is referred to as a metric century.

Chain: The chain is what allows the action of a rider pedaling to turn the rear wheel. Modern derailleur bikes use a chain with a half-inch pitch. Most of these chains are ³⁄₃₂-inch wide.

Chainring: The gears attached to the crankset are called chainrings and are measured according to the number of teeth they possess. Road bikes generally have two of them. They are paired to allow precise shifting. The most popular combinations are 53-t with 39-t, and 50-t with 34-t.

Chainstay: On a bicycle frame, two tubes extend from the bottom bracket shell to the rear dropouts; these are the chainstays.

Chamois: Many years ago the pad sewn into cycling shorts was cut from chamois leather. Today the pad is made from foam and covered with polyester or other man-made fiber, and while some people refer to the insert as a pad, many people still call it a chamois.

Chamois cream: A chamois cream is a personal lubricant of a nonromantic nature. It can be very handy in preventing discomfort caused by chafing. Some riders apply it to the chamois, while others apply it strategically to themselves.

Chrome-moly: Technically, this refers to a kind of steel in which the alloy includes chromium and molybdenum. However, it is used as a catch-all term to denote almost any formulation of steel used in bicycle frames. In fact, top-quality steel tubing is alloyed with many different materials, from vanadium to niobium. See also: steel.

Clear: Because left-hand turns can pose a hazard for a group of cyclists, riders at the front are obligated to make sure there is no approaching traffic, call "clear" before entering the intersection, and lead others on through.

Cleat: Clipless pedals use a cleat attached to the bottom of a cycling shoe that allow it to engage in the pedal, giving the rider a secure attachment to the pedal for superior power transfer and control.

Contact point: A cyclist has three contact points with a bicycle: the handlebar, the saddle and the pedals. It is through these three points that a rider controls the bicycle's direction and speed.

Control levers: The two levers mounted on the handlebars of most road bicycles control both braking and shifting.

Crankset: A crankset consists of two crank arms, left and right. The right one features five arms called the spider, to which the chainrings are bolted. Cranksets come in a variety of lengths; the length is selected according to the rider's leg length. The most common lengths are 170mm, 172.5mm, and 175mm. Some manufacturers offer cranks as short as 165mm and as long as 180mm.

Curfew: The prenegotiated time by which a rider has been ordered to be home by a significant other. See also: hall pass.

Cycling shoes: For greatest comfort and efficiency, cyclists wear special shoes that feature a stiff sole for efficient power transfer, a strong upper with either leather or plastic straps, and a cleat fixed to the bottom of the shoe that engages the pedal.

Cyclocomputer: A cyclocomputer uses a sensor mounted on a chainstay or fork blade that can detect a magnet attached to a wheel's spoke as it passes. This data gets reported in a digital readout on the cyclocomputer. At minimum, a cyclocomputer will include the following features: present speed, odometer, trip distance, elapsed time, average speed, and maximum speed.

Cyclocross: Held in the fall and winter, cyclocross races are cycling's answer to the steeplechase. Riders compete on a primarily off-road course and periodically dismount the bike, pick it up, and run over barriers before remounting the bike.

Cyclocross bike: A cyclocross bike is similar to a standard road bike, though the frame has several features specific to its use. Generally, the gearing is lower, the frame offers greater tire clearance so that wide tires can be used in muddy conditions, and cantilever brakes are used to give the bike excellent braking without crowding the tires.

D

Density: Density is a material's relationship to gravity. Expressed as pounds per cubic foot, the higher a material's density, the heavier it is. Of the three metals used in frame building, steel is the most dense. Second is titanium and aluminum is the least dense.

Derailleur, front: The front derailleur moves the chain among the different chainrings on the crankset. It is operated by a cable that runs from the left control lever.

Derailleur, rear: The rear derailleur moves the chain between the different cogs on the cassette. It is operated by a cable that runs from the right control lever.

Domestique: This French term translates as "house boy" or "errand boy." *Domestiques* are the worker bees of the professional teams. They shelter the team leader from the wind, fetch food and bottles, and either remove or retrieve jackets, vests, or other clothing when requested. The job is the very definition of unglamorous.

Down tube: The tube that runs from the bottom of the head tube to the bottom bracket shell is called the down tube.

Drafting: Drafting means riding close behind another rider. A draft is a reduction in wind resistance and can be felt as far away as 6 feet, but it becomes progressively more pronounced as the rider closes the gap to the rear wheel of the rider ahead. A rider can conserve one-third of his energy by drafting off another rider.

Drive-side: Looking down at the bike from the rider's perspective, this is everything on the right side of the bicycle, everything on the side with the drivetrain. The chainrings, derailleurs, freehub, and cassette are all designed for use on this side of the bicycle.

Dropouts: The wheels are clamped into the frame and fork at special tabs made to accept the wheels' axles and quick-release skewers. There are two at the rear of the frame to hold the rear wheel in plane with the frame and two more at the end of the fork blades to hold the front wheel in place with the fork.

Dropped: When a rider loses contact with a fast-moving group, he is said to be dropped.

E

Elongation: Elongation is the measure of a frame material's ductility— its ability to stretch without breaking. If a tube can't stretch at all, it is brittle and could break easily. Of the three metals used in frame building, titanium has the greatest elongation, while aluminum has the least, with steel coming in the middle.

Embrocation: In cold or wet conditions cyclist may sometimes massage a warming cream into their legs rather than wear tights or knee/leg warmers. The approach is popular with European pros. Also known as a Belgian knee warmer.

Existential crisis: This is what happens when you are so overtrained that you begin to wonder why you ever took up cycling.

F

False flat: Gentle grades of 1 or 2 percent are frequently referred to as false flats because though they look practically flat, they have a distinct effect on a rider's effort.

Fast-twitch muscle fiber: This is the muscle fiber that is called into use in short, powerful bursts, such as sprinting.

Fatigue strength: This is the point at which a repeatedly flexed tube fails. Steel and titanium are said to have nearly unlimited fatigue strength. However, aluminum has a finite fatigue strength and will fail after repeated flexing.

Fixed gear: A bicycle in which the rear wheel's cog is fixed to the wheel—meaning the bicycle cannot coast without pedal movement—is said to have a fixed gear.

Fork: One of the two elements of a frameset, the fork features a steerer tube that passes through the frame's head tube, a crown from which the fork blades extend, and then dropouts at the end of each fork blade into which the front wheel is clamped.

Fork rake: This is the offset, measured in millimeters, between the axis of the fork's steerer tube and the center of the dropout. More fork rake will make the bicycle steer more quickly. Less fork rake slows the bicycle's handling. Road bikes generally use a fork with between 40 and 50mm of rake.

Frame: One of the two elements of a frameset, the frame is the single most important element of a bicycle and determines more than any other component just how a bicycle will ride. It is composed of eight tubes: head tube, top tube, down tube, seat tube, two chainstays, and two seatstays, plus two dropouts, one at each of the intersection points between the seatstays and chainstays.

Frameset: Generally a frame is sold with a matching fork if a rider doesn't purchase a complete bicycle. The combination of frame and fork is referred to as a frameset. Sometimes a frameset will include a headset and/or a seatpost.

Fred: This term is a rather sophomoric way to refer to an inexperienced rider. Such a rider is usually viewed as a potential hazard within the peloton.

Freehub: The freehub is the mechanism that allows any bike equipped with derailleurs to coast. The mechanism features a ratchet and pawls that allow the wheel to turn without forcing the cogs to spin with the wheel.

Freewheel: Any time a rider coasts, he is said to freewheel. It also refers to an out-of-date mechanism that placed the ratchet mechanism within the group of cogs. The freewheel then screwed onto the rear wheel.

Front center: This is one of the dimensions a frame builder considers when designing a bike. It is the distance from the center of the bottom bracket to the center of the fork's dropouts. On small bikes this distance can be so short that toe overlap can occur. See also: toe overlap.

G

Gap: The distance from a rider's front wheel to the rear wheel of the rider ahead is called the gap. The gap isn't an issue unless that distance grows to the length of a bicycle or more. Riders will often call out "close the gap." See also: dropped.

Geometry: The relationship of each of a frame's tube lengths and design angles to each other is said to be a bike's geometry. A bike's geometry determines how it will handle and fit.

Gloves: Cycling gloves serve several functions. They insulate the hands from road shock as well as protect them in the event of a crash and give you someplace to wipe your face when you sweat.

Glucose: This simple sugar (a starch, in fact) is what your muscles use as fuel to operate.

Glutes: The glutes are made up of three muscles, and they provide the shape of the buttocks. The strongest muscles in the body, they help extend the thigh in the power phase of the pedal stroke.

Glycogen: The food you eat to power your bike rides is broken down in digestion into glycogen. Glycogen is how energy is packed until it is broken down into glucose. See also: glucose.

GPS (Global Positioning System): GPS is a navigation system based on a global network of satellites that gives the user his precise location and speed. It's ideal for cycling as it can show a rider's position on a map as well as speed and elevation, among other details.

Grade: The pitch of an uphill or downhill is called grade or gradient. It is not the same thing as angle. Grades are expressed as a percentage. A 1 percent grade means that for every 100 feet traveled horizontally, the road climbs 1 foot vertically. There are no 100 percent roads because that would mean that for every foot forward the road traveled, the road also climbed 1 foot vertically—a 45-degree angle.

Gran fondo: This Italian phrase means "big ride." These are long recreational rides that are timed. For many riders, they serve as a low-key form of racing that also allows them to enjoy long, challenging courses as found in century rides. In the U.S., the typical *gran fondo* is roughly 100 miles.

Grand Tour: There are three Grand Tours: the Tour de France, the Tour of Italy, and the Tour of Spain. They last three weeks and will dominate a cyclist's evenings as he watches them on TV. See also: TiVo.

Grand touring bike: These bikes feature relatively calm handling and a slightly higher bar position than the average sport (racing) bike. They are suited to long rides and draw their geometry from the designs that used to dominate the Grand Tours.

H

Half-wheel: In a double paceline, riders are expected to ride side-by-side. Any rider who rides ahead of or behind the rider next to him throws off the pairing of riders behind him and is said to half-wheel.

Hall pass: Cycling is a time-intensive sport, and many riders who put in 12 or more hours per week on the bike will speak of the hall pass they negotiated with their significant other. See also: curfew.

Hamstrings: The group of muscles that make up the back of the thigh are called the hamstrings. They are responsible for a great deal of the power a rider generates when in the saddle.

Handlebar: The handlebar is one of a rider's three contact points with the bicycle. It is where a rider rests his hands and how he controls the bike. The control levers are mounted on the handlebar, which generally offers three comfortable hand positions: the tops, the hoods, and the drops.

Head tube: The head tube is the shortest tube in a frame and contains two bearings called the headset, which allow the fork to turn freely and the bicycle to steer.

Head tube angle: A bicycle's head tube angle is the acute angle between the ground plane and the axis of the head tube. It helps to determine how quickly a bicycle will steer. The vast majority of all road bikes are built with a head tube angle between 72 and 75 degrees. A steeper head tube angle will cause a bike to handle more quickly, while a slacker angle will make the steering calmer.

Headset: These two bearings are mounted at the top and bottom of the head tube. The fork's steerer tube passes through them, enabling the fork to turn and the bicycle to steer.

Helmet: Other than the bicycle itself, this piece of safety equipment is the only truly necessary piece of equipment a cyclist needs when riding. See also: TBI.

Hub: Each wheel has a hub to which the spokes are laced. The hub's job is to support the bearings the axle passes through. The rear hub also includes the freehub, which allows a rider to coast on a bicycle. See also: freehub.

I

Individual time trial: Also known as the race of truth, this form of racing is generally the safest, in that it pits the rider against the clock. Riders leave the start line one-by-one (usually at 1-minute intervals), and whoever rides the fastest over the given distance wins.

J

Jersey: The shirts that cyclists wear are called jerseys. They are typically made from polyester (though some are merino wool) and have a long zipper in the front and three pockets in the back to hold food, ID, cash, and a cell phone.

K

Kilojoule: This is a measure of work and is often used to express the amount of energy a rider has burned as measured by a wattage device. A kilojoule is 1,000 joules; a single joule is the amount of work necessary to produce 1 watt for 1 second.

Knee warmers: Not to be confused with Belgian knee warmers, knee warmers are essentially snug-fitting leggings that cover the leg from midthigh to midcalf. They are made from Roubaix Lycra and extend the temperature range in which cycling shorts can be worn comfortably.

Ksi: Thousands of pounds per square inch.

KOPS: This stands for Knee Over Pedal Spindle. Most fitting systems work from the belief that positioning a rider's knee directly over the pedal spindle (when the left pedal is in the 9 o'clock position) reduces stress on the knee while helping the rider generate optimal power.

L

Lactate threshold: As a rider pedals, his muscles produce lactic acid. It is flushed away from the muscles by the bloodstream. The harder someone rides, the faster lactic acid is produced. Once the workload reaches a certain critical point, the body produces lactic acid faster than the bloodstream can flush it away. This point is the lactate threshold. Even highly trained individuals can only ride above this point for a finite period of time. Judicious training can move this number up, enabling someone to ride harder for a longer period of time. See also: blowing up.

Lanterne rouge: This French term is used to denote the rider who is last place overall in the Tour de France. Literally it means "red lantern," and the name comes from the red light that used to hang above the vehicle that picked up riders who quit the Tour. Among friends it is often used as an encouraging moniker for a slower rider who refuses to give up. See also: broom wagon.

Left-hand thread: Most threaded parts in the world feature right-hand threads, meaning to screw them in, they must be turned clockwise. Left-hand threads are tightened with counterclockwise turns. Two parts, the left pedal and the right (drive side) bottom bracket cup, feature left-hand threads.

Leg warmers: Snug-fitting leggings that cover the leg from midthigh to ankle. They are made from Roubaix Lycra and extend the temperature range in which cycling shorts can be worn comfortably.

Levers: See control levers.

Light up: When a group approaches a traffic light, should the light be yellow and turning red or already red, it is the responsibility of the riders at the front, who can most easily see ahead, to call out "light up" to alert the other riders of the need to stop. Generally, the call "light up" will precede the call "stopping."

Limit screw: Front and rear derailleurs each feature two limit screws that adjust how close to the frame and how far from the frame the derailleur may travel. The screws that adjust how close to the frame the derailleur moves are called the low-gear set screws because the small chainring and largest cassette cog are closest to the center plane of the bicycle. The screws that adjust how far from the frame the derailleur moves are called the high-gear set screws because the large chainring and smallest cassette cog are farthest from the center plane of the bicycle.

Line (a rider's line): The ability to ride a highly maneuverable road bike in a straight line is considered an elemental skill in cycling. A cyclist who can ride this way is said to be able to "hold his line." If a rider veers suddenly while in a group, other riders are likely to shout, "Hold your line!"

Liniment: This is another name for an embrocation.

Lug: A lug is a joint used to join two (or more) steel tubes together. Some framebuilders prefer to work with lugs because of the degree of control they can exercise over fit as well as allowing them to express their artistry by shaping the points of the lugs.

Lycra: Once the domain of rock stars, this ultra-stretchy material was first put to use in cycling shorts back in the 1980s and has been the backbone of all great cycling shorts ever since.

M

Macrocycle: A large block of training usually lasting nine to twelve weeks.

Mass-start event: A mass-start event is any cycling event with a predetermined start time. All riders in that event or that heat will start following a starter's gun. Races such as road races and criteriums are mass-start, as are *gran fondos*.

Maximum heart rate: The maximum rate at which your heart can beat. It is determined by age and genetics, and for older riders, their history in sport; people who have been athletic their whole lives tend to have higher max heart rates. It is not an important determiner of athletic potential.

Microcycle: A brief block of training usually lasting four to seven days.

Monuments: There are five one-day races that comprise the five Monuments. They are Milan–San Remo (Italy), the Tour of Flanders (Belgium), Paris–Roubaix (France), Liège–Bastogne–Liège (Belgium), and the Tour of Lombardy (Italy). These are the most important and prestigious cycling events next to the three Grand Tours. A rider who wins one of these is remembered for life.

N

Newbie: This is a much more polite way to refer to a new rider than Fred. A newbie is a rider who stands out due to incomplete knowledge about the sport, whether the gap is in riding skills, etiquette, or appearance. Being called a newbie is less an insult than an acknowledgement that life will be easier once the learning curve flattens out a bit.

Nondrive-side: Looking down at the bike from the rider's perspective, this is everything on the left side of the bicycle, everything on the side opposite the drive train.

O

On the rivet: The phrase "on the rivet" refers to when a rider is going especially hard and slides forward on his saddle. It used to be that a saddle had a rivet at its nose and when a rider slid forward he would literally be sitting on the rivet. If someone says he was on the rivet, he was going as hard as he could.

OTB: This phrase is short for "off the back" (of the group), meaning the rider couldn't keep up with the pace of the pack. See also: dropped.

Overtraining: A deep state of prolonged fatigue that can last for more than a week is referred to as overtraining. It is most easily achieved by exuberant and ambitious racers with an abundance of free time. See also: existential crisis.

P

Paceline: A paceline is a group of riders following each other in a line and taking turns at the front of the group in order to share the workload of riding at a given speed. A group working together in this way can ride faster for longer than any one of the riders could on his own.

Pack: This is a large group of riders that doesn't rotate in an organized fashion the way a paceline does. See also: *peloton*.

Pain cave: The pain cave is where you might find yourself following a particularly violent attack by another rider.

Patron: This French term denotes the alpha-male of the group. A *patron* is a dominant rider who is not only among the very fastest riders, but also asserts his will on the pack. Eddy Merckx, Bernard Hinault, and Lance Armstrong were legendary *patrons*. Miguel Indurain not so much. Say it with a long O and the accent on the second syllable, just like the tequila.

Pedal: The pedals are one of a rider's three contact points with the bicycle. The pedals are not only how a rider drives the chain to power the bicycle, but they offer the rider the greatest control over his weight distribution on the bicycle. Most pedals today are clipless, meaning they do not use toe clips to fix the rider's feet to the pedals.

Instead, they feature a spring-loaded retention system that locks the rider's feet to the pedals but release with a simple outward twist of the heel.

Peloton: This French term translates into English as "platoon" and denotes a large group of cyclists. In racing it refers to the main group of riders.

Polyester: The vast majority of all cycling jerseys are made from this man-made fiber. It is highly breathable, wicks sweat away from the body, and can be sublimated to display designs and sponsor logos.

Power: See wattage.

Power meter: A power meter is a type of cyclocomputer that measures the power—wattage—a cyclist puts out as he pedals. It does this via special gauges contained within the rear hub, bottom bracket, or pedals. See also: wattage.

PSI: Pounds per square inch

Pull, pulling: When a rider leads a pack or paceline he is said to be "taking a pull" or "pulling." You can compliment a rider by saying "nice pull."

Pulling off: When a rider finishes a pull the proper thing to do is to move to the left or the right of the group before slowing down. This is "pulling off."

Q

Quadriceps: Simply referred to as the quads, this is a large group of muscles at the front of the thigh. They are very handy for sprinting and other out-of-the-saddle efforts.

Quick-release skewers: The wheels are clamped to the dropouts by quick-release skewers. The skewers are tightened by cam-actuated levers that increase clamping force as they are closed. A properly closed quick-release skewer will point in toward the center plane of the frame.

R

Red kite prayer: In the last kilometer of a race, riders will often look straight down as they summon the last of their strength for a final effort to reach the line; this is a red kite prayer.

Right-hand thread: All but two threaded parts on a bicycle feature traditional right-hand threads. To screw them in, they must be turned clockwise.

Rim: The portion of the wheel onto which the tire is mounted and the brakes squeeze. It is held in place by tensioned spokes.

Road rash: Most bicycle crashes occur while a rider is moving and as a result there is usually some sliding involved. Road rash is the name for the abrasions that a rider receives. See also: Tegaderm.

Rolling: Riders at the front of a group will often call out "rolling" when entering an intersection if the light has turned yellow, as a way to let riders in back know their intention to continue through the intersection.

Roubaix Lycra: This heavy Lycra features a brushed, fleecy finish on the inside while retaining a smooth finish on the outside. It can be found most often in arm, leg, and knee warmers. It is named for the city in which the race Paris–Roubaix (one of the five Monuments) finishes.

S

Saddle (or seat): The saddle is one of a rider's three contact points with the bicycle.

Sag: Stops along the course of an organized ride, such as a century, are called sags. They are usually equipped with lots of food and water, and sometimes drink mixes and even soda.

Seat tube: The seat tube extends from the bottom bracket shell to the intersection of the top tube and seatstays. On older steel frames, the seat tube length was one of the indicators of a frame's potential fit.

Seat tube angle: A bicycle's seat tube angle is the acute angle between the ground plane and the axis of the seat tube. It helps to determine how a bicycle will fit a rider. The vast majority of all road bikes are built with a seat tube angle between 72 and 75 degrees.

Seatpost: The seatpost is a component to which the saddle is mounted and extends into the frame's seat tube. Saddle height is set by either raising or lowering the seatpost.

Seatstays: The seatstays are the two tubes that run from the top of the seat tube (or near it) down to where they meet the chainstays at the dropouts. They are the smallest, thinnest tubes in a frame.

Shifter: See control lever.

Shorts: Cycling shorts are critical to a pleasant cycling experience. The key to a good pair of shorts is the pad, or chamois, that places the cushioning right where a cyclist needs it. The stretchy shorts hold the pad in place and reduce chafing. See also: bib shorts.

Skirt: When a cyclist wears a jersey that is so long it covers his rear and catches on the saddle, the jersey gets called a skirt.

Slow-twitch muscle fiber: This is the muscle fiber that is called into use for lower-intensity repeated use.

Slumming it: Taking it easy and riding at the back of the pack.

Snot rocket: Riding hard can not only cause a rider to sweat, but it can make for a runny nose as well. Riders will frequently close one nostril with a free hand, aim down and give a hard blow. Aiming down is critical to keeping the riders behind happy.

Spoke: Spokes help give wheels shape by securing the rim to the hub. The spokes are spaced evenly and tensioned to give the wheel strength and consistent handling.

Spoke nipple: In most wheels, small nuts called spoke nipples are inserted into the rim and threaded onto the spokes in order to give the wheel shape and strength under tension.

Sport bike: Of the various types of road bikes, sport bikes are the ones used for racing and feature the sharpest, most agile handling.

Squirrel, squirrelly: If a rider has difficulty holding his line or following a line in a group, he is said to be squirrelly.

Stem: The stem attaches the handlebar to the fork's steerer tube. To help size a bicycle to the rider, stems come in a variety of lengths. The most common ones are 80, 90, 100, 110, 120, and 130mm.

Steel: More bicycle frames have been made from steel than any other frame material. There are nearly countless formulations for steel, so it may also be referred to as 4130 or chrome-moly. The material is very strong and can give a custom builder a palette with which to create an artful bike.

Stiffness: More properly known as Young's Modulus (E), the modulus of elasticity tells just how stiff a frame material is. Tubes drawn from different materials to the same dimensions will vary in stiffness. Young's Modulus quantifies that difference.

Sunscreen: Because cyclists can spend 2 hours or more per day in the sun, sunscreen is an indispensable element in good skin care. It also happens to be a great way to get grease off of hands, should they get dirty when fixing a flat.

T

TBI: This is the abbreviation for "traumatic brain injury," which is what can happen if a rider hits his head during an accident. A concussion is one of several kinds of TBIs. A helmet can't completely prevent a TBI, but it will lessen the severity of one. Repeated TBIs are known to cause cognitive and emotional disturbances in people.

Team time trial: In the Grand Tours, teams often compete in a time trial where the nine riders will work together, riding in a paceline. The finishing time is usually taken when the rear wheel of the fifth rider crosses the line.

Tegaderm: Tegaderm is a clear bandage that can be used to cover road rash wounds. It speeds healing and does not require frequent changing like gauze pads. If cyclists were songwriters, there would be love songs devoted to Tegaderm.

TIG welding: This stands for "tungsten inert gas welding." It is one of the primary methods used for joining tubes when building a frame out of steel, titanium, or aluminum. An electric arc is used to join the two sections of tubing together by fusing the two tubes together one pinpoint zap at a time.

Time trial: Time trials come in two forms: individual and team. Individual time trials are far more common than team time trials, but a team time trial can be a spectacular event to watch on TV or in person. See also: individual time trial and team time trial.

Time trial bike: A time trial bike is a road bike optimized with aerodynamic equipment. The most advanced time trial bikes will feature specially shaped frames, special aerodynamic wheels, and aerodynamic bars, and will place the rider in an especially aerodynamic position.

Tire, clincher: The majority of all bicycle tires made are clinchers. They feature a center tread, sidewalls, and a bead that secures the tire to the rim once the tube is inflated.

Tire, tubular: A tubular tire is a special tire used almost exclusively by racers. It is also referred to as a sew-up because the tire casing is literally sewn around the tube. Tubulars must be glued to special tubular rims. They are valued for their supple ride and cornering performance. They are, however, difficult to change in the event of a flat.

Titanium: Titanium is an excellent material for frame construction due to its corrosion resistance and high strength; it's nearly indestructible as a result. It is often referred to by its composition; 3/2.5 means the alloy is 94.5 percent titanium with 3 percent aluminum and 2.5 percent vanadium. Less common is 6/4, which means the alloy is composed of 90 percent titanium with 6 percent aluminum and 4 percent vanadium. Titanium doesn't make for cheap frames, unfortunately.

TiVo: In the homes of cyclists, this television recording device will usually be found to be at capacity with the Monuments and stages of the Tour de France.

Toe clip: Prior to the advent of clipless pedals, toe clips combined with a toe strap were used to secure a rider's foot to the pedal. Clipless pedals are called clipless because they lack a toe clip.

Toe overlap: On relatively small-framed bicycles, sometimes the front center of a bicycle will be short enough that the front of a rider's shoe can make contact with the front wheel. While the contact can be disconcerting, the front wheel never turns enough for it to occur at normal riding speeds.

Top tube: The top tube extends from the top of the head tube to the top of the seat tube. The length of a frame's top tube is one of a bicycle's greatest indicators of a frame's potential fit. See also: virtual top tube.

Touring bike: A touring bike is the backpacker of the cycling world. A fully outfitted touring bike can carry four bags called panniers, plus a handlebar bag. Though heavy, a touring bike offers the rider exceptional independence.

Town-line sprint: Many training rides will feature a sprint to the sign that designates a town line, or some other easily noticeable landmark.

Track: See velodrome.

Track bike: A track bike is the simplest of all bicycles. It features no brakes, no lever, and no derailleurs, and has but one direct-drive gear, making it what is called a fixed-gear bicycle. If the bicycle is moving, the pedals are turning; there is no coasting.

Track stand: A track stand is the act of balancing on a bicycle while at a standstill. Its name comes from the use of the technique in sprint events on the track, but roadies find it handy to use at stop lights to make a quick getaway.

Trail: The combination of a bicycle's head tube angle and its fork rake results in what is called trail. It is the difference between the point where the steering axis meets the ground and the point where a line perpendicular to the front wheel's axis meets the ground. Trail is expressed in centimeters. More trail means calmer handling while less trail means greater agility. Most road bikes will have between 5.6 and 6.2cm of trail.

Training cycles: The body gets stronger as a result of periods of stress followed by periods of recovery. This cycle works at the micro level as with an interval workout, as well as on the macro level by planning weeks of hard work followed by a week of rest. It also works on a super-macro level with months of hard work followed by a month of recovery.

Tube: Clincher tires require an inner tube in order to be inflated. Tubes come in a variety of diameters, widths, and valve lengths based on the wheel diameter, tire width, and rim depth.

U

Über-geek: Any cyclist who can produce more facts about bicycles than watts is considered an über-geek. See also: author's bio.

Ultimate tensile strength (UTS): This is the absolute strength of a tube, the point at which so much force has been applied that it simply breaks, measured in ksi. It determines how thin a tube can be, and therefore, how light a steel, titanium, or aluminum frame can be.

V

Velodrome: Also called the track, a velodrome is a special venue for bicycle races featuring a short loop generally either 250 or 333 meters long (though other lengths do exist) and featuring a banked surface.

Virtual top tube: Today, with most frames featuring a sloping top tube, frame size will be determined by the "virtual" length of a top tube, a measurement taken from the center of the seat tube to the center of the top tube on a line parallel to the ground plane.

VO$_2$ max: This number is a measure of how quickly your body can process oxygen. It is a number determined by genetics, and unlike lactate threshold or power, it is not a number that a relatively healthy person can change.

W

Wattage: Wattage is an absolute measure of the power a cyclist puts out. It is the clearest indicator of just how strong a cyclist is and can also be one of the leading indicators of overtraining by showing falling wattage numbers through continued training. Wattage is equal to work divided by time or Joules per second.

Weight weenie: The most obvious objective measure of a bike's superiority is its weight. Weight, however isn't the only important feature of a bicycle, and a rider overly concerned with a bike's weight is called a "weight weenie."

Wheel: Sizes include: 700C, 650B, 650C.

Wheel-sucker: In the spirit of camaraderie, sharing the workload among the riders on a hard ride is expected. Any rider who avoids taking pulls and, instead, sits on the wheel of another rider is called a "wheel-sucker."

Wheelbase: The distance from the center of the rear dropouts to the center of the front dropouts, measured on a line parallel to the ground plane is a bicycle's wheelbase. Most road bikes will have a wheelbase within +/−5cm of 100 cm. The shorter a bike's wheelbase, the greater its agility. The longer a bike's wheelbase, the calmer its handling.

X

X: Cyclocross is often referred to as 'cross, or sometimes just as "X."

Y

Yield strength: This is the force required (measured in ksi) to bend a tube permanently.

Z

Zinc oxide: Because sunscreen can run when a rider gets sweaty, zinc oxides that dry clear can be a better way to protect the face.

Appendix

A. The Trail-o-Matic

A number of factors determine how a bicycle handles. Bottom bracket height, wheelbase length, and trail are the three most influential factors. However, manufacturers almost never give trail figures; you're lucky if you can get both head tube angle and fork rake. You can use the chart below to better compare the geometry of various bicycles. Generally, the "sweet spot" for road bike handling (where the bike feels racing-bike-quick without feeling skittish) is believed to be around 5.9cm, though the higher the bottom bracket, the more a bike's trail must decrease to keep handling sharp.

FORK RAKE

HEAD TUBE ANGLE	3.3	3.4	3.5	3.6	3.7	3.8	3.9	4.0	4.1	4.2	4.3	4.4	4.5	4.6	4.7	4.8	4.9	5.0	5.1	5.2	5.3	5.4	5.5	HEAD TUBE ANGLE
70	8.86	8.76	8.65	8.54	8.44	8.33	8.22	8.12	8.01	7.91	7.80	7.69	7.59	7.48	7.37	7.27	7.16	7.05	6.95	6.84	6.73	6.63	6.52	70
70.5	8.54	8.44	8.33	8.22	8.12	8.01	7.91	7.80	7.69	7.59	7.48	7.37	7.27	7.16	7.05	6.95	6.84	6.73	6.63	6.52	6.42	6.31	6.21	70.5
71	8.22	8.12	8.01	7.91	7.80	7.69	7.59	7.48	7.37	7.27	7.16	7.05	6.95	6.84	6.73	6.63	6.52	6.42	6.31	6.21	6.10	6.00	5.89	71
71.5	7.90	7.79	7.69	7.58	7.47	7.37	7.26	7.16	7.05	6.95	6.84	6.74	6.63	6.53	6.42	6.31	6.21	6.10	6.00	5.89	5.79	5.68	5.58	71.5
72	7.58	7.47	7.37	7.26	7.16	7.05	6.95	6.84	6.74	6.63	6.53	6.42	6.31	6.21	6.10	6.00	5.90	5.79	5.68	5.58	5.47	5.37	5.26	72
72.5	7.26	7.16	7.05	6.95	6.84	6.74	6.63	6.53	6.42	6.31	6.21	6.10	6.00	5.89	5.79	5.68	5.58	5.48	5.38	5.28	5.17	5.06	4.96	72.5
73	6.94	6.84	6.73	6.63	6.53	6.42	6.32	6.21	6.11	6.00	5.90	5.79	5.69	5.58	5.48	5.38	5.28	5.17	5.06	4.96	4.85	4.75	4.64	73
73.5	6.63	6.53	6.42	6.32	6.21	6.11	6.00	5.90	5.80	5.69	5.59	5.48	5.38	5.27	5.17	5.07	4.96	4.86	4.75	4.65	4.54	4.44	4.34	73.5
74	6.32	6.21	6.11	6.00	5.90	5.80	5.69	5.59	5.48	5.38	5.27	5.17	5.07	4.96	4.86	4.75	4.65	4.54	4.44	4.34	4.24	4.13	4.03	74
74.5	6.00	5.90	5.80	5.69	5.59	5.49	5.38	5.28	5.17	5.07	4.97	4.86	4.76	4.66	4.55	4.45	4.34	4.24	4.14	4.03	3.92	3.83	3.72	74.5
75	5.69	5.59	5.49	5.38	5.28	5.18	5.07	4.97	4.87	4.76	4.66	4.56	4.45	4.35	4.24	4.14	4.04	3.93	3.83	3.73	3.62	3.52	3.42	75
75.5	5.38	5.28	5.18	5.07	4.97	4.87	4.76	4.66	4.56	4.45	4.35	4.25	4.14	4.04	3.94	3.84	3.73	3.63	3.53	3.42	3.32	3.22	3.11	75.5
76	5.08	4.97	4.87	4.77	4.66	4.56	4.46	4.35	4.25	4.15	4.05	3.94	3.84	3.74	3.63	3.53	3.43	3.32	3.22	3.12	3.01	2.91	2.81	76
	3.3	3.4	3.5	3.6	3.7	3.8	3.9	4.0	4.1	4.2	4.3	4.4	4.5	4.6	4.7	4.8	4.9	5.0	5.1	5.2	5.3	5.4	5.5	

FORK RAKE

Courtesy Bill McGann, bikeraceinfo.com

B. Gear-Repetition Charts

The following tables show how gears get repeated in drivetrains and demonstrate why a compact drivetrain offers more practical gearing for the average cyclist: It eliminates a number of repeated gears found in a triple while giving riders a broader range of gears than available with a standard 53/39 combination.

Shaded areas indicate gear duplication. Each redundant gear cuts the number of different gears a drivetrain offers the rider.

Gear inches for traditional gearing

	# OF CHAINRING TEETH	
	39	**53**
23	45.8	62.2
21	50.1	68.1
19	55.4	75.3
18	58.5	79.5
17	61.9	84.2
16	65.8	89.4
15	70.2	95.4
14	75.2	102.2
13	81.0	110.1
12	87.8	119.3

(# OF CASSETTE COG TEETH)

Gear inches for 53/39/30 triple combination—6 overlapping gears

	# OF CHAINRING TEETH		
	30	**39**	**53**
27	29.3	38.1	51.8
24	33.0	42.9	58.3
21	37.7	49.0	66.6
19	41.7	54.1	73.6
17	46.6	60.5	82.2
15	52.8	68.6	93.2
14	56.5	73.5	99.9
13	60.9	79.1	107.5
12	66.0	85.7	116.5
11	71.9	93.5	127.1

(# OF CASSETTE COG TEETH)

Gear inches for 53/42/30 triple combination—9 overlapping gears

	# OF CHAINRING TEETH		
	30	**42**	**53**
27	30.0	42.0	53.0
24	33.8	47.2	59.6
21	38.6	54.0	68.1
19	42.6	59.7	75.3
17	47.6	66.7	84.2
15	54.0	75.6	95.4
14	57.9	81.0	102.2
13	62.3	87.2	110.1
12	67.5	94.5	119.3
11	73.6	103.1	130.1

(# OF CASSETTE COG TEETH)

Gear inches for 52/42/32 triple—5 overlapping gears

	# OF CHAINRING TEETH		
	32	**42**	**52**
27	31.3	41.0	50.8
24	35.2	46.2	57.2
21	40.2	52.8	65.3
19	44.4	58.3	72.2
17	49.7	65.2	80.7
15	52.8	69.2	85.7
14	56.3	73.9	91.5
13	60.3	79.1	98.0
12	64.9	85.2	105.5
11	70.3	92.3	114.3

(# OF CASSETTE COG TEETH)

Gear inches for 50/34 compact gearing—
2 and 3 overlapping gears, respectively

 # OF CHAINRING TEETH

# OF CASSETTE COG TEETH	34	50
23	38.8	57.1
1	42.5	62.6
9	47.0	69.2
17	52.6	77.3
16	55.8	82.1
15	59.6	87.6
4	63.8	93.9
13	68.7	101.1
12	74.5	109.5
11	81.2	119.5

 # OF CHAINRING TEETH

# OF CASSETTE COG TEETH	34	50
28	31.9	46.9
25	35.7	52.6
23	38.8	57.1
21	42.5	62.6
9	47.0	69.2
7	52.6	77.3
5	59.6	87.6
3	68.7	101.1
2	74.5	109.5
11	81.2	119.5

Speed in mph for each gear combination at 100 rpm

 # OF CHAINRING TEETH

# OF CASSETTE COG TEETH	34	50
23	11.6	17.1
21	12.7	18.7
19	14.0	20.7
17	15.7	23.1
16	16.7	24.5
15	17.8	26.2
14	19.1	28.0
13	20.5	30.2
12	22.2	32.7
11	24.3	35.7

c. Gear-Range Chart

This chart will give you some insight into how different gear combinations compare and help you in choosing the appropriate cassette for your local terrain.

Legend:
- 53/39 chainring options
- 50/34 compact chainring options
- Third (triple) chainring option

CHAINRING	COG	GEAR INCHES
30	27	30.00
30	25	32.40
34	28	32.79
34	27	34.00
30	23	35.22
34	25	36.72
30	21	38.57
39	27	39.00
34	23	39.91
39	25	42.12
30	19	42.63
34	21	43.71
30	18	45.00
39	23	45.78
30	17	47.65
34	19	48.32
50	27	50.00
39	21	50.14
34	18	51.00
53	27	53.00
50	25	54.00
34	17	54.00
39	19	55.42
53	25	57.24
34	16	57.38
39	18	58.50
50	23	58.70
34	15	61.20
39	17	61.94
53	23	62.22

CHAINRING	COG	GEAR INCHES
50	21	64.29
34	14	65.57
39	16	65.81
53	21	68.14
39	15	70.20
34	13	70.62
50	19	71.05
50	18	75.00
39	14	75.21
53	19	75.32
34	12	76.50
50	17	79.41
53	18	79.50
39	13	81.00
34	11	83.45
53	17	84.18
50	16	84.38
39	12	87.75
53	16	89.44
50	15	90.00
53	15	95.40
39	11	95.73
50	14	96.43
53	14	102.21
50	13	103.85
53	13	110.08
50	12	112.50
53	12	119.25
50	11	122.73
53	11	130.09

D. Periodized Century Training Plan

	MONDAY	TUESDAY	WEDNESDAY	THURSDAY	FRIDAY	SATURDAY	SUNDAY
1	Off	1 hour hills or intervals	1.5 hours easy	1 hour moderate	1 hour easy	1.5-hour group ride	2 hours easy
2	Off	1 hour hills or intervals	1.5 hours easy	1 hour moderate	1 hour easy	1.5-hour group ride	2.5 hours easy
3	Off	1 hours hills or intervals	1.5 hours easy	1 hour moderate	1 hour easy	1.5-hour group ride	3 hours easy
4	Off	45 min. hills or intervals	1 hour easy	45 min. moderate	45 min. easy	1-hour group ride	2 hours easy
5	Off	1.5 hours hills or intervals	2 hours easy	1.5 hours moderate	1.5 hours easy	2-hour group ride	2.5 hours easy
6	Off	1.5 hours hills or intervals	2 hours easy	1.5 hours moderate	1.5 hours easy	2-hour group ride	3 hours easy
7	Off	1.5 hours hills or intervals	2 hours easy	1.5 hours moderate	1.5 hours easy	2-hour group ride	3.5 hours easy
8	Off	1 hour hills or intervals	1.5 hours easy	1 hour moderate	1 hour easy	1.5-hour group ride	2.5 hours easy
9	Off	2 hours hills or intervals	2.5 hours easy	2 hours moderate	2 hours easy	2.5-hour group ride	3 hours easy
10	Off	2 hours hills or intervals	2.5 hours easy	2 hours moderate	2 hours easy	2.5-hour group ride	3.5 hours easy
11	Off	2 hours hills or intervals	2.5 hours easy	2 hours moderate	2 hours easy	2.5-hour group ride	4 hours easy
12	Off	1 hour hills or intervals	1.5 hours easy	1 hour moderate	1 hour easy	Event or 1.5-hour group ride	Event or 1 hour easy

E. The Conconi Test

Most of us took up cycling because it was fun, not because we like lactic acid. Even so, part of the fun is going fast, and if fast equals fun, then more fast must equal more fun. But getting truly fast means suffering for the clock to find out just how to fit you are.

Knowing your lactate threshold (LT) won't make you faster, but it can teach you when to either go harder or easier. If you regularly train with a heart rate monitor or wattage-measuring device, this little tidbit can mean the difference between trying to eat sand and a sandwich. Oh, and by the way, knowing your max HR, which you may or may not find out while doing this test, doesn't mean much. Most riders don't have the aerobic fitness required to push themselves to the point that they hit their max HR; you're likely to blow long before you hit that point, which is why your LT is much more important.

To do a Conconi Test, you'll need your bike, a stationary trainer, a cyclocomputer with rear wheel sensor, a heart rate monitor (HRM) with a memory (some of units sample your HR every five seconds), some graph paper, and a pen. On a day when your are well rested, set your bike up on the trainer and climb on. If you want motivational tunes, fine, but it won't make a bit of difference—the Conconi test is all about what you've done in training lately, not how motivated you are today. Select a gear you would do intervals in, say 53x16. Begin pedaling at 12 mph, and every 30 seconds increase your speed by one-half mile per hour. The level of effort you make at the beginning will leave you suspicious that this test could take all afternoon. However, your heart rate will steadily climb until you begin to hurt. You will continue to pedal and you will hurt more. Eventually, you'll pop with lactic acid searing your blood like olive oil in a pan. You may stop pedaling.

On the graph paper you will create an X-axis and a Y-axis. The X-axis will show time and the Y-axis will show your heart rate. As you review the HRM data, you will see the values climb steadily, until suddenly there will be a break where the line flattens out and a few seconds later it will begin to climb again, only more sharply. That plateau is what you are looking for.

Depending on your HRM's sampling rate, you should be able to get two to four readings per minute. Near your break point you may see readings something like this: 172, 172, 173, 173, 174, 174, 174, 174, 175, 176, 177, KABOOM! The 174 reading is the break point that represents lactate threshold. If you are diligent in your interval training, you will be able to hover around this mark, pushing it up further with careful training.

It is unlikely you will wish to perform this test more than once a month.

Index

A

accessories. *See also* clothing
    arm, leg, knee warmers, 136
    bike fenders, 144
    club discounts, 211
    cyclocomputer, 142
    eyewear, 141–42
    gloves, 118, 136–37, 241
    GPS devices, 144
    heart rate monitor, 144
    helmet mirrors, 45
    helmets, 127–29
    lights, 142, 143
    maintenance necessities, 147–48
    toe covers and booties, 137
    water bottles/water-bottle cages, 141
    wattage-measuring devices, 143–44
accident reports, 48–49
accordion effect, pack, 25
Active.com (cycling events site), 55
ad hoc training, 237
Adventure Cycling Association, 212
Adventure Cyclist (magazine), 212
age classes, racing, 62
alcohol, cycling and, 187
Allen wrench, 237
alloys
    aluminum frames, 74
    defined, 237
    steel frames, 72
    titanium frames, 75
aluminum frames

basics, 69–70
    construction, 73–74
    material specifics, 73, 237
    metallurgy properties, 70–71
    place in today's market, 74
    ride quality, 74
American Bicycle Racing, 62
American top-tier races, 219
Amgen Tour of California, 219
amphetamines, 228
anabolic steroids, 228
Andy Pruitt's Complete Medical Guide for Cyclists
    (Pruitt), 234
ankling, 237
Anquetil, Jacques, 221, 228
arm, leg, knee warmers, 136, 237, 243
Armstrong, Lance, 7, 78, 143, 175, 220–21, 229, 244
Asphalt magazine, 265
"Assometer," 117
Atlanta, 1996 Olympic Games, 219
attack, 237
au bloc ("all-out"), 237
axle, 237

B

backsliding, in a pack, 25–26
balance, determining dominant foot, 9–10
bar height, xi, 107
bar top, 15, 117–18
base-layer clothing, 134

base miles, 180
Bausch, Dotsie, 37, 179
beach cruisers, 99
bearings, 237
Belgian knee warmers (embrocations), 199
Belgium Knee Warmers (website), 265
bell bottoms (shorts), 192, 237
Bellows Falls and Vicinity Illustrated (Gobie), viii
bib shorts, 237
bicycle-advocacy organizations, 212–13
bicycle components. *See specific component by name*
bicycle design. *See also* construction methods
    components identified, 64
    evolution over time, 4, 102–06
    finding comfort and efficiency, 115
    metric measurements, 66, 83
    weight distribution, 107
    women's issues, 37–38
bicycle dimensions/geometry
    about, 99–100
    bottom bracket height, 100
    chainstay length, 102
    front center length, 102
    height and center of gravity, 100
    tube angles/lengths, 101–02
    wheel size, 100
    wheelbase, 100
bicycle fit
    fitting the bike to the rider, xi–xii
    frame dimensions, 66
    women's issues, 38–39
Bicycle Guide (magazine), xiii, 265

bicycle models/manufacturers
   about production vs. custom, 112
   Alan, 73–74
   Cannondale, 74, 103, 104
   Felt, 77, 103, 104
   Giant, 77, 96, 103, 104
   Guerciotti, 73–74
   Kestrel, 77
   Klein, 74
   Litespeed, 75
   Merlin Metalworks, 75
   Moots, 75
   Odonata (Seven Cycles), 79
   Ridley, 96
   Seven Cycles, 75–76
   Specialized Bicycles, 4, 82, 103
   Time, 96
   Trek Bicycles, 74, 78, 96, 103, 104
Bicycle motocross. *See* BMX bikes
bicycle racing
   author's introduction to, xiii
   governing bodies, 62
   kinds of races, 59–61
   licensing, classes, categories, 62
Bicycle Road Racing: The Complete Program for
   Training and Competition (Borysewicz), 233
Bicycle: The History (Herlihy), 235
bicycle touring
   going alone or with friends, 204
   guided tours and travel companies, 205–06
   overdoing it, 206–07
   schedule flexibility, 207
   transporting your bike, 203–04
bicycle types. *See also specific bicycle*
   beach cruisers, 99
   BMX bikes, 5
   city bikes, 7
   cruiser bikes, 5
   cyclocross bikes, 67, 106, 110
   designed for women, 37–39
   enthusiast bikes, 111

   entry-level bikes, 111
   grand touring bikes, 67, 104
   hybrid bikes, 6
   mountain bikes, 6
   racing bikes, 111
   recreational bikes, 111
   road bikes, 4, 64–67
   sport road bikes, 103, 109
   tandem bikes, 67, 106, 110
   three-speed bikes, 99
   time trial bikes, 67, 105, 109
   touring bikes, 66, 104, 109
   track bikes ("fixies"), 67, 105, 109
bicycle upgrades
   cranks/crankset/crank arms, 167
   fork, 167
   handlebars, 165–66
   rims, 164
   saddle, 165
   seatpost, 166–67
   tires and tubes, 165
   wheels, 163–64
Bicycling (magazine), 232
Bicycling and the Law (Mionske), 236
Bicycling Los Angeles County (Brady), 265
Bicycling Science (Wilson), 236
Big Blue Book of Bicycle Repair (Jones), 233
"big ring," 238
bike racks, 203–04
"bikers," xiv
Bikes Belong Coalition, 212
blades (fork), 83–84
blinking lights, 142
"blowing up," 238
BMX bikes, 5
Bobet, Louison, 222
bonding, 80
"bonk"/"bonking," 33, 54, 185, 189, 200, 238
Borg Rating of Perceived Exertion (RPE), 178
bottom bracket, 64–65, 89, 238
bottom bracket height, 238

boutique builders, 112
Boyer, Jonathan, 226
Brady, Gabriel Martin, viii
brakes, front/rear
   brake barrel adjustment, 159
   calipers and pads, 238
   control levers, 94–95
   described/defined, 64–65
   design/purpose, 94
   using the quick release, 151
braking, basics of "how to," 14
brass brazing, 72
brazing, 238
breakaway, 238
Breaking the Chain (Voet), 234
brinelling, 86
broken bones, 48
broom wagon, 238
Bruyneel, Johann, 227, 229
bumping, recovery from, 32
butted, 238

C

cables, 150
cadence, 238
calf (muscles), 238
calories, 185, 188, 238
Campagnolo (Facchinetti and Rubino), 235
Campagnolo, Tullio, 89
cantilever brake, 238
"car back"/"car up," 238, 239
carbohydrates, diet and, 185–86
carbon fiber, 239
carbon fiber components
   cranksets, 168
   forks, 168
   handlebars, 165–66
   rims, 164
   seatposts, 166–67
carbon fiber frames

basics, 69–70
construction, 77–78
material specifics, 76–77
metallurgy properties, 70–71
place in today's market, 78
ride quality, 78
Carmichael, Chris, 175, 179, 181
carpal tunnel syndrome, 118
cassette
described/defined, 64–65, 239
design/purpose, 86–87, 93
gearing options, 171–72
spares for different terrain, 150
categories, racing, 62
center of gravity, 100, 239
century bikes. *See* grand touring bikes
century rides (100 miles), 54, 239
century training plan, 253
chainring tattoo, 192
chainrings
described/defined, 239
gearing options, 171
size/configuration, 90
when to shift, 14
chains
described/defined, 64–65, 239
design/purpose, 93–94
how to lubricate, 152
maintenance necessities, 147–48
spares on hand, 150
wear indicator, 149
chainstays, 65–66, 70, 102, 239
chamois, 239
chamois cream, 198, 239
charity rides, 53–54
checklists, cycling-event, 56
choosing your position, pack, 26
Chrome-Moly (alloy), 239
city bikes, 7
"clear," 23, 239
cleat, 239

climbers (cycling team), 228
climbing hills, 16–17
clincher rims/tires, 86, 87–88, 247
clothing. *See also* accessories
about styling and colors, 43, 131
appropriate to the weather, 138–39
base layer, 134
bell bottoms, 192
checklist, 56
club-coordinated designs, 211
cycling shorts, 117, 132–33, 246
dressing/undressing while riding, 33
fabric choices, 131–32
"Fred," 192
jackets, 135
jerseys, 133–34, 192, 242, 246
Lycra clothing, 132, 243, 245
selection and colors for women, 41
shoes, 116, 239
socks, 137
tights and knickers, 135
vests, 136
coaching
keeping track of the numbers, 179
training plans and, 182
Colorado Springs, 1986 World Championships, 219
commitment, training, 182
competition bikes, 66
computers
cyclocomputer, 142
GPS devices, 144
monitoring fitness, 177
workout-analysis software, 145
Conconi Test, 179, 254
construction methods
bonding, 80
brass brazing, 72
carbon fiber, 76–78
fillet brazing, 72, 80
hydroforming, 74

lugged construction, 72, 73, 79
monocoque molding, 81
net molding, 77–78
silver brazing, 72
TIG welding, 72, 73, 75, 80, 246–47
contact. *See* bumping; touching; touching wheels
contact point, 239
contre le montre ("against the clock"), 105
control levers, 64–65, 94–95, 239
Coors Classic race, 219
Coors Light team, 33
Coppi, Fausto, 220, 228
cornering, 17–18, 91
corporate sponsorship, 219
corticosteroids, 228
countersteering, 17–18, 29–30
cranks/crankset/crank arms
described/defined, 64–65, 239
design/purpose, 90
fitting the bike to the rider, 125
gearing options, 171
upgrade options, 167
crashes. *See also* safety on the road
accident report, 48–49
accordion effect, 25
common injuries, 48
dealing with police, 49
debris on the road, 193–94
emergency items to carry, 47–48
gloves as protection, 118
healing your body takes time, 50
protect your front wheel, 24
repairing your bike, 50
replacing the helmet, 129
riding skills to avoid, 35
rule of falling, 48
criterium (crit) racing, 60
crown (fork), 83–84
cruiser bikes, 5
The CTS Collection: Training Tips for Cyclists and Triathletes (Carmichael), 233

curfew, 239
custom-built bicycles, 112
Cycle Sport (magazine), 232
cycling clubs, benefits, 210–12
cycling etiquette, 193–95
cycling events
    about finding, 55
    charity rides, 53–54
    destination rides, 53
    distance rides, 54
    planning and packing for, 55–56
cycling groups/organizations, 212–13
cycling hazards, 199–201
cycling resources
    books, 233–36
    clubs and organizations, 210–13
    Internet (websites), 231–32
    magazines, 232
cycling rituals/practices, 197–99
cycling shorts, 117, 132–33, 237, 246
cycling teams, 228, 240
Cycling's Golden Age: Heroes of the Postwar Era,
   1947–1967 (Horton and Mulholland), 235
The Cyclist's Training Bible (Friel), 233
cyclocomputer, 142, 177, 239–40, 245
cyclocross bikes, 67, 106, 110, 240
cyclocross races, 61, 240

D

De Vlaeminck, Roger, 223
density, 240
derailleur, front/rear
    control levers, 94–95
    described/defined, 64–65, 240
    design/purpose, 91–92
    gearing and, 170
descending, body position and countersteering,
   29–30
destination rides, 53–54
diet

alcohol, 187
author's philosophy on, xii
calories, 185, 188
carbs, 185–86
eating while riding, 33, 188
fats, 186–87
hydration, 187
protein, 186
weight loss, 188–89
distance rides, 54
A Dog in a Hat (Parkin), 234
domestique (cycling team), 228, 240
dominant foot, balance, 9–10
doping, 228–29
double century rides (200 miles), 54
double-metric century rides (200 km, 124 miles),
  54
double paclines, 22
down tube, 65–66, 70, 240
downhill skiing, road racing is like, x
downshifting. *See* shifting
drafting
    cycling etiquette, 195
    described, 4, 240
    maintaining distance, 22
dressing/undressing while riding, 33
drinking on the bike, 26–27
drive-side, 240
dropouts, front/rear, 65–66, 70, 83–84, 240
dropped/getting dropped
    defined, 240
    "off the back" (OTB), 244
    riding in a pack, 24
drops, 16, 118, 125
drug scandals/testing, 229
drugs/drug use, 228–29

E

Easton, Peter, 204, 205
eating/food. *See* diet

echelon (paceline), 30–31
Eddie B. (Borysewicz), xi, xii
Eddy Merckx (Vanwalleghem), 234
elongation, 240
embrocations, 199, 240
endurance limit, 71, 73
enthusiast bikes, price points, 111
entry-level bikes, 111
erectile dysfunction, 97, 117
erythropoietin (EPO), 228–29
events. *See* cycling events
Every Second Counts (Armstrong), 234
exertion rating scale, 178
existential crisis, 240
eyewear, 142

F

falls and crashes. *See* crashes
false flat (uphill grade), 22, 240
fast-twitch muscle fiber, 241
fatigue and overtraining, 181
fatigue strength (tube), 241
fenders, 144
Festina Affair, 1998, 229
fillet brazing, 72, 80
first-aid kit, 49
fitness. *See also* training
    Conconi Test, 179, 254
    defining a racing cyclist, 176
    exertion rating scale, 178
    heart rate, 178
    keeping track of the numbers, 179
    lactic acid/lactate threshold, 178–79
    muscle fibers/groups, 176–77
    training aids, 177
    types of, 177
    VO_2 max, 248
fitting the bike to the rider
    adjusting the bike, 123–24
    bike dimensions and geometry, 99–102

bike-type considerations, 109–10
body dimensions and flexibility, 122–23
component choices, 125
elements of fit, 124
frame dimensions, 66
production vs. custom bikes, 121–22
purchasing considerations, 112
riding habits and, xi–xii
women's issues, 38–39
fixed gear, 241
"fixies." *See* track bikes
flexibility training, 181
food. *See* diet
fork
   component parts, 70, 83
   described/defined, 64–65, 241
   design/purpose, 84
   front rake/front center dimensions, 101–02
   repairs from a crash, 84
   upgrade options, 167
fork rake, 241
frame
   described/defined, 64–65, 70, 241
   geometry of tube angles/lengths, 101–02
   repairs from a crash, 50
   sizes for women cyclists, 37–39
frame materials and construction
   aluminum frames, 73–74
   basics for the beginner, 69–70
   beyond the basics, 70–71
   carbon fiber frames, 76–78
   hybrid designs, 79–81
   steel frames, 72–73
   titanium frames, 75–76
frameset, 241
"Fred" (newbie). *See also* cycling etiquette
   avoiding the label of, 191
   defined, 241, 244
   telltale signs, 191–92
freehub, 93, 241
freewheel, 241

front rake/front center, 101, 102, 241
Fuentes, Eufemiano (Dr.), 229

G

"gap," closing the, 26, 241
gear bag, 56
gearing/gearing changes. *See also* cassette; shifting
   adaptations and options for, 169
   brief history of, 170
   cassette options, 171–72
   chainring/crank options, 171
   derailleurs and, 91–92
   gear development/combinations, 170–71
   maintenance adjustments, 155–59
   range charts, 252
   repetition charts, 250–51
   spare cassettes on hand for, 150
   women's issues, 39
genitalia, health issues, 97, 117
geometry, 241
George M. Cohan, the Original Yankee Doodle Dandy (Brady), viii
Giro d'Italia, x
gloves, 118, 136–37, 241
glucose, 241
glutes (muscle), 241
glycogen, 241
Gobie, Henry Philip, vii
Gobie, Philip Henry, vii
Goldstein, Irwin (Dr.), 97, 117
governing bodies, cycling, 62
GPS devices, 144, 177, 241
grade, 242
gran fondo ("big ride"), 242
grand touring bikes (century bikes), 67, 104, 109, 242
The Grand Tours, 215–16, 242
grassroots cycling associations, 62
group rides

cycling etiquette, 193–95
difficulties of women, 40
double pacelines, 22
ride meeting point, 197
riding in a pack, 23–27
"roadies" culture, xiv
rotating paceline, 23
single pacelines, 21–22
training for, 175
guided tours and travel companies, 205–06

H

half-wheel, 242
"half-wheeling," 22
"hall pass," 182, 242
Hamilton, Tyler, 224–25
Hampsten, Andy, 224
Hampsten Cycles, xi–xii
hamstrings, 242
hand positions, 15–16, 117–18
hand signals, cycling etiquette, 193–95
handlebar tape, 119, 150, 160
handlebars
   described/defined, 64–65, 242
   design/purpose, 85
   finding comfort and efficiency, 117–19
   fitting the bike to the rider, xi, 125
   upgrade options, 165–66
   wrapping, 160
hands-free riding, 33
head tube/head tube angle, 65–66, 70, 101, 242
headlights, 143
headset, 64–65, 85–86, 242
health issues. *See also* "bonk"/"bonking"; diet; injuries
   books, 233–34
   carpal tunnel syndrome, 118
   genitalia, 97, 117
   medical information, 47–48
   road rash, 48, 245

saddle sores, 199
   Tegaderm, 246
heart rate
   Conconi Test, 179, 254
   defined, 244
   monitors, 144, 177
   scale, 178
helmet mirrors, 45
helmets
   evolution over time, 127–28
   features, 128–29, 242
   helmets, 127–29
   how it works, 45
   sizing/fitting, 129
   when to replace, 129
high-wheeler bikes, 4
hill repeats, 180
Hinault, Bernard, 221, 244
Hincapie, George, 225
"holding your line"
   described, 11–12, 243
   receiving a push, 31
   riding in a pack, 24
hoods, hand positions, 118
hormone use, 228–29
hubs, front/rear, 86–87, 93, 242
hybrid bikes, 6
hybrid frames, 79–81
hybrid tires, 88
hydration, importance of, 187
hydroforming, 74
Hyperglide system, 90, 93

I

I.C.E. ("in case of emergency"), 47–48
indexed shifting, adjusting, 155–59
individual racing events, 59
individual time trial, 242
Indurain, Miguel, 73, 222
injuries. *See also* health issues

falls and crashes, 48
first aid kit, 49
   take time to heal, 50
Internet. *See* websites
intervals, 180
It's Not About the Bike: My Journey Back to Life
   (Armstrong), 234

J

jackets, 135
jerseys, 133–34, 192, 242, 246
Julich, Bobby, 225
Junior age class (age 18 and under), 62
Junior Worlds team, xi

K

Kelly, Sean, xii, 74, 223
kilojoule, 243
ksi (thousand pounds per square inch), 243

L

lacing patterns, spoke, 87
lactic acid/lactate threshold, 178–79, 243, 254
Lance Armstrong's War (Coyle), 234
Landis, Floyd, 229
Landscapes of Cycling (Watson), 236
lanterne rouge ("red lantern"), 243
"last," riding a paceline, 23
leader (cycling team), 228
League of American Bicyclists, 213
left-hand thread, 243
leg shaving, 197–98
Leipheimer, Levi, 225
LeMond, Greg, xiii, 78, 222
lever hoods, hand positions, 15
licensing, racing, 62
Liège–Bastogne–Liège race, 218

lifestyle, fitness, 182
Liggett, Phil, 227
"light up," 243
lights (blinking lights/headlights), 142, 143
limit screw, 243
line. *See* "holding your line"
liniment, 243
looking over your shoulder
   basics of "why"/"how," 18–19
   common sense safety, 45
lug/lugged construction, 72, 79, 243
Lycra clothing, 132, 243, 245

M

macrocycles/microcycles, 180, 244
main triangle, frame, 70
maintenance
   about the importance of, xi
   basic tools and supplies, 149–50
   beyond the basic tools, 150–51
   necessities to have on hand, 147–48
   repair manuals, 233
maintenance, basic procedures
   brake barrel adjustment, 159
   chain lubrication, 152
   fixing a flat, 152–54
   indexed shifting adjustment, 155–59
   using a brake quick release, 151
   using a wheel quick release, 152
   washing your bicycle, 154–55
   wrapping handlebar tape, 160
massage, 198
mass-start racing events, 59, 244
Master class (age 30 and up), 62
medical information, 47–48
Merckx, Eddy, xii, xiii, 220, 244
metallurgy properties, frame, 70–71
metric century rides (100 km, 62 miles), 54
metric measurements, 66, 83

Mike and the Bike (Ward, Thomson and Liggett), 236
Milan–San Remo race, 216–17
monocoque molding, 81
The Monuments, 216–18, 244
Mount, George, 226
mountain bikes, 6
"moving up," in a pack, 26

N

National Collegiate Cycling Association (NCCC), 62
Neel, Mike, 226
net molding, 77–78
newbie. *See* "Fred"
Nijdam, Jelle, 32
noise distraction, 194
nondrive-side, 244
"noodles," 74
nose blowing and spitting, 194

O

"off the back" (OTB), 244
"on the rivet," 244
Operation Puerto, 2006, 229
opiates, 228
overtraining and fatigue, 181, 244

P

pacelines
    avoiding road debris, 193–94
    defined, 244
    double paceline, 22
    echelon, 30–31
    learning to ride, xiii, 3
    riding in a pack, 23
    rotating paceline, 23
single paceline, 21–22
pack, riding in a
    accordion effect, 25
    backsliding, 25–26
    choosing your position, 26
    closing a "gap," 26
    defined, 244
    drinking on the bike, 26–27
    getting dropped, 24
    holding your line, 24
    moving up, 26
    pacelines, 23
    protecting your front wheel, 24
"pain cave," 244
Paris–Roubaix: A Journey Through Hell (Bouvet, Callewaert, Gatellier and Serge), 235
Paris–Roubaix race, 217–18
Parkin, Joe, 30
"patron" (cycling team), 244
pedaling cadence, 13
pedaling in circles, 12–13
pedals/clipless pedals
    clipping in/out, 10–11
    design/purpose, 90–91, 244–45
    fitting the bike to the rider, 115–16
peloton ("platoon")
    defined, 245
    thrill of riding in, x
peloton magazine, 265
People Powered Movement, 213
performance-enhancing drugs (PEDs), 228
periodized century training plan, 253
peripheral vision, 19
permits, race, 62
Phinney, Davis, 226
police, accident reports, 48–49
polyester clothing, 132
power meter. *See* cyclocomputer
practicing riding skills, avoiding crashes by, 35
price points, 110–11
production vs. custom bikes
fitting the bike to the rider, 123–24
    purchasing considerations, 112
Professional Ski Instructors of America, xiii
protect your front wheel, 24
proteins, diet and, 186
PSI (pounds per square inch), 245
"pull"/"pull off"/"taking a pull"
    defined, 245
    double pacelines, 22
    single pacelines, 21
    "wheel-sucker," 248
pump, floor/frame, 147–48
purchasing a bicycle
    choosing the right type, 109–10
    price points, 110
    production vs. boutique, 112
    riding styles and, 111
pushing, 31, 40

Q

quadriceps (quads), 245
quick-release skewers, 89, 152, 245

R

racing. *See* bicycle racing
racing bikes, price points, 110–11
rain, riding in the, 200
rear triangle, frame, 70
recovery rides, 180
recreational bikes, price points, 111
red kite prayer, 245
Red Kite Prayer (blog), 232, 265
regional cycling associations, 62
repair manuals, 233
The Ride (magazine), 265
ride-meeting point, 197
ride quality
    aluminum frames, 74

carbon fiber frames, 78
steel frames, 73
"sweet spot," 249
titanium frames, 76
Young's Modulus (E), 71, 246
The Rider (Krabbe), 236
riding habits, fitting the bike to the rider, xi–xii
riding on city streets
being seen, 43
commonsense rules, 43
dealing with traffic, 44
parked cars, 44–45
riding skills, advanced
bumping, 32
descending, 29–30
dressing/undressing while riding, 34
eating while riding, 33
echelons, 30–31
hands-free riding, 33
practicing, 35
touching, 31–32, 40
touching wheels, 32
riding skills, basic
balance, 9–10
braking, 14
climbing hills, 16
clipping in/out, 10–11
cornering, 17–18
"holding your line," 11–12
looking over your shoulder, 18–19
pedaling cadence, 13
pedaling in circles, 12–13
shifting, 13–14
standing up from the saddle, 17
starting/stopping, 10–11
using hand positions, 15–16
riding skills, group
riding in a paceline, 21–23
riding in a pack, 23–27
right-hand thread, 245
rims, wheel, 86–87, 164, 245

Road (magazine), 232
Road Bike Action (magazine), 232
road bikes. *See also* bicycle design and
construction
basic characteristics, 4
description and types, 66–67
design and purpose, 7
finding comfort and efficiency, 115
price points and riding style, 110–11
as sports cars, 99
variations of type, 104–06
road cycling, described, 3–4
road debris, 193–94
road racing, 60
road rash, 48, 245, 246
road speeds
basics of shifting, 13
evolution over time, 7, 102
"roadies," understanding the culture of, xiv
Roll, Bob, 32, 227
"rolling," 245
roof racks, 203–04
rotating paceline. *See* pacelines
Roubaix Lycra, 245

S

saddle
described/defined, 64–65, 245
design/purpose, 96–97
finding comfort and efficiency, 116–17
fitting the bike to the rider, 125
height/setback, 107
upgrade options, 165
saddle sores, 199
safety on the road. *See also* crashes
dealing with traffic, 43–45
"holding your line," 11–12
looking over your shoulder, 18–19, 45
practicing riding skills, 35
toe overlap, 37–38

"sag," 245
sanctioned races, 62
seat tube/seat tube angle, 70, 101–02, 245–46
seatpost
described/defined, 64–65, 246
design/purpose, 96
fitting the bike to the rider, 125
upgrade options, 166–67
seatstays, 65–66, 70, 246
Senior class (age 23-29), 62
Serious Cycling (Burke), 233
7-Eleven/Motorola team, x
Sherwen, Paul, 227
shifting. *See also* control levers; gearing/gearing
changes
basics of "when to," 13–14
maintenance adjustments, 155–59
shoes, 116, 239
short ride events (20–30 miles), 54
shoving, 32
silver brazing, 72
single pacelines, 21–22
"skirt," 192, 246
"slipping out," 200
slow-twitch muscle fiber, 246
"slumming it," 246
snot rocket, 194, 246
soccer, road racing is like, x
socks, 137
*The Speedy: A history of the U.S. special delivery
service* (Gobie), viii
spitting, cycling etiquette, 194
spokes, 86–87, 246. *See also* wheels
sponsorships, club, 211
sport road bikes, 103, 109, 246
sprinter (cycling team), 228
sprints/sprinting, 17, 180
squirrel/squirrelly, 246
stage racing, 61
standing up from the saddle, 17
starting/stopping, clipping in/out, 10–11

steel frames
    basics, 69–70
    construction, 72
    material specifics, 72, 246
    metallurgy properties, 70–71
    place in today's market, 73
    ride quality, 73
steerer tube (fork), 70, 83–84
stem/stem post/stem length
    changing weight distribution, 107
    described/defined, 64–65, 246
    design/purpose, 84–85
    fitting the bike to the rider, xi, 125
steroids, 228
stiffness (modulus of elasticity). See ride quality
The Story of the Tour de France Vol. 1 & 2 (McGann
    and McGann), 235
sunburn, 199
sunscreen, 197, 246
Sutherland's Handbook of Bicycle Mechanics
    (Sutherland), 233
"sweet spot," 249
Swiss Phonak cycling team, 229

T

"taking a pull"/"pull off," 71–72
tandem bikes, 67, 106, 110
tapping, 31
team time trial, 246
Tegaderm, 246
testosterone, 228
three-speed bikes, 99
Thunderhead Alliance (renamed People Powered
    Movement), 213
TIG welding, 72, 73, 75, 80, 246–47
tights and knickers, 135
time trial bikes, 67, 105, 109, 247
time trials ("race of truth")
    defined, 247
    described, 59–60

individual, 242
    team, 246
    tires and tubes
    avoiding road debris, 193–94
    clincher tires, 87–88, 247, 248
    fixing a flat, 152–54
    flat-tire etiquette, 194
    maintenance necessities, 147–48
    riding in the rain ("slipping out"), 200
    spares, 150
    tubular tires, 87–88, 247, 248
    upgrade options, 165
titanium frames
    basics, 69–70
    construction, 75
    material specifics, 75, 247
    metallurgy properties, 70–71
    place in today's market, 76
    ride quality, 76
TiVo, 247
toe clips, 247
toe covers and booties, 137
toe overlap, 37–38, 137, 247
tools and supplies
    basic necessities, 149–50
    beyond the necessities, 150–51
top tube, 65–66, 70, 101, 247
touching
    bumping, 32
    pushing, 31, 40
    shoving, 32
    tapping, 31
touching wheels, 32
Tour de France, xiii, 7, 73, 74, 76, 78, 215–16, 229
Tour de France: The 2005 Tour de France in
    Photography (Startt), 236
Tour DuPont, 33, 219
Tour of California, 219
Tour of Flanders, 217
Tour of Georgia, 219
Tour of Italy, 216

Tour of Lombardy, 218
Tour of Spain, 216
touring bikes, 66, 104, 109, 247
town-line sprint, 247
track bikes ("fixies"), 67, 105, 109
track racing, 61. See velodrome
traffic, riding in
    being seen on the street, 43
    cycling etiquette, 193–95
    parked car hazards, 44–45
    riding in the rain, 200
    riding legally, 43
    road surface hazards, 200–201
    where/when to ride, 43
trail (steering/handling), 38, 66, 101, 102, 247
Trail-o-Matic chart, 249
training. See also fitness
    about the benefits, 175
    about the commitment to, 182
    basic considerations, 179
    basic workouts, 180
    books, 233–34
    fatigue and overtraining, 181
    flexibility, 181
    as lifestyle, 182
    macrocycles/microcycles, 180
    town-line sprint, 247
training aids
    cyclocomputer, 142, 239–40
    monitoring fitness, 177
    wattage-measuring devices, 143–44
    workout analysis software, 145
training cycles, 247
training plans
    about the basics, 181
    coaching and, 182
    periodized, 253
    using a "hall pass," 182, 242
traumatic brain injury (TBI), 246
traveling with a bike. See bicycle touring
triathlon bikes, 67

tubes. *See* tires and tubes
tubular rims/tires, 86, 87–88, 247
turning radius, 18

U

"über-geek," 248
Ullrich, Jan, 223–24, 229
ultimate tensile strength (UTS), 248
Under-23 class (age 19-22), 62
Union Cycliste Internationale, 62
United States Cycling Federation (USCF), 62
United States Olympic Committee (USOC), 62
United States top-tier races, 219
upgrade options
    cranks/crankset/crank arms, 167
    fork, 167
    handlebars, 165–66
    rims, wheel, 164
    saddle, 165
    seatpost, 166–67
    tires and tubes, 165
    wheels, front/rear, 163–64
upshifting. *See* shifting
U.S. Bicycle Route System, 212
U.S. Postal Service cycling team, xii, 229
USA Cycling, 62, 213

V

vacationing. *See* bicycle touring
valve stems, tube, 88
Van Looy, Rik, 222
Vaughters, Jonathan, 227
Velo Classic Tours, 204
velodrome, track racing, 61, 248
VeloNews (magazine), 232
Verbruggen, Hein, 229
vests, 136
Virenque, Richard, 224

virtual top tube, 248
VO$_2$ max, 248
Voet, Willy, 229

W

washing your bicycle, 154–55
water bottles/water-bottle cages, 141
wattage-measuring devices, 143–44, 177, 248
weather
    dressing in layers, 138–39
    wind/crosswinds, 30–31
websites
    bicycle advocacy, 212–13
    cycling information and blogs, 231–32
    finding a bicycle club, 212
    finding cycling events, 55
weight distribution, 107
weight loss, cycling and, 188–89
"weight weenie," 248
wheelbase, 66, 100, 248
wheels, front/rear
    described/defined, 64–65
    design/purpose, 86–87
    fixing a flat, 152–54
    quick-release skewers, 89
    size/dimensions, 100, 248
    sizes for women cyclists, 38
    tires/tubes, 87–88
    upgrade options, 163–64
    using the quick releases, 151–52
"wheel-sucker," 248
wind/crosswinds, 30–31
women cyclists, issues of
    bike fit, 38–39
    bike frames, 74
    bike geometry and wheel size, 37–38
    clothing, 41
    gearing, 39
    pushing, 40
    racing categories, 62

riding in a group, 40
wool/merino wool clothing, 131–32
workout analysis software, 145, 177
World Championships, 29, 218–19

X

"X." *See* cyclocross races
X Games, 6

Y

yield strength, 248
Young's Modulus (E), 71, 246

Z

Zabel, Erik, 224
zinc oxide, 248
Zinn and the Art of Road Bike Maintenance (Zinn), 233
Zoetemelk, Joop, 223

Patrick Brady

Patrick Brady has been an avid cyclist for more than 20 years. He has toured the U.S. and Europe and raced from Vermont to California. He was the publisher of the highly regarded *Asphalt* magazine and served as an editor for *Bicycle Guide* and *The Ride*. His first book, *Bicycling Los Angeles County,* was published by Menasha Ridge Press in 2007. His groundbreaking work at the Belgium Knee Warmers blog led to the launch of his blog, Red Kite Prayer, and his role as a contributing editor for *peloton* magazine.